FEAST

Daily Saints

DAILY SAINTS WHOSE ANCESTRY IS KNOWN

Daily Saints Whose Ancestry is Known

ISBN: 1453749187
EAN-13 is 9781453749180

Starr, Brian Daniel is the owner of this work with all rights and responsibilities related to this work.

Copyright 2007

All Rights Reserved. No part of this book may be reproduced in any form without permission in writing from the author, except in the case of brief quotations embodied in critical articles or reviews.

Printed in the United States of America

SAINTS DAILY
Kings, Queens, Popes, Princes, Princesses, Emperors, Hermits, Bishops

Daily Saints Whose Ancestry is Known

AUTHOR
Brian Daniel Starr

Copyright 2007
First Printing May, 20th 2007
Second Printing August 5, 2010

SAINTS DAILY
Kings, Queens, Popes, Princes, Princesses, Emperors, Hermits, Bishops

DEDICATION

To My Loving Wife and Lovely Daughter

Julieta Starr

Gabriella Maria Starr

Who have given me the patience and fortitude to complete this work.

SAINTS DAILY
Kings, Queens, Popes, Princes, Princesses, Emperors, Hermits, Bishops

DAILY SAINTS WHOSE ANCESTRY IS KNOWN

CHART OF CONTENTS

FEASTDAY	SAINT	COUNTRY	BORN	DIED
1-Jan	Saint Fanchea	Ireland		c 530
1-Jan	Blessed Adalbero	France		1128
2-Jan	Saint Adalhard	France	753	827
2-Jan	Blessed Ayrald	France		1146
2-Jan	Saint Adelard	France	753	827
3-Jan	Saint Wenodog	Wales		6th
4-Jan	Saint Gregory Bishop of Langres	France		539
6-Jan	Saint Wiltrude	France	937	986
7-Jan	Saint Canute the Pious	Denmark	1096	1130
7-Jan	Saint Kentigerna	Ireland		734
8-Jan	Saint Gudula	Belgium		712
10-Jan	Saint Pietro I Orseolo	Italy	935	987
10-Jan	Blessed Gregory X	Italy	1210	1276
11-Jan	Saint Fidelmia	Ireland		c. 250
11-Jan	Saint Ethenia	Ireland		c. 250
11-Jan	Saint Hyginus	Rome		140

SAINTS DAILY
Kings, Queens, Popes, Princes, Princesses, Emperors, Hermits, Bishops

DAILY SAINTS WHOSE ANCESTRY IS KNOWN

13-Jan	Saint Kentigern	England	518	603
15-Jan	Saint Tarsicia Saint	France		600
15-Jan	Saint Ceolwulf	Britain		c. 764
15-Jan	Saint Emebert	Belgium		715
15-Jan	Saint Teath	Wales		6th
16-Jan	Saint Fulgentius	Spain		c 633
17-Jan	Saint Mildgytha	England		c 676
19-Jan	Saint Canute IV of Ostrevant	King	1048	1086
19-Jan	Saint Fillan	Ireland		8th
24-Jan	Saint Cadoc	Wales		c 580
25-Jan	Saint Dwynwen	Wales		c. 460
26-Jan	Saint Margaret of Hungary	Hungary	1242	1270
26-Jan	Saint Paula	Rome	347	404
28-Jan	Saint Thomas d'Aquino	Italy	1225	1273
28-Jan	Blessed Charlemange	Franks		814
30-Jan	Saint Bathildis	Franks		680
30-Jan	Saint Adelgundis	France	630	684
31-Jan	Saint Judoc	England		c 668
31-Jan	Saint Aidan	Ireland		626

SAINTS DAILY
Kings, Queens, Popes, Princes, Princesses, Emperors, Hermits, Bishops

6

DAILY SAINTS WHOSE ANCESTRY IS KNOWN

1-Feb	Saint Sigebert of East Anglia	Franks	631	656
1-Feb	Saint Siagre of Austrasie	France		Late 8th
1-Feb	Saint Brigid	Ireland	c 453	c 523
2-Feb	Saint Adalbald		600	652
3-Feb	Saint Werberga	England	661	699
4-Feb	Saint Adele of Blois	England		1137
4-Feb	Saint Joan of Valois	France	1464	1505
5-Feb	Saint Avitus Of Vienne Bishop	Rome	451	525
6-Feb	Saint Melchu	Ireland		
6-Feb	Saint Mel	Ireland		c 490
8-Feb	Saint Wethoc	Brittany		5th
8-Feb	Saint Jacut	Brittany		5th
8-Feb	Saint Elfleda	England		714
9-Feb	Saint Teilo	Britain		c. 500
11-Feb	Saint Theodora	Byzantine		867
11-Feb	Saint Benedict of Aniane	France	750	821
12-Feb	Saint Humberline			1135
14-Feb	Blessed Conrad of Bavaria	Germany	C.1105	C.1154

SAINTS DAILY
Kings, Queens, Popes, Princes, Princesses, Emperors, Hermits, Bishops

7

DAILY SAINTS WHOSE ANCESTRY IS KNOWN

Date	Saint	Country	Born	Died
16-Feb	Saint Gilbert of Sempringham	England	1083	1189
17-Feb	Saint Loman	Ireland		c 450
18-Feb	Saint Angilbert	France	c 740	814
18-Feb	Saint Simon Apostle	Israel		1st
18-Feb	Saint Simeon	Israel		1st
21-Feb	Blessed Pepin of Landen	France		c 639
21-Feb	Saint Robert Southwell	England	1561	1593
23-Feb	Saint Milburga	England		c 715
23-Feb	Saint Jurmin	England		8th
25-Feb	Saint Aldeltrudis de Hainault	Belgium	bef 670	
25-Feb	Saint Aethelbert of Kent	England	560	616
25-Feb	Saint Bertha of Kent	Frankish		612
26-Feb	Saint Isabel of France	France		1270
27-Feb	Saint Leander of Seville	Spain	534	600
28-Feb	Blessed Hedwig of Poland	Poland	1374	1399
1-Mar	Saint Dewi	England		600
2-Mar	Saint Charles the Good	Denmark	1081	1127

SAINTS DAILY
Kings, Queens, Popes, Princes, Princesses, Emperors, Hermits, Bishops

DAILY SAINTS WHOSE ANCESTRY IS KNOWN

3-Mar	Saint Cunigunda of Luxemburg	Luxemberg	978	1033
3-Mar	Saint Non Saint	Wales		6th
3-Mar	Saint Anselm of Nonantola			803
3-Mar	Saint Winaloe	France		6th
4-Mar	Blessed Humbert III	France	1136	1189
4-Mar	Saint Casimir	France	1458	1484
5-Mar	Saint Piran	England	480	6th
6-Mar	Saint Chrodegang of Metz	France	712	766
6-Mar	Saint Kyneburga	England		c 680
6-Mar	Saint Kyneswide	England		c 680
6-Mar	Saint Agnes of Bohemia	Armenia	1205	1282
7-Mar	Saint Enodoch	Wales		6th
11-Mar	Saint Custennin ap Cadwy	Dumnonia	520	
11-Mar	Saint Constantine II of Scotland	Scotland	836	877
14-Mar	Saint Mathilda of Germany	Germany	892	967/68

SAINTS DAILY
Kings, Queens, Popes, Princes, Princesses, Emperors, Hermits, Bishops

DAILY SAINTS WHOSE ANCESTRY IS KNOWN

15-Mar	Saint Raymond Fitero	Aragon	1113	1162
16-Mar	Saint Dentlin	England		7th
16-Mar	Saint Eusebia	France		c 680
16-Mar	Saint Abban	Ireland		620
17-Mar	Saint Ceneu	Britain	374	
17-Mar	Saint Joseph of Arimathea	Israel		
17-Mar	Saint Paternus Pasrut	Scotland	305	
17-Mar	Saint Helen of the Host	Wales	330	
17-Mar	Saint Gertrude of Nivelles	France		659
17-Mar	Saint Gertrude	France	632	7th
17-Mar	Saint Patrick Saccatus	Ireland	385	461
18-Mar	Saint Edward "the martyr"	England		c 978
20-Mar	Saint Tetricus Bishop	France		572
21-Mar	Saint Enda	Ireland		c 530
22-Mar	Saint Darerca	Ireland	310	5th
24-Mar	Saint Catherine of Sweden	Sweden	1331	1381
26-Mar	Saint Margaret Clitherow	England	1556	1586
29-Mar	Saint Gwladys	Wales		5th

SAINTS DAILY
Kings, Queens, Popes, Princes, Princesses, Emperors, Hermits, Bishops

10

DAILY SAINTS WHOSE ANCESTRY IS KNOWN

29-Mar	Saint Gwynllyw Farfog	Wales	466	523
4-Apr	Blessed Aleth		1069	
4-Apr	Saint Isadore	Spain	c 500	c 600
5-Apr	Saint Derfel Gadarn	England		6th
5-Apr	Saint Ethelburga	Northumbria		647
6-Apr	Saint Brychan King of Brycheiniog	Wales	419	
9-Apr	Saint Madrun ferch Gwerthefyr	Gwent	440	
9-Apr	Saint Waldetrudis	France		640
9-Apr	Saint Hugo Bishop of Rouen	France		730
9-Apr	Saint Mary Cleopas	Israel		1st
13-Apr	Saint Ida of Loraine or Boulogne	Boulogne	1040	1113
13-Apr	Saint Hermengild	Spain		585
17-Apr	Saint Landericus	England		c. 660
19-Apr	Saint Geraud	France		c 1000
19-Apr	Saint Pope Leo IX,	France	1002	11th
21-Apr	Saint Beuno	England		?
22-Apr	Saint Opportuna	France		770

SAINTS DAILY
Kings, Queens, Popes, Princes, Princesses, Emperors, Hermits, Bishops

DAILY SAINTS WHOSE ANCESTRY IS KNOWN

27-Apr	Saint Floribert	France		746
27-Apr	Saint Enoder	Wales		6th
29-Apr	Saint Endellion	Wales		6th
30-Apr	Blessed Hildegard	France	754	783
1-May	Saint Joseph	Israel		1st
1-May	Saint Asaph	Wales		6th
1-May	Saint Sigismund de Bourgogne	France		523
2-May	Saint Mafalda	Portugal	1204	1252
3-May	Saint James the Lesser	Israel		1st
5-May	Saint Mauront	France		701
5-May	Saint Pius V Pope	Italy		1572
6-May	Saint Elizabeth of Hungary	Hungary	1207	
6-May	Saint Agnes of Bohemia	Armenia	1205	1282
6- May	Saint Eadbert	Great Britain		698
7-May	Saint Liudhard	France		c 602
10-May	Blessed Beatrice D'Este	Italy	1206	1226
11-May	Saint Walbert	Belgium		c 678
12-May	Blessed Joan of Portugal	Portugal	1452	1490
12-May	Saint Domitilla	Italy		1st
12-May	Saint Rictrudis	France		c 688
13-May	Saint Erconwald	England		693

SAINTS DAILY
Kings, Queens, Popes, Princes, Princesses, Emperors, Hermits, Bishops

DAILY SAINTS WHOSE ANCESTRY IS KNOWN

16-May	Saint Carranog	Wales		6th
18-May	Saint Elgiva of Wessex	England	942	944
18-May	Saint Eric IX of Sweden	Sweden		1160
19-May	Saint Dunstan	England	900	988
19-May	Saint Prudentiana	Rome		1st
21-May	Saint Contantine the Great	Rome		337
23-May	Saint Euphrosyne of Polotsk	Russia		1173
24-May	Saint David of Scotland	Scotland	1085	1153
26-May	Saint Dyfan	Wales		6th
27-May	Saint Bruno Bishop of Wurzburg	France		1045
28-May	Blessed Margaret Pole	England	1471	1541
30-May	Saint Fernando of Spain	Spain	1199	1252
31-May	Saint Mechildis	Holland	1125	1160
1-Jun	Saint Gracia	Cordoba	1071	
1-Jun	Saint Wistan	Prince	835	892
1-Jun	Saint Mary	Spain		1180
1-Jun	Saint Bernard	Spain		1180
3-Jun	Saint Clotilde of the Franks	Franks	475	545
5-Jun	Blessed Ferdinand	Portugal	1402	1443

SAINTS DAILY
Kings, Queens, Popes, Princes, Princesses, Emperors, Hermits, Bishops

13

DAILY SAINTS WHOSE ANCESTRY IS KNOWN

8-Jun	Saint Edgar the Peaceful	England	943	975
8-Jun	Saint Clodulphe Bishop	Metz	615	690
8-Jun	Saint William of York	England	c 1100	1154
9-Jun	Saint Columba	Ireland	c. 521	c 579
12-Jun	Blessed Jolenta	Hungary		1299
14-Jun	Saint Dogmael	Wales		6th
15-Jun	Saint Trillo	Wales		6th
15-Jun	Saint Edburga of Winchester	England		960
17-Jun	Saint Sanchia of Portugal	Portugal	1182	1229
17-Jun	Saint Nectan	Wales	468	510
17-Jun	Saint Teresa	Portugal	1181	13th
20-Jun	Saint Novatus	Rome		137
20-Jun	Saint Florentina	Spain		c 636
22-Jun	Saint Pulcheria	Italy	399	453
22-Jun	Saint Pontius Meropius Anicius Paulinus	Italy	354	431
22-Jun	Saint Thomas More	England	1477	1534
22-Jun	Saint Flavius	Italy		c. 96

SAINTS DAILY
Kings, Queens, Popes, Princes, Princesses, Emperors, Hermits, Bishops

DAILY SAINTS WHOSE ANCESTRY IS KNOWN

	Clemens			
23-Jun	Saint Etheldreda	England		679
27-Jun	Saint Lazlo of Hungary (d 1095)	Hungary		1095
28-Jun	Saint John Southworth	England	1592	1654
28-Jun	Saint Austell	Wales		6th
29-Jun	Saint Paul	Israel		c 67
30-Jun	Saint Eurgen of Llan Ilid	BRITAIN		6th
30-Jun	Saint Clotsind	France		714
1-Jul	Saint Leonorius			c. 570
1-Jul	Saint Veep	Wales		6th
2-Jul	Blessed Peter of Luxemborg	Luxemborg	1371	1399
2-Jul	Saint Oudoceus		536	625
4-Jul	Saint Isabel of Aragon	Portugal	1271	1336
5-Jul	Saint Gwen	Brittany		5th
5-Jul	Saint Morwenna	Wales		6th
5-Jul	Saint Fracan	Brittany		5th
6-Jul	Saint Sexburga	Kent		c 699
7-Jul	Saint Aubierge (Ethelburga)	England		c 647
7-Jul	Saint Ethelburga	England		664
7-Jul	Saint Ercongotha	England		660

SAINTS DAILY
Kings, Queens, Popes, Princes, Princesses, Emperors, Hermits, Bishops

15

DAILY SAINTS WHOSE ANCESTRY IS KNOWN

8-Jul	Saint Withburga	England		c 743
11-Jul	Saint Pius	Rome		155
11-Jul	Saint Olga of Kiev	Russia	879	969
13-Jul	Saint Henry II of Germany	Germany	972	1024
13-Jul	Saint Mildred Of Thanet	England		c 700
14-Jul	Blessed Boniface of Savoy	France		1270
15-Jul	Blessed Bernard of Baden	France	1429	1458
15-Jul	Saint Vladimir of Kiev	Russia	956	1015
15-Jul	Saint Edith of Polesworth	Viking		
16-Jul	Blessed Ermengard	Germany	c. 832	c. 866
16-Jul	Saint Reineldis	Belgium		680
17-Jul	Saint Cynwl	Wales		6th
17-Jul	Saint Kenelm	England		821
18-Jul	Saint Arnulf Bishop of Metz	Metz		635
18-Jul	Saint Edburga of Bicester	England		7th
20-Jul	Saint Etheldwitha	England	852	905
20-Jul	Saint Joseph Barsabas Apostle	Israel		1st
21-Jul	Saint Praxedes	Rome		mid 2nd

SAINTS DAILY
Kings, Queens, Popes, Princes, Princesses, Emperors, Hermits, Bishops

DAILY SAINTS WHOSE ANCESTRY IS KNOWN

22-Jul	Saint Mary Magdalene	Israel		1st
22-Jul	Saint Wandrille	France	635	665
23-Jul	Blessed Cunegund	Hungary	1224	1292
23-Jul	Saint Bridget of Sweden	Sweden	1303	1373
24-Jul	Blessed Louisa of Savoi	France	1461	1503
24-Jul	Saint Boris	Russia		1010
24-Jul	Saint Gleb	Russia		1010
24-Jul	Saint Menefrida	Wales		6th
25-Jul	Saint James the Greater	Israel		1st
28-Jul	Saint Sampson	Britain		565
29-Jul	Blessed Urban II Pope		1042	1099
29-Jul	Saint Olaf of Norway	Norway		1030
30-Jul	Saint Olaf of Skottkonung	Sweden	c 950	c 1024
30-Jul	Blessed Mannes	Spain		c. 1230
31-Jul	Saint Germannus d'Auxerre	Britain		6th
31-Jul	Saint Neot	Britain		9th
1-Aug	Saint Rioch	Ireland		c 480
1-Aug	Saint Almedha	Wales		6th
2-Aug	Saint Ethelritha	England		835
3-Aug	Saint Waltheof	Scotland		1160
7-Aug	Saint Claudia	Rome		1st

SAINTS DAILY
Kings, Queens, Popes, Princes, Princesses, Emperors, Hermits, Bishops

17

DAILY SAINTS WHOSE ANCESTRY IS KNOWN

8-Aug	Blessed Joan of Aza	Spain		c 1190
8-Aug	Saint Dominic	Spain	1170	1221
9-Aug	Saint Oswald	England	c. 605	642
12-Aug	Saint Merewenna	Wales		6th
13-Aug	Saint Radegund	Franks	499	
13-Aug	Blessed Gertrude of Altenburg	Hungary	1227	1297
16-Aug	Saint Stephen of Hungary	Hungary	977	1038
18-Aug	Saint Helena of Rome	Rome	250	330
19-Aug	Saint Louis of Toulouse	France		1297
20-Aug	Saint Oswin	England		651
20-Aug	Saint Bernard of Clairvaux	France	1090	1153
21-Aug	Saint Apollinaris Sidonius	Rome		480
22-Aug	Saint John Wall	England		1679
22-Aug	Saint Tydfil	Wales		6th
23-Aug	Saint Zaccaeus	Israel		116
24-Aug	Saint Batholomew	Israel		1st
25-Aug	Saint Louis IX of France	France	1214	1270
25-Aug	Saint Ebbe	England		683
28-Aug	Saint Rumwald	England		c 650
29-Aug	Saint Sebbi	England		695
30-Aug	Saint Pammachius	Italy		410
31-Aug	Saint Waltheof of Huntington	Northumbria	1045	1076

SAINTS DAILY
Kings, Queens, Popes, Princes, Princesses, Emperors, Hermits, Bishops

DAILY SAINTS WHOSE ANCESTRY IS KNOWN

1-Sep	Saint Nivard	France		c 670
3-Sep	Saint Hereswitha	Wessex		690
3-Sep	Saint Cuthburga	England		c. 725
4-Sep	Saint Ida d'Autun of Herzfeld	England	770	840
7-Sep	Saint Alchmund	Britain		781
7-Sep	Saint Madelberta	England		7th
7-Sep	Saint Clodoald	France	c 520	560
8-Sep	Saint Adela	Flanders	1009	1077
9-Sept	Blessed Seraphina Sforza	Italy	1432	1478
9-Sep	Saint Isaac Pahlav the Great	Armenia	351	438
10-Sep	Saint Edward Ambrose Barlow	England	1585	1681
11-Sep	Saint Deniol	Wales	c 535	584
12-Sep	Saint Eanswida	England		c. 640
12-Sep	Saint Eanswythe	England		640
16-Sep	Saint Ludmilla of Bohemia	Bohemia		
16-Sep	Saint Edith of Wilton	England		984
16-Sep	Saint Victor III	Italy	c 1027	1087

SAINTS DAILY
Kings, Queens, Popes, Princes, Princesses, Emperors, Hermits, Bishops

DAILY SAINTS WHOSE ANCESTRY IS KNOWN

18-Sep	Saint Richardis	Franks		c 895
20-Sep	Saint Vincent Madelgaire de Hainault	Hainault	635	677
21-Sep	Saint Michael of Cheringov	Russia		1246
21-Sep	Saint Mathew Apostle	Israel		1st
23-Sep	Saint Linus Bishop of Rome	Rome		c 76
28-Sep	Saint Wenceslaus I Vaclav	England	907	10th
28-Sep	Saint Blesilla	Rome	363	383
28-Sep	Saint Eustochium Julia	Rome	c 368	491
30-Sep	Saint Gregory the Enlightened	Armenia	c 240	c 326
1-Oct	Saint Umbrafael	England		505
1-Oct	Saint Remi	France	730	770
1-Oct	Saint Bavo	France		7th
2-Oct	Saint Leodegar	France	616	679
2-Oct	Saint Thomas de Cantelou	Italy	1218	1282
3-Oct	Saint Hesychius of Vienne	Italy		c. 6th

SAINTS DAILY
Kings, Queens, Popes, Princes, Princesses, Emperors, Hermits, Bishops

DAILY SAINTS WHOSE ANCESTRY IS KNOWN

5-Oct	Saint Apollinaris of Vienne	Rome		520
5-Oct	Saint Galla			c. 550
6-Oct	Saint Ephipanes	France		800
6-Oct	Saint Gregory of Utrecht	Austrasia		800
6-Oct	Blessed Adalbero		1045	1090
7-Oct	Saint Osyth of Penda	Penda	650	700
7-Oct	Saint Osyth	England	650	699
10-Oct	Saint Francis Borgia	Italy		16th
11-Oct	Saint Firminus of Uzes	France		553
12-Oct	Saint Edwin of Wessex	Northumbria	584	633
13-Oct	Saint Comgan	England		8th
13-Oct	Saint Gerald of Aurillac	France		909
13-Oct	Saint Edward the Confessor	England		1066
16-Oct	Saint Hedwig	Silesia		
16-Oct	Saint Balderic	France		7th
17-Oct	Saint Ethelred	Kent		670
17-Oct	Saint Ethelbricht	Kent		670
18-Oct	Saint Keyna	Wales		
18-Oct	Saint Gwen	Wales		5th

SAINTS DAILY
Kings, Queens, Popes, Princes, Princesses, Emperors, Hermits, Bishops

DAILY SAINTS WHOSE ANCESTRY IS KNOWN

19-Oct	Saint Elfleda	England		1000
19-Oct	Saint Phillip Howard	England	1556	1595
21-Oct	Saint Ursula	Dumonia	305	
22-Oct	Saint Mary Salome	Israel		1st
23-Oct	Saint Anicius Manlius Severius	Italy	480	524
23-Oct	Saint Ignatius of Constaninople		799	877
23-Oct	Saint Ode	Aquitaine		688
23-Oct	Saint Clether	Wales		6th
24-Oct	Saint Maglor	England		6th
26-Oct	Saint Alfred the Great	England		899
26-Oct	Saint Eadfrid	Great Britain		675
26-Oct	Saint Evatistus	Rome		105
28-Oct	Saint Judas Apostle	Israel		1st
1-Nov	Saint Dingad	Wales		
1-Nov	Saint Cadfan	Wales	530	590
2-Nov	Saint Maura	Ireland		5th
3-Nov	Saint Hubert	France		727
3-Nov	Saint Winifred	England	565	
4-Nov	Saint Emeric	Hungary		1031
4-Nov	Saint Charles Borromeo	Italy	1538	1584

SAINTS DAILY
Kings, Queens, Popes, Princes, Princesses, Emperors, Hermits, Bishops

DAILY SAINTS WHOSE ANCESTRY IS KNOWN

4-Nov	Blessed Francis D' Amboise	France	1427	1485
5-Nov	Saint Bertilia	Belgium		c 687
6-Nov	Saint Margaret of Lorraine	France	1463	1521
6-Nov	Saint Edwen	England		600
6-Nov	Saint Illtud Saint	Britain		c 535
6-Nov	Saint Winnoc	England		c 717
6-Nov	Blessed Nonius	Portugal	1360	1431
6-Nov	Blessed Joan Mary de Maille	France		1414
7-Nov	Saint Engelbert	England	1187	1225
8-Nov	Saint Cybi	England	490	555
8-Nov	Saint Tysilio	England		c 640
9-Nov	Saint Pabo	England		530
12-Nov	Saint Kadwalladyr of North Wales	Wales		664
12-Nov	Saint Cadwaladr	England	c. 615	664
14-Nov	Saint Alberic	France		784

SAINTS DAILY
Kings, Queens, Popes, Princes, Princesses, Emperors, Hermits, Bishops

DAILY SAINTS WHOSE ANCESTRY IS KNOWN

14-Nov	Saint Laurence O'Toole	England	1128	1180
15-Nov	Saint Leopold III of Austria	Austria	1073	1136
16-Nov	Saint Eucherius	France		449
16-Nov	Saint Margaret of Scotland	Scotland	1046	1093
17-Nov	Saint Gregory Bishop Of Tours	France	583	594
17-Nov	Saint Hilda	England	614	680
17-Nov	Blessed Salome	Poland	1202	1268
18-Nov	Saint Mabyn	Wales		6th
19-Nov	Saint Narses Pahlav the I	Armenia	335	373
19-Nov	Saint Ermenburga	England		c 650
21-Nov	Saint Albert of Louvain	France		1193
22-Nov	Saint Tigrida	Spain		11th
24-Nov	Saint Eanfleda	England		c 700
27-Nov	Saint Guntramus	France	c. 488	592
27-Nov	Saint Cungar	Britain	c. 488	550
29-Nov	Saint Sadwrn Farchog	Britain		6th
29-Nov	Saint Ethelwin	Britain		7th

SAINTS DAILY
Kings, Queens, Popes, Princes, Princesses, Emperors, Hermits, Bishops

DAILY SAINTS WHOSE ANCESTRY IS KNOWN

29-Nov	Saint Egelwine	Britain		7th
30-Nov	Saint Tudwal	Britain		400
1-Dec	Saint Tudwal	Britain		c. 564
4-Dec	Saint Osmund	France		1099
6-Dec	Saint Gertrude of Hamage	Prussia	540	
9-Dec	Saint Budoc	England		7th
9-Dec	Saint Ethelgiva	England		896
13-Dec	Saint Odile	France		c. 720
16-Dec	Saint Adelaide of Italy	Italy		999
17-Dec	Saint Judicael of Domnonee	Domnonee		658
17-Dec	Saint Tydecho	Britain		6th
17-Dec	Saint Begga	Landen		694
18-Dec	Saint Gondolfus Bishop de d'Aquitaine	Aquitaine	530	c 599
18-Dec	Saint Flannan	Ireland		7th
22-Dec	Blessed Jutta	Germany	1111	1136
23-Dec	Blessed Margaret of Savoy	Italy	1382	1464
23-Dec	Saint Dagobert II of Franks	Franks		679
24-Dec	Saint Irmina	France		708
24-Dec	Saint Adele of Austrasia	France		8th

SAINTS DAILY
Kings, Queens, Popes, Princes, Princesses, Emperors, Hermits, Bishops

DAILY SAINTS WHOSE ANCESTRY IS KNOWN

25-Dec	Saint Alburga	England	777	c 800
25-Dec	Saint Adalsind	France		c 715
27-Dec	Saint John Zebedee	Israel		1st
29-Dec	Saint Thomas Beckett	England	1118	1170
29-Dec	Blessed William Howard	England	1614	1680
31-Dec	Saint Offa	England		709

SAINTS DAILY
Kings, Queens, Popes, Princes, Princesses, Emperors, Hermits, Bishops

DAILY SAINTS WHOSE ANCESTRY IS KNOWN

Saints of January

FEAST DAY	SAINT	COUNTRY	BORN	DIED
1-Jan	Saint Fanchea	Ireland		c 530
1-Jan	Blessed Adalbero	France		1128
2-Jan	Saint Adalhard	France	753	827
2-Jan	Blessed Ayrald	France		1146
2-Jan	Saint Adelard	France	753	827
3-Jan	Saint Wenodog	Wales		6th
4-Jan	Saint Gregory Bishop of Langres	France		539
6-Jan	Saint Wiltrude	France	937	986
7-Jan	Saint Canute the Pious	Denmark	1096	1130
7-Jan	Saint Kentigerna	Ireland		734
8-Jan	Saint Gudula	Belgium		712
10-Jan	Saint Pietro I Orseolo	Italy	935	987
10-Jan	Blessed Gregory X	Italy	1210	1276
11-Jan	Saint Fidelmia	Ireland		c. 250

SAINTS DAILY
Kings, Queens, Popes, Princes, Princesses, Emperors, Hermits, Bishops

DAILY SAINTS WHOSE ANCESTRY IS KNOWN

11-Jan	Saint Ethenia	Ireland		c. 250
11-Jan	Saint Hyginus	Rome		140
13-Jan	Saint Kentigern	England	518	603
15-Jan	Saint Tarsicia Saint	France		600
15-Jan	Saint Ceolwulf	Britain		c. 764
15-Jan	Saint Emebert	Belgium		715
15-Jan	Saint Teath	Wales		6th
16-Jan	Saint Fulgentius	Spain		c 633
17-Jan	Saint Mildgytha	England		c 676
19-Jan	Saint Canute IV of Ostrevant	King	1048	1086
19-Jan	Saint Fillan	Ireland		8th
24-Jan	Saint Cadoc	Wales		c 580
25-Jan	Saint Dwynwen	Wales		c. 460
26-Jan	Saint Margaret of Hungary	Hungary	1242	1270
26-Jan	Saint Paula	Rome	347	404
28-Jan	Saint Thomas d'Aquino	Italy	1225	1273
28-Jan	Blessed Charlemange	Franks		814
30-Jan	Saint Bathildis	Franks		680
30-Jan	Saint Adelgundis	France	630	684
31-Jan	Saint Judoc	England		c 668
31-Jan	Saint Aidan	Ireland		626

SAINTS DAILY
Kings, Queens, Popes, Princes, Princesses, Emperors, Hermits, Bishops

28

DAILY SAINTS WHOSE ANCESTRY IS KNOWN

TABLE TWO SAINTS OF JANUARY

January 1 Saint Fanchea
Country: Ireland   **Date:** 585

Father: Ainmire De Ireland   Mother: Brigid
Spouse: Unknown   Siblings: Unknown

Ancestors: Fergus De Meath; Tuathal Teachtmar King of Ireland. And so Magog the son of Japeth the son of Noah.

Branches of the Tree: Fergus De Meath who was Saint Enda Great Grandfather had a son Dermot who was a King of Ireland.

Biography: Saint Fanchea was the sister of Saint Ends, or Endeus. She was born in Clogher and founded Rossary Convent in Fermanagh Ireland. Also was called Garbh Fanchea. She was buried at Killane.

January 1   *Blessed Adalbero*
Feastday: January 1   Date: d.1128

Family: Father: Godfrey I, The Bearded, Earl of Brussels
Mother: Ida De Nemur, De Chiny
Spouse: Unknown   Siblings: GodfreyII, Count of Louvain

Country: France

Ancestors: Ancestors include Odin, Kings of Denmark,

SAINTS DAILY
Kings, Queens, Popes, Princes, Princesses, Emperors, Hermits, Bishops

DAILY SAINTS WHOSE ANCESTRY IS KNOWN

Branches of the Tree This is the branch of the tree near those who went on the First Crusade. The noble Brabant and the Louvain Dukes and Counts are near in this branch.

Biography: Blessed Adalbero was brother to Godfrey Le Barbu of Louvain. He founded the St. Giles Monastery and was Bishop of Liege.

January 2   *Saint Adalhard*

Date: 827

Family: Father: Bernard   Mother: Unknown
Spouse: Unknown   Siblings: Pippin II

Country: Austrasia

Ancestors: Charles Martel is the Grandfather of Saint Adalhard.

Branches of the Tree: Charles Martel is the Grandfather of Charlemagne as well as Saint Adalhard.

Biography: Saint Adalhard was the brother of Pippin II. He is patron of French churches and towns. He was the nephew of Charles Martel and cousin of Charlemagne. Therefore he was raised as a nobleman at the court of his cousin Charlemagne. He stayed in court until age twenty when he entered a monastery of Corbie in Picardy. He then went to Monte Cassino, until Charlemagne asked him to return to court. While at Corbie he was elected abbot and then became Prime Minister to Pepin, the son of Charlemagne, King of Italy. He was banished to Hermoutier when involved in the political struggles of the royal family in 814. He returned to the court of Louis the Pious after seven years of exile. Adelard died on January 2, 827.

SAINTS DAILY
Kings, Queens, Popes, Princes, Princesses, Emperors, Hermits, Bishops

DAILY SAINTS WHOSE ANCESTRY IS KNOWN

January 2 *Blessed Ayrald*
Feastday: Jan 2   **Date:** d 1146

Family:
Parents: Father: William II The Great Count of Burgundy
         Mother: Stephanie De Longwy
Spouse: None   Children: None   Siblings: Sibylle of Burgundy, Etienne I "Tete-hardi De Macon, Raymond of Burgundy Conde de Galicia y Coimbr, Gisele Burgundy of, Callistus II Pope

Ancestry: King Louis I of France is eleven generations Blessed Ayrald's Ancestor. Because King Louis I of France was Charlemange's son Blessed Ayrald has similar ancestry.

Branch of the Tree: The rulers of Burgundy France seem to intermarry with the Kings of Italy in this branch of the tree and after twelve generations to Charlemange.

Biography: Blessed Ayrald was brother to Pope CallistusII and son of Count William II. King Raymond of Castile and Count Henry of Portugal were also his brothers. At Portes he joined the Cartusians and in time became prior. He was appointed bishop of Maurienne.

January 2   *Saint Adelard*
Country: France   **Date:** 827   **Patron:** Gardeners

Family: Father: Bernard   Mother: Unknown
Spouse: Unknown   Siblings: Pippin II

Ancestors: Charles Martel is the Grandfather of Saint Adalhard.

SAINTS DAILY
Kings, Queens, Popes, Princes, Princesses, Emperors, Hermits, Bishops

DAILY SAINTS WHOSE ANCESTRY IS KNOWN

Branches of the Tree: Charles Martel is the Grandfather of Charlemagne as well as Saint Adalhard.

Biography:
Saint Adalhard was the brother of Pippin II. He is patron of French churches and towns. He was the nephew of Charles Martel and cousin of Charlemagne. Therefore he was raised as a nobleman at the court of his cousin Charlemagne. He stayed in court until age twenty when he entered a monastery of Corbie in Picardy. He then went to Monte Cassino, until Charlemagne asked him to return to court. While at Corbie he was elected abbot and then became Prime Minister to Pepin, the son of Charlemagne, King of Italy. He was banished to Hermoutier when involved in the political struggles of the royal family in 814. He returned to the court of Louis the Pious after seven years of exile. Adelard died on January 2, 827.

January 3   Saint Wenodog

Family:
Parents: Father-Saint Brychan   Mother- Rigrawst b: 0450
Husband: Unknown
Children: Unknown

Biography:
There is a Saint Wenog listed as a Saint of Wales with no details of his life known. This may be Saint Wenodog.

January 4   Saint Gregory Bishop of Langres

Country: France   *Date:* d. 539

Family: Father: Unknown   Mother: Unknown
Spouse: Unknown   Siblings: Unknown
Offspring: Georgia; Tetricus Bishop Of Langres

SAINTS DAILY
 Kings, Queens, Popes, Princes, Princesses, Emperors, Hermits, Bishops

DAILY SAINTS WHOSE ANCESTRY IS KNOWN

Ancestors: None known.

Branches of the Tree: Offspring Georgia is the Grandfather of Saint Gregory Bishop of Tours. Georgia married Leocardia, who had a different husband Mundéric des Francs Ripuaires. He is the father of Gondolfus who is a saint in his own right. Saint Gondolfus has descendents such as Saint Ladislaus of Hungary, Saint Louis IX of France, Saint Leopold III of Austria, Saint Leutwinus, Saint Margaret, Saint William of Toulouse, Saint Ansigisel, Saint Hedwig, Saint Clotilde, Saint Fernando III of Spain, Saint Ida, Saint Irene of Hungary, Saint Isabelle of Aragon, and Saint Nithard the Chronicler are all Descendents also King of England Edward III Plantagenet, King of Naples Charles II, King of France Louis VIII are also Descendents.

Biography: Saint Gregory ruled the area wisely as Count of Autun, France. He ruled well for forty years until Armentaris, his wife died, so he devoted himself to a religious life. He became Bishop of Langres by election, was devoted to duty, and known for his austerities and charities. He had his epitaph written by Venantius Forunatus and his great grandson St. Gregory of Tours wrote his biography.

January 6 — *Saint Wiltrude*

Feastday: January 6   Date: b. 937 d. 986

Family: Father: Giselbert Duc de Lorraine   Mother: Gerberge of Saxony Abbess of Notre Dame
Spouse: Duke Berthold of Bavaria   Siblings: Gerberge Princess of Lorraine, Henri Duke of Lorraine, Alberade de Lorraine

Country: France

Ancestors: Henry the Fowler is a grandfather and Saint Matilda is her grandmother. Blessed Charlemange is a six generation ancestor. Therefore King David of Judah and Israel is an

SAINTS DAILY
Kings, Queens, Popes, Princes, Princesses, Emperors, Hermits, Bishops

DAILY SAINTS WHOSE ANCESTRY IS KNOWN

ancestor and the line of the franks to Joseph the Israelite. Also Israelites Benjamin, Levi, Zebulon, and Judah lines from King David of Judah and Israel and his decendent on the line of Solomon to Reheboam.

Branches of the Tree: This is the Emperors lines of France and Germany.

Biography: Saint Wiltrudis became a nun when her husband Duke Berthold of Bavaria died about 947. She was noted for her piety. She founded a convent called Bergen in 976.

January 7   Saint Canute The Pious of Wendon

Country: Denmark   *Date:* c 1096- 1130

Family: Parents: Father- Erik I The Ever good King of Denmark Mother- Bothilde Thorgautsdottir
Wife: Ingeborg of Novgorod of Kiev   Children: Valdermar Knutsson I "The Great" King of Denmark

Ancestry: King of Denmark ancestry is not known.

Descendents: Valdermar Knutsson I "The Great" King of Denmark
Otto I Duke Of Brunswick-Lhuneburg
Stefan II Duke Of Bavaria-Landshut

Biography: Born at Roskilde, he stayed in the Saxon Court as he was the good king Eric's second son. He was the Duke of Southern Jutland with ideals of feudalism and military organization. He was murdered by two of his cousins, after

SAINTS DAILY
Kings, Queens, Popes, Princes, Princesses, Emperors, Hermits, Bishops

DAILY SAINTS WHOSE ANCESTRY IS KNOWN

becoming a rival of his Uncle King Niels. Canute's son Valdemar I requested his father's canonization after becoming the King of Denmark. Alexander III canonized him in 1169. Archbishops of Lund and Uppsala presented evidence about Canute's life and miracles. He is regarded as a martyr in Denmark.

January 7   Saint Kentigerna Of Loch Lomond

Country: Leinster, Ireland   **Date:** 734

Family: Father: Cellach Cualann King Of Leinster
       Mother: Mugain
Spouse: Unknown   Siblings: Conchenn

Ancestors: Saint Ethelburga mother is Saint Hereswitha. Further back ancestry is not known. Woden and Frigg are Ancestors. Saint Cyllin is an Ancestor. Ancestors that were the Kings of Siluria. Generations previous to this they were the Kings of Britain. The line then goes back to Zerah, whose father is Judah. This line also marries Anna Arimathea who is the daughter of Joseph of Arimathea. A little know fact of the biblical character of Joseph of Arimathea is that he is the son of Mathat, who is in the line of Nathan that is listed in the New Testament book of Luke. So Saint Cyllin is descended from the Davidic line of Nathan and so from Judah thru Perez, and also as previously mentioned thru Judah's son Zerah.

Branches of the Tree: Kings of East Anglia

Biography: Saint Kentigerna was a widowed hermitess. She was the mother of St. Coellan and daughter of Cellach the prince of Leinster, Ireland. She went to Ichebroida Island in Loch Lomond, Scotland. A church there is dedicated to her memory.

SAINTS DAILY
Kings, Queens, Popes, Princes, Princesses, Emperors, Hermits, Bishops

DAILY SAINTS WHOSE ANCESTRY IS KNOWN

January 8 *Saint Gudula*
Country: Belgium   **Date:** 712

Family: Father: Theuderic (Thierry) III (King of Neustria)
Mother: Saint Amalaberga de Neustria Saint
Spouse: Unknown   Siblings: Chrotlind des Francs; Saint Reinildis

Ancestors: Saint Bathildis is the grandmother, and Saint Amalberga is the mother. Notable ancestors include Clovis I and Saint Clotidle who started the merovigian dynasty.

Branches of the Tree: This is the branch of Clovis the Frankish King and Saint Bathildis.

Biography: Saint Gudula was the sister of Saint Reinildis. Her mother was Saint Amalbera. She was the daughter of Count Witger, and had a sibling Chrotlind des Francs. She was the patroness of Brussels, Belgium. She was also called Ergoule. Saint Gudula was educated by Saint Gertrude of Nivelles. Saint Gudula was fortunate to live at the family castle of Morzelles, until Gertrude died. In 664 she then dedicated herself to God. Saint Gudula was known for her great charity.

January 10 *Saint Pietro I Orseolo*
Country: Italy   *Date:* 928-987

Family: Parents: Father- Pietro Orseolo Mother- Unknown
Wife: Felicita di Malpiero   Children: Pietro II Orseolo (Doge of Venice)

Ancestry: Ancestry past father unknown.

Descendents: Saint Isabella of Aragon and Saint Leopold III of Austria are descendents.

SAINTS DAILY
Kings, Queens, Popes, Princes, Princesses, Emperors, Hermits, Bishops

DAILY SAINTS WHOSE ANCESTRY IS KNOWN

Ryksa Princess of Silesia, and King Edward IV of England are descendents.

Biography: Also called Peter Orseolo he was a Benedictine hermit. As a member of one of the most noble houses of Venice and, at the age of twenty, became an admiral in the Venetian Navy. He was elected Doge of Venice in 967 after a series of successful campaigns against the Dalmatian pirates. He supposedly secured his elevation by poisoning his predecessor Peter Candiani IV, as St. Peter Damian charged. Peter ruled with consummate skill for two years assisting Venice to get thru a series of political crises. He disappeared from Venice and secretly, without any warning and without informing his family he entered the Benedictine abbey of Cuxa, in the Spanish Pyrenees. He worked as a humble sacrist devoting himself to a life of severe austerity and asceticism, until St. Romuald suggested that he become a hermit. He lived alone until his death.

January 10   *Blessed Gregory X*
Country: Italy   **Date:** 1210-1276

Family: Father: Unknown   Mother: Unknown
Spouse: Unknown   Siblings: Unknown

Ancestors: Unknown

Branches of the Tree: This branch of the tree will lead directly down to the Valois Family of the royalty of France.

Biography: Christened Theobald Visconti he was born of a distinguished family at Piacenza Italy. At Paris and Liege he studied canon law and became archdeacon of Liege. He accompanied Cardinal Ottonboni on a mission to England. He was at Acre on pilgrimage to the Holy Land when he was informed that though he was not yet ordained, he had been selected as Pope. This selection was done by a committee of six

SAINTS DAILY
Kings, Queens, Popes, Princes, Princesses, Emperors, Hermits, Bishops

DAILY SAINTS WHOSE ANCESTRY IS KNOWN

cardinals who had been chosen to select a Pope when a candidate had not been selected by the cardinals at Vitervo to fill the pontifical throne, which had been vacant for three years. So he returned to Rome and was ordained a priest on March 19, and then was consecrated pope on March 27, 1272, taking the name Gregory X. There was warfare between the Guelphs and the Guilbellines, which he labored to end. Florence became under interdict at his orders for refusing efforts at reconciliation with its neighbors. Blessed Gregory X also approved Rudolph of Hapsburg as German Emperor. Blessed Gregory convoked the fourteenth General Council at Lyons in 1274, Which effected a short-lived reunion of the Eastern churches with Rome. He was however unsuccessful at launching a crusade. He died at Tezzo, Italy, on his was back from the Council on January 10. His cult was approved in 1713.

January 11 *Saint Fidelmia*

Country: Ireland **Date:** 1st Century

Family: Father: King Laoghaire Of Ireland
Mother: Unknown
Spouse: Unknown Siblings: Saint Ethenea

Ancestors: Marcomir IV and also the Kings of Britain leading to Tros, and then Zerah the son of Judah the Israelite.

Branches of the Tree: This is the branch of the tree of the Kings of Ireland and Scotland, Fergus is quite close in this branch of the tree.

Biography: One of the two of the first converts of St. Patrick, one of the daughters of King Laoghaire. Tradition states that St. Patrick gave her the veil and then died after taking holy communion.

SAINTS DAILY
Kings, Queens, Popes, Princes, Princesses, Emperors, Hermits, Bishops

DAILY SAINTS WHOSE ANCESTRY IS KNOWN

January 11 *Saint Ethenea*

Country: Ireland **Date:** 1st Century

Family: Father: King Laoghaire Of Ireland
　　Mother: Unknown
Spouse: Unknown   Siblings: Saint Fidelmia

Ancestors: Marcomir IV and also the Kings of Britain leading to Tros, and then Zerah the son of Judah the Israelite.

Branches of the Tree: This is the branch of the tree of the Kings of Ireland and Scotland, Fergus is quite close in this branch of the tree.

Biography: One of the two of the first converts of St. Patrick, one of the daughters of King Laoghaire. Tradition states that St. Patrick gave her the veil and then died after taking holy communion.

January 11 *Saint Hyginus*

Date: ruled the papacy 136-140

Family: Father: Saint Evaristus   Mother: Unknown
Unknown Spouse: Unknown   Siblings: unknown
Children: Unknown

Country: Israel

Ancestors: See James the Lesser Apostles ancestry.

Branches of the Tree: This is the branch of the tree right on the descent of Saint James the Lesser Apostle.

Biography: Saint Hyginus organized the degrees of the clergy. Antoniunus Pius ordered that Christians should be left alone during his pontificate. He was forced to excommunicate Cerdo who taught there was two Gods. (dualistic Gnosticism). Despite the emperor Antoniunus Pius's policy Saint Hyginus was

SAINTS DAILY
Kings, Queens, Popes, Princes, Princesses, Emperors, Hermits, Bishops

DAILY SAINTS WHOSE ANCESTRY IS KNOWN

martyred after four years. Feastday Rome, January 11. Feastday Athens, January 19.

January 13   *Saint Kentigern*

Country: Ireland   **Date:** d. 603   **Patron:** Glasgow
Scotland

Family: Father: Garthrwys   Mother: Denyw
Spouse: None   Siblings: Saint Comgan

Ancestors: King Pharamond of France about 370 AD is an ancestors also Sunno and the line to Joseph the Israelite and so a descendent of Abraham.

Branches of the Tree: The Frankish kings about 350 years before Charlemagne is where the branch ties into the tree.

Biography: The Strathclyde Britons's first Bishop was Saint Kentigern Mungo his nickname means "dear one" or "darling" he was the son of the British princess. Tradition states raised by Saint Serf he became a hermit near Glasgow Scotland. consecrated a Bishop about 540 he was driven into exile. Saint Kentigern went to speak with Saint David in Wales possibly there he founded Asaph Monastery at Llanelwy. Returning to Scotland in 553 to continue his labors he is a patron of Glasgow. He is also venerated as the apostle of Northwest England and South Western Scotland.

January 15   *Saint Emebert*

Country: Belgium   **Date:** 710

Family: Father: Theuderic (Thierry) III (King of Neustria)
          Mother: Saint Amalaberga de Neustria Saint

SAINTS DAILY
Kings, Queens, Popes, Princes, Princesses, Emperors, Hermits, Bishops

DAILY SAINTS WHOSE ANCESTRY IS KNOWN

Spouse: Unknown   Siblings: Chrotlind des Francs; Saint Reinildis; Saint Gudula

Ancestors: Saint Bathildis is the grandmother, and Saint Amalberga is the mother. Notable ancestors include Clovis I and Saint Clotidle who started the merovigian dynasty.

Branches of the Tree: This is the branch of Clovis the Frankish King and Saint Bathildis.

Biography: A bishop of Cambrai, in Flanders, Belgium. His father was the King of Neustria and his mother was Saint Amalaberga. He was a brother of Sts. Gudula and Reineldi.

January 15 *Saint Ceolwulf*

Feastday: January 15   Date: d. c 764

Family: Father: Cuthwine   Mother: unknown
Spouse: unknown   Siblings Cenred   Children: unknown

Country: Britain

Ancestors: A few generations back the fathers of Northumbria are found

Branches of the Tree: A few generations back the line becomes close to King Aelli the father of Saint Edwin. This is the area of the Northumbria Saints of Britain.

Biography: Saint Ceolwulf was a king in Northumbria. He resigned in 738 after reigning eight years to become a monk. He became a monk at Lindesfarne. Father Bede dedicated his Ecclesiastical History to the "Most Glorius King Ceolwulf".

SAINTS DAILY
Kings, Queens, Popes, Princes, Princesses, Emperors, Hermits, Bishops

DAILY SAINTS WHOSE ANCESTRY IS KNOWN

January 15 *Saint Tarsicia*
Country: France   **Date:** 600

Family: Father: Ansbertus Of Moselle   Mother: Blithildes Of France
Spouse: Theodegotho Princess   Siblings: Ferrolus Saint; Arnoul Margrave Of Schelde

Ancestors: Ancestors include Faramund, and so the line of Joseph the Israelite. Also found is a line of Ancient Britain which goes to Priam, and so to Zerah son of Judah the Israelite.

Biography: Saint Tarsicia was the sister of Saint Ferroulus. She was a hermit and a Virgin. The Frankish king Clotaire I was her Grandfather. She spent most of her life as a hermit near Rode, France.

January 15 *Saint Teath*
Date: d. Sixth   Feastday: January 15

Family:
Parents: Father-Saint Brychan Mother- Rigrawst b: 0450

Children: Unknown

Biography:
A Cornwall Church bears her name. She may also be Saint Ita.

January 16 *Saint Fulgentius*
Country: Cartagena Spain   **Date:** 633

Family: Father: Severinum , Count Of Cartagena   Mother: Theodora
Spouse: None   Siblings: Theodosia; Leander of Seville Saint; Florentina Saint; Isadore Saint

Ancestors: Not much Ancestry is Known

SAINTS DAILY
 Kings, Queens, Popes, Princes, Princesses, Emperors, Hermits, Bishops

DAILY SAINTS WHOSE ANCESTRY IS KNOWN

Biography: Saint Fulgentius was from a large family of Saints. He was brother of St. Isidore, St. Leander, and St. Florentina. Fulgentius was the bishop of Elijah, in Andalusia, Spain.

January 17 *Saint Mildgytha*
Country: Great Britain   **Date:** 676

Family: Father: Merewald of Mercia   Mother: Saint Ermenburga
Spouse: Unknown   Siblings: Milburga Saint; Mildregytha Saint;

Ancestors: The line of the King of Mercia Penda who is the grandfather goes to Woden and Frigg.

Biography: Saint Mildgytha was from a family of Saints, her mother and two siblings became saints. She was a Benedictine nun, the daughter of Saint Ermenburga. She was a princess of Mercia. Her mother presented her the veil on the Isle of Thanet. In later years she became abbess of a Northumbrian convent.

January 19 *Saint Canute IV Svendsson*
Country: Denmark   *Date: c. 1186*

Family: Parents: Father- Svend II Ulfsson (Estridssen) King Of Denmark
Mother- Concubine Rannveig Tordsdatter Wife: Adele Flandern
Children: Carl,"The Dane" Knutsson Prince Of Denmark; Cecilie Knudsdatter Princess Of Denmark; Ingegard Knudsatter Princess Of Denmark

Ancestry: Kings of Sweden and Denmark are present as well as the line that goes to Asgard to Odin and Frigg.

SAINTS DAILY
Kings, Queens, Popes, Princes, Princesses, Emperors, Hermits, Bishops

DAILY SAINTS WHOSE ANCESTRY IS KNOWN

Descendents: Ingegard Knutsdatter Princess Of Denmark.; Cecilia Knutsdatter Princess Of Denmark Carl The Dane Prince Of Denmark

Biography: Sometimes called Knud Saint Canute was the martyred King of Denmark. The son of King Sven II Estridson of Denmark he was born from a concubine and is illegitimate. His brother Harald III Hen held the crown until 1081 when Saint Canute succeeded him. Canute built churches and monasteries then the sister of Count Robert of Flanders captivated him and he married her, the fair Adela. In 1085, he planned an invasion of England, but the nobles of the court rebelled against him when in 1085 he planned to invade England. The isle of Funen is where he then fled to away from the nobles of the court. There, were slain there in the church of St. Alban were Canute, his brother Benedict, and seventeen companions. Saint Canute's cult was authorized in 1101 by Pope Paschal II.

January 19   *Saint Fillan*

Country: Ireland   **Date:** 8th Century

Father: Feriach Saint   Mother: Kentigerna Of Loch Lomond
Spouse: Unknown   Siblings: Unknown

Ancestors: Only about two generations are unknown

Branches of the Tree: Saint Kentigerna sibling has descendents that are the Irish People.

Biography: Saint Fillan, son of Feriach and St. Kentigerna, also is known as using the name of Foelan. He accompanied his mother from Ireland to Scotland after becoming a monk. He lived near Saint Andrew's monastery as a hermit for many years, and then Saint Fillan was elected Abbot. He resumed his eremitical life at Glendochart Pertchire after resigning being Abbot. Here he built a church and was known for his miracles.

SAINTS DAILY
 Kings, Queens, Popes, Princes, Princesses, Emperors, Hermits, Bishops

DAILY SAINTS WHOSE ANCESTRY IS KNOWN

A Legend states that a wolf killed his Ox that was hauling supplies to build his church. He used prayer and the wolf took the Ox's place. On January 19 Saint Fillian died.

January 24   *Saint Cadoc*

Country: English Wales   **Date:** 580

Family: Father: Gwynllyw Farfog (King of Gwynllwg) Saint
Mother: Gwladys verch Brychan Saint
Spouse: Unknown   Siblings: Cadog Ddoeth (King of Gwynllwg) Saint; Maches Saint

Ancestors: Saint Brychan is an Ancestor, of which only a few generations are known on father's side. Saint Helen of the Host is known as Brychan's Mother's Ancestor.

Branches of the Tree: This is the branch of the tree in the vicinity of Saint Brychan

Biography: Saint Cadoc is also known and Cadvael, Docus, and Cathmael. He was a welsh bishop and martyr. He founded Llancarfan Monastery near Cardiff, Wales. After this he became a missionary on the coast of Brittany in France. He was martyred by the Saxons near Weedon England after returning to Britain during the Saxon occupation of the British lands.

January 25   *Saint Dwynwen verch Brychan*

Date: d. c. 460. Feastday: January 25

Family:
Parents: Father-Saint Brychan   Mother- Rigrawst b: 0450

Children: Unknown

SAINTS DAILY
 Kings, Queens, Popes, Princes, Princesses, Emperors, Hermits, Bishops

45

DAILY SAINTS WHOSE ANCESTRY IS KNOWN

Biography:
She is credited with the saying "Nothing wins hearts like Cheerfulness". Saint Dwynwen settled in Anglesey where her name is retained in Llanddwyn and Porthddwyn. Her church was the goal of the sick and especially young men and maidens. Saint Dwynwen is the Welsh patron of lovers. There is a legend that says that a certain young man Maelon wished to marry, however she rejected him and prayed to be delivered. She dreamt that she was given a drink which cured her, but it turned Maelon to ice. She made three requests, that Maelon be unfrozen, that all true hearted lovers should either succeed in their quest or else be cured of their passion, and that she should never wish to be married. Therefore Saint Dwynwen became a nun. In the Middle Ages Llanddwyn was rich due to the offerings at the shrine and the holy well, where the movements of the fish were believed to indicate the destiny of those who consulted it. Saint Dwynwen name was invoked to cure sick animals this practice continued past the reformation. The popular superstitions survived possibly due to the remote location of Llanddwyn.

January 26   Saint Margaret of Hungary

Country: Hungary   **Date:** 1242-1270

Family: Father: Bela IV (King of Hungary)
         Mother: Marie Lascarina
Spouse: Unknown   Siblings: Stephen V (King of Hungary); Blessed Jolenta; Blessed Cunegunda

Ancestors: Ancestors include thru Turkey to Armenia Saint Isaac Pahlav and Saint Gregory the Enlightened.

Branches of the Tree: This branch contains Stephen of Hungary and Margaret of Hungary.

SAINTS DAILY
Kings, Queens, Popes, Princes, Princesses, Emperors, Hermits, Bishops

DAILY SAINTS WHOSE ANCESTRY IS KNOWN

Biography: Saint Margaret of Hungary was the daughter of King Bela IV. She was the sister of King Stephen V and Blessed Jolenta, and Blessed Cunegunda. When she was twelve she became a novice in a royal convent built on an island on the Danube. She was a princess among nuns, however she did go accept any special treatment. She went out of her way to perform the most menial tasks and the most exacting labors for the poor. Due to her labors and fasting and hours of prayer, she became fatigued and died of this fatigue on January 18.
Her feast day is January 26th.

January 26   Saint Paula

Country: Italy (Rome)   **Date:** 347-404
    Patron: Widows

Family: Father: Rogatus   Mother: (Mæcia) PLACIDA (Blessilla)
Spouse: Julius Toxotius , Roman senator   Siblings: Unknown

Ancestors: Very few generations known.

Branches of the Tree: Go up the tree three generations and down ten to find Saint Arnulf Bishop of Metz.

Biography: Born to a noble family Saint Paula married Toxotius. Her birthday was May 5, 347. She had five children by Toxotius, named Toxotius, Blesella, Paulina Eustochium and Rufina. When Toxotius died in 379 she renounced the world, and devoted herself to helping the poor. She lived in the greatest austerity. Her marriage to Toxotius was regarded as an ideal marriage. In 382 she met Saint Jerome through St. Epiphanius and Paulinus of Antioch. She was closely associated with Jerome in his work while he was in Rome. She became heartbroken upon the death of her daughter Blesilla in 384 and in 385 she traveled to the Holy Land with Jerome and Eustochium. She settled in Bethlehem under his spiritual direction. She governed

SAINTS DAILY
 Kings, Queens, Popes, Princes, Princesses, Emperors, Hermits, Bishops

DAILY SAINTS WHOSE ANCESTRY IS KNOWN

a hospice, a monastery, and a convent which she built. She was the closest confidante and assistant to Saint Jerome while he did his biblical work. She built numerous churches in her old age. Some of these caused her financial difficulty in her old age. On January 26 she died in Bethlehem. She is the patroness of widows. The feast day on which she is celebrated is January 26.

January 28   Blessed Charlemagne

Family: Parents: Father-Pepin III "The Short" King of France
    Mother- Berthe (Bertrade) Countess of Laon
Wives: Hildegarde; Himiltrude: Galiena de France; Luitgard de France; Regina (Reginopycrha), Holy Roman Empire; Desideri; Madelgard de France; Gersvind de France; Adelheid Adelinde de France

Sons: Hugh L' Abbe Abbot of St Quentin by Regina; Louis I by Hildegarde; Pepin I de Lombardy King of Italy by Hildegarde; Charles the Younger Duc de Ingelheim by Hildegard;

Daughter: Aupais by Himiltrude

Ancestry:
(A Saint by an Anti-Pope, recognized as a Blessed by Rome.) Ancestry is directly traceable to Zerah brother of Perez and son of Judah. Also the Israelite Joseph is a direct ancestor. Tiberius Claudius Caesar, Emperor of Rome. Gaius Julius Caesar, Consul of Rome. Saint Joseph of Arimathea and so the Line of Nathan Son of David King of Israel and Judah. King David's ancestors include the Israelites, Zebulon, Levi, Joseph, and Judah. Also Anna of Arimathea, daughter to Joseph of Aramathea married Bran the Blessed whose line goes to Tros and so to Epraim son of Joseph the Israelite. Also the line from Anna of Arimathea's mother goes thru Simon the Just thru many High Priests to Judah the Israelite.

Descendents:

SAINTS DAILY
Kings, Queens, Popes, Princes, Princesses, Emperors, Hermits, Bishops

DAILY SAINTS WHOSE ANCESTRY IS KNOWN

Descendents of Charlemange include the Kings of France, Saint Margaret of Scotland, King Edward III of England. There are societies that are concerned with his descendents, and it is safe to say almost all nobles from most of Europe can claim him as an ancestor.

Biography:
King of the Franks from 768-814 and Frankish Emperor from 800, defender of the Pope and a central famous figure of European History. The Son of Pepin the Short born in 742 he became the sole ruler after the death of his brother Carloman. He waged war throughout Europe, defended Rome with the sword, and established a Christian Empire which was his goal. At the time of his death his realm stretched from the Pyrenees through France, Italy, and Switzerland into Bavaria, Germany and the Balkans. The Church played an important role and he was a patron of Christian learning, monasteries, and churches. He caused the Carolingian Renaissance reviving Europe intellectually, politically, and culturally. Crowned the first Holy Roman Emperor on Christmas Day in 800 by Pope Leo III the relationship between the Franks and Rome was founded thus ending Rome's dependence on the Byantine Empire. He was the Rex Pater Europa (King Father of Europe) well educated in theology, philosophy, mathematics, and languages. The Vita Carolini was written by Einhard, a biography of Charlemange, and his age was looked on well past his time as a golden age thus adding to his reputation. The title of blessed was allowed by Pope Benedict XIV in 1475. An Anti-Pope declared him a saint, although to this point Rome has not. His feast day is January 28 and there is a shrine in Aachen.

STUDY OF CHARLEMANGE and HIS RELATIONS
Family:
Parents: Father-Pepin III "The Short" King of France
          Mother- Berthe (Bertrade) Countess of Laon
Wives: Hildegarde; Himiltrude: Galiena de France; Luitgard de France; Regina (Reginopycrha), Holy Roman Empire;

SAINTS DAILY
Kings, Queens, Popes, Princes, Princesses, Emperors, Hermits, Bishops

DAILY SAINTS WHOSE ANCESTRY IS KNOWN

Desideri; Madelgard de France; Gersvind de France; Adelheid Adelinde de France

Sons: Hugh L' Abbe Abbot of St Quentin by Regina; Louis I by Hildegarde; Pepin I de Lombardy King of Italy by Hildegarde; Charles the Younger Duc de Ingelheim by Hildegard;

Daughter: Aupais by Himiltrude

Ancestry:
(A Saint by an Anti-Pope, recognized as a Blessed by Rome.) Ancestry is directly traceable to Zerah brother of Perez and son of Judah. Also the Israelite Joseph is a direct ancestor. Tiberius Claudius Caesar, Emperor of Rome. Gaius Julius Caesar, Consul of Rome. Saint Joseph of Arimathea and so the Line of Nathan Son of David King of Israel and Judah. King David's ancestors include the Israelites, Zebulon, Levi, Joseph, and Judah. Also Anna of Arimathea, daughter to Joseph of Aramathea married Bran the Blessed whose line goes to Tros and so to Epraim son of Joseph the Israelite. Also the line from Anna of Arimathea's mother goes thru Simon the Just thru many High Priests to Judah the Israelite.

Ancestry: Charlemange may not be descended from Saint Brychan, however his wife Hildegard is and so are all his descendents from Hildegard.

Descendents:
Descendents of Charlemange include the Kings of France, Saint Margaret of Scotland, King Edward III of England. There are societies that are concerned with his descendents, and it is safe to say almost all nobles from most of Europe can claim him as an ancestor.

Relationship to Saints and Blesseds:
- Charlemange's Sister Isberga was a Saint.
- Charlemange's Wife Himiltrude was a blessed (Beatus).

SAINTS DAILY
Kings, Queens, Popes, Princes, Princesses, Emperors, Hermits, Bishops

DAILY SAINTS WHOSE ANCESTRY IS KNOWN

- Great Grandfather Bishop of Treves was Saint Lievin
- Charlemange's Niece was Siagre of Austrasie Saint
- Thru Charlemange's Mother Bertha his Great Great Grandparents were Saint Angisel and Saint Begga. Saint Angisel and Saint Begga were the parents of Clotilde d'Heristal von Metz Saint. Saint Begga was the Daughter of Blessed Pepin Mayor of the Palace and Saint Itta of Metz whose daughter was Saint Gertrude (she would be the sister of Saint Begga.) Saint Itta's Brothers were Saint Arnulf Bishop of Metz and Saint Moald.
- Thru Charlemange's Father his Great Grandparents were Saint Angisel and Saint Begga.
- Saint Angisel had a son Pepin II, Count Of Heristal , who was the father of Drogo of Champagne, Duke Of Champagne who was the father of Hugo Bishop Of Rouen Saint. Pepin II, Count Of Heristal had a relationship with Alpaida Of Saxony and the son was Charles Martel. Charles Martel's son Pepin III "The Short" was the father of Charlemange.
- Blessed Pepin Mayor of the Palace was the Great Grandfather of Charlemange thru his Father's side of the family and Great Grandfather of Charlemange thru his Mother's side.
- Blessed Pepin Mayor of the Palace was the father of Saint Begue.
- Saint Angisel was the son of Blessed Pepin Mayor of the Palace and the Brother to Saint Clodulf who was the Grandfather of Saint Leutwinus.
- Saint Angisel was the son of Saint Arnulf Bishop of Metz whose GrandFather was Saint Gondolphus.

SAINTS DAILY
Kings, Queens, Popes, Princes, Princesses, Emperors, Hermits, Bishops

DAILY SAINTS WHOSE ANCESTRY IS KNOWN

- Charlemange's Wife Fastrada was the Sister of Saint Epiphania.
- Charlemange's Great Grandson Charles III of France married Saint Elgiva thru his daughter Aupais.
- Duke of Friuli Eberhard the Saint was the husband of Gisela of France, Granddaughter of Charlemange by his son Louis I.
- Saint Lothaire was the Grandson of Charlemange thru son Louis I and his wife Ermengarde.
- Saint Anglibert was the son of Charlemange thru his Blessed wife Hildegarde.
- Nithard the Cronicler the Saint was the grandson of Charlemange thru Saint Anglibert.
- Saint Matilda married the son of his Great Granddaughter Hedwig. She was the mother of Henry I of Germany who married Saint Mathilda of Ringelheim.
- Saint Matilda's son was Otto I who married Saint Adelaide.

Title of Charlemagne:

Karolus serenissimus augustus a Deo coronatus magnus, pacificus imperator, Romanum gubernans imperium, qui et per misericordiam Die rex Francorum atque Langobardorum

"Charles, the most merciful, awe-inspiring, great, and pacific emperor crowned by God, who rules the Roman Empire and who [is] king of the Franks and Lombards by the grace of God."

SAINTS DAILY
Kings, Queens, Popes, Princes, Princesses, Emperors, Hermits, Bishops

DAILY SAINTS WHOSE ANCESTRY IS KNOWN

January 28 *Saint Thomas d'Aquino (Aquinas)*

Country: Italy   **Date:** c. 1225-1274
  Patron: Roman Catholic Academies; Apologists; Booksellers; Scholars; Theologians; Catholic Universities

Family: Father: Landolfo (Landone) V d'Aquino
  Mother: Teodora di Caracciola (Contessa di Teano)
  Spouse: None   Siblings: Unknown

Ancestors: Ancestry goes thru Bavaria to Flanders and Baldwin V who married Adele Princess of France is an ancestors.

Branches of the Tree: The branch of the tree to get to Saint Thomas d'Aquino is thru Flanders and the kings of France and Belgium.

Biography: St. Thomas Aquinas, was a priest and doctor of the Church, and also patron of all universities and of students. Landulph, Count of Aquino, was his father who, when St. Thomas was five years old, placed him under the care of the Benedictines of Monte Casino. He surpassed all his fellow pupils in learning as well as in the practice of virtue and his teachers were surprised at the progress he made. He was born toward the end of the year 1226.

St. Thomas joined the order of St. Dominic and as soon as he was of age, although his family opposed this decision. When he was 17 in 1243, he joined the Dominicans of Naples. Over a two-year period, all members of his family resorted to break his constancy and even sent a impure women to tempt him. St. Thomas preserved his vocation in spite of all their efforts. All their efforts did not stop St. Thomas. St. Thomas was given the gift of perfect chastity which merited a title of angelic doctor.

SAINTS DAILY
Kings, Queens, Popes, Princes, Princesses, Emperors, Hermits, Bishops

DAILY SAINTS WHOSE ANCESTRY IS KNOWN

He studied at Cologne under Saint Albertus Magnus the great after making his profession (ordination) A dumb ox was his nick name due to his large-size and silent ways. However, he was really a brilliant student. St. Thomas was appointed to teach at Cologne. Here he began to publish his first works. He was sent to Paris. He received his doctor. He was then a priest. St. Louis, The King of France became his friend and dined together often in 1261. Urban the fourth who was Pope, called him to Rome. He was appointed to teach in Rome. St. Thomas wrote many books and his thoughts were brilliant. He preached often. Clement the fourth offered him the Archbishop position of Naples, which he refused.

In 1261, Urban IV called him to Rome where he was appointed to teach, but he positively declined to accept any ecclesiastical dignity. St. Thomas not only wrote (his writings filled twenty hefty tomes characterized by brilliance of thought and lucidity of language), but he preached often and with greatest fruit. Clement IV offered him the archbishopric of Naples which he also refused. He left the last work of his learning, was unfinished because he fell sick and died at the Cistercian monastery of Fosse Nuova in 1274.

His work was "Summa Theologica", he was ordered by Gregory X two Council of Lyons, St. Thomas was one of the greatest and most influential theologians of all time. He was canonized in 1323 and declared Doctor of the Church by Pope Pius V.
Date: d 814

January 30 *Saint Bathildis*
Country: Franks   *Date:* d 680

Family: Parents: Unknown   Husband: Clovis II (Chodovech) King of the Franks
Children: Theuderic III King of the Franks

SAINTS DAILY
Kings, Queens, Popes, Princes, Princesses, Emperors, Hermits, Bishops

DAILY SAINTS WHOSE ANCESTRY IS KNOWN

Ancestry: Saint Bathildis married Clovis II King of the Franks and her ancestry is not known.

Descendents: Descendants include Saint Adelaide of Italy, Saint Louis IX of France, Saint Fernando III of Spain, Saint Cunigunda of Luxemborg, Saint Leopold III of Austria, Saint Henry II of Germany, and Saint David and Saint Margaret of Scotland. Royal descendents include King Edward III Plantagenet of England, King of Naples Charles II, King of France Philip IV, Casimir King of Poland and Henry IV Holy Roman Emperor of Germany.

Biography: Born in England, where she was enslaved and taken to Neustria a part of the Frankish kingdom. In time Bathildis became a trusted member of the court and married King Clovis II in 649. Three sons, Clotaire III, Childeric II and Thierry III where all destined to become Kings. Bathildis served as regent for Clotaire III when Clovis died in 657. She founded a Benedictine convent at Chelles, and St. Denis Monastery and Corbie. Bathildis retired to Chelles, when Clotaire III assumed the throne, where she died on January 30.

January 30   *Saint Aldegundis*
Country: France   **Date:** 684

Family: Father: Saint Walbert   Mother: Saint Bertilla
Spouse: None   Siblings: Saint Waldetrudis de Loomis

Ancestors: None known past parentage

Branches of the Tree: This is the branch of the tree that Saint Vincent Madelgaire de Hainault who would be the brother in law to Saint Aldegundis.

Biography: Saint Adelgundis was a member of royal family of Merovingians. She was a Virgin and Abbess. Saint Walberg and St. Fratello, were her parents. On all region of Flanders, a region

SAINTS DAILY
Kings, Queens, Popes, Princes, Princesses, Emperors, Hermits, Bishops

DAILY SAINTS WHOSE ANCESTRY IS KNOWN

of the low countries was where the family lived many nobles offered to marry her. Saint Adelgundis received the veil from St. Amadeus, the bishop of Maastricht. The years, the Sandburg River at a desert site called malbode a convent was founded. She followed this ceremony of acceptance into the religious life, a convent and Mons was founded by her sister, Saint Waldetrudis. At the age of 54 Saint Aldegundis died of cancer.

January 31   *Saint Judoc*
Country: Britain   **Date:** 626

Family: Father: Hoel III King of Bretons   Mother: Pritelle
Spouse: None   Siblings: Saint Judicael

Ancestors: Saint Judicael ancestors include Saint Patrick, Saint Cyllinus, Blessed Bran and Anna of Arimathea Anna of Armimathea's father is Saint Joseph of Arimathea and so the Line of Nathan Son of David King of Israel and Judah. King David's ancestors include the Israelites, Zebulon, Levi, Joseph, and Judah. Also Anna of Arimathea, daughter to Joseph of Aramathea married Bran the Blessed whose line goes to Tros and so to Epraim son of Joseph the Israelite. Also the line from Anna of Arimathea's mother goes thru Simon the Just thru many High Priests to Judah the Israelite.

Branches of the Tree: This is the branch containing Saint Judoc brother Saint Judicael whose descendents are known.

Biography: Saint Judicael is a sibling of Saint Judoc and he was the son of Hoel III who was the King of Bretons.

January 31   *Saint Aidan*
Country: Ireland   **Date:** 626

Family: Father: Tairdelbach   Mother: Unknown

SAINTS DAILY
Kings, Queens, Popes, Princes, Princesses, Emperors, Hermits, Bishops

DAILY SAINTS WHOSE ANCESTRY IS KNOWN

Spouse: None   Siblings: Saint Flannan

Ancestors: A line of Irish for nine generations ending in Conall.

Branches of the Tree: The King of Ireland Brian Boroimhe is in this branch of the tree. Saints in the branch of King Brian include Saint Flannan, Saint Breacan. A related branch of the tree of King Brian's wife Gormflaith Of Nass is the Saint Cumne, Saint Sodelb, Saint Ethne, Saint Dar-Carthaind, Saint Fedelm, Saint Coeman Santlethan and Saint Mugain, all in the branch of the tree of King Brian's wife Gormflaith Of Nass

Biography: Saint Aidan was a miracle worker, bishop, and monastic founder. He was known for his kindness to animals. Born in Connaught Ireland signs and omens heralded his birth. According to tradition as a small child he showed signs of piety. Leinster was where Saint Aidan was educated, and he went to St. David monastery in Wales. He studied Scriptures and remained there for several years, and his presence saved St. David from disaster.   During his stay Saxon war parties attacked the monastery, and he be repelled them miraculously. He founded a monastery in Wexford in Ferns and returned to Ireland where he became the bishop of the region in Ireland. Many people came to the Church due to his miracles. He is represented with this a stag in religious art. There is a legend that a beautiful stag was attacked by pounds and Saint Aidan made this stag invisible in order to save the stag.

SAINTS DAILY
Kings, Queens, Popes, Princes, Princesses, Emperors, Hermits, Bishops

DAILY SAINTS WHOSE ANCESTRY IS KNOWN

Saints of February

FEAST DAY	SAINT	COUNTRY	BORN	DIED
1-Feb	Saint Sigebert of East Anglia	Franks	631	656
1-Feb	Saint Siagre of Austrasie	France		Late 8th
1-Feb	Saint Brigid	Ireland	c 453	c 523
2-Feb	Saint Adalbald		600	652
3-Feb	Saint Werberga	England	661	699
4-Feb	Saint Adele of Blois	England		1137
4-Feb	Saint Joan of Valois	France	1464	1505
5-Feb	Saint Avitus Of Vienne Bishop	Rome	451	525
6-Feb	Saint Melchu	Ireland		
6-Feb	Saint Mel	Ireland		c 490
8-Feb	Saint Wethoc	Brittany		5th
8-Feb	Saint Jacut	Brittany		5th
8-Feb	Saint Elfleda	England		714
9-Feb	Saint Teilo	Britain		c. 500
11-Feb	Saint Theodora	Byzantine		867
11-Feb	Saint Benedict of Aniane	France	750	821
12-Feb	Saint Humberline			1135
14-Feb	Blessed Conrad of Bavaria	Germany	C.1105	C.1154
16-Feb	Saint Gilbert of Sempringham	England	1083	1189
17-Feb	Saint Loman	Ireland		c 450
18-Feb	Saint Angilbert	France	c 740	814

SAINTS DAILY
Kings, Queens, Popes, Princes, Princesses, Emperors, Hermits, Bishops

58

DAILY SAINTS WHOSE ANCESTRY IS KNOWN

18-Feb	Saint Simon Apostle	Israel		1st
18-Feb	Saint Simeon	Israel		1st
21-Feb	Blessed Pepin of Landen	France		c 639
21-Feb	Saint Robert Southwell	England	1561	1593
23-Feb	Saint Milburga	England		c 715
23-Feb	Saint Jurmin	England		8th
25-Feb	Saint Aldeltrudis de Hainault	Belgium	bef 670	
25-Feb	Saint Aethelbert of Kent	England	560	616
25-Feb	Saint Bertha of Kent	Frankish		612
26-Feb	Saint Isabel of France	France		1270
27-Feb	Saint Leander of Seville	Spain	534	600
28-Feb	Blessed Hedwig of Poland	Poland	1374	1399

TABLE THREE SAINTS OF FEBRUARY

February 1   *Saint Siegeberht*

Country: East Anglia, England   **Date:** 634

Family: Father: Raedwald   Mother: Unknown
Spouse: Unknown   Siblings: Unknown

Ancestors: Woden or Odin and Frigg are ancestors of Asgard.

Branches of the Tree: This is the top of the Branch very near to Odin and Frigg.

Biography : King of East Anglia from 631 – 634 he was the son of Raedwald. This is very old England. Not much other than the

SAINTS DAILY
Kings, Queens, Popes, Princes, Princesses, Emperors, Hermits, Bishops

59

DAILY SAINTS WHOSE ANCESTRY IS KNOWN

relationships found in the Saints in the Tree are known about Saint Siegeberht.

February 1   Saint Siagre of Austrasie

Feastday: Feb 1   Date: b. Abt. 730 d. 14 Jan 770/71

Family: Father: Carloman (King of the Franks - 768-771)
Mother: Gerberge Di Lombardi
Spouse: Unknown   Siblings: Unknown

Country: France (Austrasia)

Ancestors: This Ancestry contains Walter, Sunno, Joshua son of Non, and Joseph the Israelite.

Branches of the Tree: This is the branch that is the Frankish Kings, as Charles Martel is the Descendent of Pharamond, the early King of France. This line eventually leads to the Israelite Joseph and contains Joshua son of Non.

Biography: Very Little is known of the son of Carloman who was King of the Franks. His lineage back to Joseph the Israelite is known from Saints in the Tree as are his other lineage relationships.

February 1   Saint Seiriol

Feastday: Feb 1   Date: Sixth Century

Family: Father: Owain ab   Mother: Unknown
Spouse: Unknown   Siblings: Unknown

Country: Wales

Ancestors: Owain DanWyn who was Saint Seiriol's Father was son of Einion Yrth who was son of Cunneda. Cunneda is an Ancestor of Saint Dewi and his lineage leads to a Sister of the Virgin Mary.

SAINTS DAILY
 Kings, Queens, Popes, Princes, Princesses, Emperors, Hermits, Bishops

60

DAILY SAINTS WHOSE ANCESTRY IS KNOWN

Branches of the Tree: This is a branch of Wales near Saint Brychan and Saint Cadwallon.
Biography: Very Little is known of the son of Owain DanWyn, Saint Seiriol who is honored in the Puffin Islands. He was a welsh hermit and monk. Puffin Island is off the coast of Anglesey Wales.

February 1   *Saint Bridgid of Kildare*

Country: Ireland   **Date:** c. 453 c. 523 **Patron:** Dairy Workers; Ireland;Scholars

Family: Father: Dubtach   Mother: Unknown
Spouse: Unknown   Siblings: Unknown

Ancestors: Tuathal Teachtmar, King of Ireland is an ancestor, and so the line that goes back to Japeth, son of Noah thru the son Magog.

Branches of the Tree: This is the branch of the tree of the Irish Kings.

Biography: Saint Brigid was born at Faughart near Dundalk, Louth, Ireland. Saint Patrick baptized her parents, and she developed a close friendship with Saint Patrick. According to legend, her father was Dubtach. Her mother Brocca was a slave at the court of the chieftain. As a young girl Saint Brigid was interested in a religious life. In her youth she took the veil from Saint Macaille at Croghan and was likely professed by Saint Mel of Armagh. She and seven of her virgins settled at the foot of Croghan Hill for a time. This occurred about 468. In 470 she founded a double monastery at Cill-Dara (Kildare) and was Abbess of the convent. This was the first in Ireland. The Cathedral city of Kildare grew around the monastery. A school of art at Kildare was founded by Saint Brigid, and its illuminated

SAINTS DAILY
Kings, Queens, Popes, Princes, Princesses, Emperors, Hermits, Bishops

DAILY SAINTS WHOSE ANCESTRY IS KNOWN

manuscripts became famous. Three centuries ago the Book of Kildare disappeared, however it was there at the School of art in Kildare before it disappeared. On February 1 she died at Kildare. She is buried at Downpatrick with Saint Columba and Saint Patrick. She is the patron of Ireland with Saint Columba and Saint Patrick. She is sometimes called Bridget and Bride.

February 2   *Saint Adalbald I De Artois*

Country: *Date:* b 600 d. 652

Family: Parents: Father- Richemeres von Franconia
Mother- Gertrude of Hamage Saint
Wife: Saint Rictrudis Children: Adalbald II De Artois; Eusibia Saint, Clotsind Saint, Adalsind Saint, and Mauront Saint

Ancestry: Parents unknown as well as any other ancestor.

Descendents: Sainted Descendents include Saint Adelaide Empress of Italy, Saint Henry II, Saint Louis IX, Saint Adele Countess of Blois, Saint Cunigunda of Luxemborg, Saint David of Scotland, Saint Margaret of Scotland, Saint Ferdinand III of Spain, Saint Leopold III of Austria, Saint Leutwinus, and Saint Raymond Berenger IV. Blessed Charlemagne, blessed Humbert III, and Blessed Gisele are also Descendents. Royal Descendents Include King of Aragon Pedro II, King of Castile Alphonso VIII, King of England William the Conqueror, King of France Hugh Capet, King of Hungary Andreas II, King of Italy Berenger I, King of Naples Charles II, King of Navarre Teobaldo, King of Jerusalem Fulk V, King of Scotland William the Lion.

Biography: Saint Adabald of Ostrevant faced some of the most vicious in-laws ever recorded. He was a martyr and noble. St. Gertrude of Hamage was his mother and was born in Flanders. In Dagobert I of France's court he was a nobleman. Going to Gascony, in France, to put down a local rebellion, Meeting a

SAINTS DAILY
Kings, Queens, Popes, Princes, Princesses, Emperors, Hermits, Bishops

DAILY SAINTS WHOSE ANCESTRY IS KNOWN

noblewoman, Rictrudis, daughter of Ernold while going to France, specifically Gascony he fell in love and married her. He was traveling to put down a revolt. Many of her relatives objected due to his warring in that region. Dedicated to acts of mercy and religious projects, Adalbald and Rictrudis lived happily. His inlaws however killed him upon his return to Gascony, thus making Adalbald a martyr. At his tomb many miracles have been reported.

February 3   *Saint Werberga*
Country: Kent England   **Date:** 661

Family: Father: King Wulfhere Of Mercia Mother: Princess Eormengild of Kent
Spouse: Unknown Siblings: King Coenred of Mercia; Prince Behrtwald of Mercia

Ancestors: Saint Sexberga and King Earconbert are ancestors.

Branches of the Tree: Saint Cyllin is an Ancestor. Ancestors include the Kings of Siluria. Generations previous to this they were the Kings of Britain. The line then goes back to Zerah, whose father is Judah. This line also marries Anna Arimathea who is the daughter of Joseph of Arimathea. A little know fact of the biblical character of Joseph of Arimathea is that he is the son of Mathat, who is in the line of Nathan that is listed in the New Testament book of Luke. So Saint Cyllin is descended from the Davidic line of Nathan and so from Judah thru Perez, and also as previously mentioned thru Judah's son Zerah.

Biography: Saint Werberga was a Benedictine nun. She was the daughter of King Wulfhere of Mercia and Saint Ermenilda. She is the patroness of Chester, England and she was born in Staffordshire. She insisted on being a nun at Ely and refused to marry. After studying under Saint Etheldreda in 675 she began reforming the convents of the realm. She did this to assist her uncle King Ethelred. In Northhamptonshire she also founded

SAINTS DAILY
Kings, Queens, Popes, Princes, Princesses, Emperors, Hermits, Bishops

DAILY SAINTS WHOSE ANCESTRY IS KNOWN

communities at Hanbury, Wedon, and Trentham. She became venerated as the patron saint of the city of Chester after her remains were transferred from Trentham to Chester. She was reputed to have the ability to read the minds of others. During her life she was revered for miracles.

February 4 *Saint Adele of Blois*
Country: England   *Date:* d 1137

Family: Parents: Father- Dagobert II King Of Franks Saint Mother- Ragnetrude
Husband: Unknown   Children: Aubrey I Count of Blois

Ancestry: Ancestors include Charlemagne, Joseph of Arimathea, and Helena of Rome.
Also King David of Judah and Israel is an ancestor thru Nathan his son. King Solomon of Israel and Judah is also an ancestor. Sainted ancestors include Saint Ethelbert, Saint Arnulf, Blessed Pepin, Saint Clodulf, Saint Matilda, Saint Itta, Saint Sigebert, Saint Dagobert, Saint Beggue, and Saint Sexburga.

Descendents: Descendents include Earl Thomas De Beauchamp of Warwick and Edward Stafford 3rd Duke of Buckingham.

Biography: English Princess and Benefactor. She was the youngest daughter of William the Conqueror. Adela married Stephen of Blois in 1080. She always lead an active role in English politics. Endowing churches and monastic institutions gave her fame.

February 4 *Saint Joan of Valois*
Country: France   *Date:* 1464- 1505

Family: Father: Louis XI de Valois   Mother: Charlotte de Savoy

SAINTS DAILY
Kings, Queens, Popes, Princes, Princesses, Emperors, Hermits, Bishops

DAILY SAINTS WHOSE ANCESTRY IS KNOWN

Spouse: Unknown Siblings: Charles VIII De Valois; Anne De Valois

Ancestors: Ancestors include thru Turkey to Armenia Saint Isaac Pahlav and Saint Gregory the Enlightened.

Branches of the Tree: This branch contains Stephen of Hungary and Margaret of Hungary.

Biography: Saint Joan of Valois was the second daughter of King Louis XI and Charlotte of Savoy. She was betrothed to the Duke of Orleans at the age of two months. The marriage took place 1n 1476. Saint Joan was born on April 23, 1464. The marriage may have been invalid because it was said that Louis of Orleans married her in fear of his life to comply with the King's order. Joan was by no means a prepossessing figure. She was pock-marked and hunch-backed. On her husband's succession to the throne Joan's marriage was declared invalid and she was given the title of Duchess of Berry. Saint Joan was not to occupy the throne of the Queen of France. She founded the Order of the Annunciation. The King Louis XII approved of the Order readily enough, however the Pope was unwilling to give his approval. The foundation was made at Bouges, and the remains of the house may still be seen there. Joan died at the age of 41 on February 4, 1505. Saint Joan was canonized in 1950. Her feast day is February 4.

February 5   Saint Avitus Of Vienne Bishop

Country: Italy   **Date:** 520

Family: Father: Hesychius of Vienne Saint   Mother: Audentia of Rome
Spouse: Unknown   Siblings: Apollinaris Saint, Fuscina Of Vienne

SAINTS DAILY
Kings, Queens, Popes, Princes, Princesses, Emperors, Hermits, Bishops

DAILY SAINTS WHOSE ANCESTRY IS KNOWN

Ancestors: Unknown

Branches of the Tree: Family of Saints including Hesychius of Vienne and Apollinaris

Biography: Saint Avitus was the Bishop of Vienne. His father was Bishop Isychius, a former Roman senator. He succeeded his father in the see of Vienneg in 490. He converted members of the Frankish tribes, ransomed captives, and became known for his wisdom and charity. He also presided over the Council of Epaon in 517. He was noted for his elegant writings, including an allegory, a poem on chastiy, his many sermons, and he wrote letters.

February 6   *Saint Mel*

Country: Ireland   **Date:** d.c.490

Family: Father: Conan (Cynan) Meriadoc (King of Dumnonia) Mother: Saint Darerca
Spouse: Unknown Siblings: Gradlon Maw ('the Great') (King of Bretagne); Ystrafael; Melchu, Munis, Rioch Saint

Ancestors: Saint Joseph of Arimathea is an Ancestor, as is Bran the Blessed King of Britain around 10 AD. Bran the Blessed ancestors include Camber and Tros, sons of Dardanus, who is the son of Zerah son of the Isralite Judah. Dardanus mother is also listed as Electra wife of Tarah, son of Ephriam who is the son of Joseph the Israelite. Saint Patrick is then descended from both Joseph and Judah, thru Dardanus and from David the King of Israel and Judah thru his son Nathan and the line leading to Matthat, father of Saint Joseph of Arimathea.

Branches of the Tree: The line of ancestry of Saint Patrick is sixteen generations from his ancestor Joseph of Arimathea, and fifteen generations from Bran the Blessed, whose ancestors are from the Israelites.

SAINTS DAILY
Kings, Queens, Popes, Princes, Princesses, Emperors, Hermits, Bishops

DAILY SAINTS WHOSE ANCESTRY IS KNOWN

Biography: Saint Mel was the son of Conis and Saint Darerca, the sister of St. Patrick. Saint Mel worked with the St. Patrick in Ireland and held to evangelize all of Ireland. He is said to have had no fixed See. According to the Life of St. Brigid, which might fit in his being a missionary, St. Patrick appointed his nephew the church at Ardagh that St. Patrick had built. Saint Mel supported himself by working with his hands. Anything he made beyond his bare necessities he gave to the poor. Slanderous tongues spread serious accusations against Saint Mel when he lived with his Aunt Lupait. Saint Patrick himself came to investigate their conduct. Saint Mel cleared himself of the charge by miraculously picking up a live fish from the ground as if from a net when he was plowing when St. Patrick arrived. Aunt Lupait carried glowing coals without burning herself or her clothing thus establishing her innocence. Saint Patrick believed in their innocence and told his nephew in the future to do these fishing in the water and his plowing on the land. He asked them to avoid scandal by separating and living in praying far part. St. Mel's feast day is February 6.

February 6 *Saint Melchu*

Feastday: February 6   Date: d.c.490

Family: Father: Conan (Cynan) Meriadoc (King of Dumnonia)   Mother: Saint Darerca
Spouse: Unknown   Siblings: Gradlon Maw ('the Great') (King of Bretagne); Ystrafael; Saint Mel, Munis, Rioch Saint

Country: Ireland

Ancestors:
Saint Joseph of Arimathea is an Ancestor, as is Bran the Blessed King of Britain around 10 AD. Bran the Blessed ancestors include Camber and Tros, sons of Dardanus, who is the son of Zerah son of the Israelite Judah. Dardanus mother is also listed as Electra wife of Tarah, son of Ephriam who is the son of Joseph

SAINTS DAILY
Kings, Queens, Popes, Princes, Princesses, Emperors, Hermits, Bishops

DAILY SAINTS WHOSE ANCESTRY IS KNOWN

the Israelite. Saint Patrick is then descended from both Joseph and Judah, thru Dardanus and from David the King of Israel and Judah thru his son Nathan and the line leading to Matthat, father of Saint Joseph of Arimathea.

Branches of the Tree: The line of ancestry of Saint Patrick is sixteen generations from his ancestor Joseph of Arimathea, and fifteen generations from Bran the Blessed, whose ancestors are from the Israelites.

Biography: One of the sons of Conan and Saint Darerca Saint Melchu may have been a missionary. He was a Bishop that had no fixed see. Possibly was the Bishop of Ardagh. He is said to have accompanied Saint Patrick on the evangelization of Ireland. Several Hagiograhers have supposed that Melchu was a mistaken interpolation of Mel and that they are one and the same person.

February 8   *Saint Elfleda*
Country: England   **Date:** 714

Family: Father: Aethelfrith Of Northumbria
         Mother: Acha Of Deira
Spouse: Unknown   Siblings: Eanfrith; Oswiu; Saint Ebbe

Ancestors: Aethelfrith line is unknown, but Acha of Deira goes back many generations to Woden (Norse God of ancient legend.) Ancestors go back to the Anglo-Saxons around the year 100 AD. Also the line of the Kings of Deira lead to the Lords of the Anglo Saxons.

Branches of the Tree : This branch of the tree connects to the Mercia Kings, and the Kings of Penda. Also Acha of Deira the Saints mother is the sister to Saint Edwin of Northumbria. His line is known

SAINTS DAILY
Kings, Queens, Popes, Princes, Princesses, Emperors, Hermits, Bishops

DAILY SAINTS WHOSE ANCESTRY IS KNOWN

Biography: Saint Elfleda was the head of the abbey at Whitby. Other names she has been called are Edifleda, Elfeda, Elgiva, or Ethelfieda. Elfleda was powerful in Church affairs. She was the sister of King Oswy of Northumbria, England, as well as Saint Ebbe and Saint Oswald. Saint Elfleda was placed in the convent of Harlepool as an infant. The previous abbess, St. Hilda took Elfieda to Whitby. St. Cuthbert was aided by Saint Elfleda. After a time Saint Elfleda succeeded Hilda there as abbess. There was a dispute between Sts. Wilfrid and Theodore. Saint Elfleda mediated this dispute. Elfieda died at Whitby.

February 8   *Saint Wethoc*

Country: Brittany France   **Date:** 5th

Family: Father: Saint Fracan Mother: Saint Gwen Spouse: Unknown Siblings: Saint Wethoc, Saint Iocab, Chreirbia

Ancestors: James the son of Saint Joseph is an Ancestor, so is Conan.

Branches of the Tree: This is the branch that leads to Saint Judicael

Biography: Son of Fragan and Gwen. Forced to flee England and travel to France. Disiple of Saint Budoc.

February 8   *Saint Jacut*

Country: Brittany France   **Date:** 5th

Family: Father: Saint Fracan Mother: Saint Gwen Spouse: Unknown Siblings: Saint Wethoc, Saint Iocab, Chreirbia

SAINTS DAILY
Kings, Queens, Popes, Princes, Princesses, Emperors, Hermits, Bishops

DAILY SAINTS WHOSE ANCESTRY IS KNOWN

Ancestors: James the son of Saint Joseph is an Ancestor, so is Conan.

Branches of the Tree: This is the branch that leads to Saint Judicael

Biography: Son of Fragan and Gwen. Forced to flee England and travel to France. Disiple of Saint Budoc.

February 9 *Saint Teilo*

Feastday: February 9   Date: b. c. 500

Family: Father: Ensich ap Hydwn   Mother: None   Spouse: Unknown   Siblings: Anowed verch Ensich   Children: None

Country: Britain

Ancestors: Saint Brychan is four generations Saint Teilo's ancestor thru the daughter Saint Meriri. Therefore Conan, Saint Dareca, Saint Ursula, and all the ancestors of the marriage of Saint Brychan, including the five Israelites Joseph, Benjamin, Levi, Zebulon, and Judah.

Branches of the Tree: This is a branch of the tree near Saint Brychan and his wife Prawst.

Biography: In Wales near Penally Pembrokeshire Saint Teilo was born. He is known as Eliud there. St Dubricius as the intellect he studied under and he went to Jerusalem with Saint David. Seven years were spent with Saint Samson at Dol in Brittany. In 554 he returned to Wales and preached with great success. At Llandeilo Fawr, Carmarthenshire, he established Monasteries where he was abbot bishop.

SAINTS DAILY
Kings, Queens, Popes, Princes, Princesses, Emperors, Hermits, Bishops

DAILY SAINTS WHOSE ANCESTRY IS KNOWN

February 9 *Saint Ansbert Bishop of Rouen*

Feastday: February 9   Date: d 695

Family: Father: Sigoen Industrus   Mother: Magnafildis
Spouse: Unknown   Siblings: Ferreolus Bishop of Autun
Children: None

Country: Britain

Ancestors: Godin Cahors brother to Saint Goeric, Papanilla, Emperor Avitus, Tonance Ferreol Senator of Narbonne

Branches of the Tree: This is the branch of the tree near Saint Leger and Saint Leiutwinus.

Biography: King Clotaire III of France was whom Saint Ansbert Bishop of Rouen served as Bishop and Chancellor. Saint Ansbert was named abbot of Fontenelle. He was a noted courtier in Rouen France. Saint Ansbert was the confessor to a king of the Ostrogoths. Saint Quen was succeeded as Bishop of Rouen by Saint Ansbert. Pepin the mayor of the Royal Palace exiled Ansbert to Hautmont monastery. Saint Ansbert had gotten caught up in the political upheavals of his time. Saint Ansbert died in the monastery.

February 11 Saint Theodora

Country: Byzantine   *Date:* 867

Family: Parents: Father- Marinos   Mother- Theoctiste Florine
Husband: Theophilus Byzantine Emperor   Children: Michael III the Drunkard

SAINTS DAILY
Kings, Queens, Popes, Princes, Princesses, Emperors, Hermits, Bishops

71

DAILY SAINTS WHOSE ANCESTRY IS KNOWN

Ancestry The Mamikonians line is her ancestry, which includes the Saints Gregory the Illuminator, Saint Narses, Saint Isaac all of Armenia.

Descendents: Saint Louis IX of France and Saint Fernando of Spain are descendents. King Edward III Plantagenet is a descendent as well as Boleslaw III of Poland. Premsyll King of Bohemia is a descendent, as well as Charles VI King of France.

Biography: Wife of Emperor Theophilus Saint Theodora was a Byzantine empress. She was the mother of Michael III called the Drunkard. The Icononclast policy of the Byzantine Emperors was promoted by Saint Theodora, and so ended the policy of not having any Icons in the empire. She acted as regent for her son until he turned 18 upon which she was sent to a convent. Because of her defense of the icons, she is venerated as a saint, although sanctity claims are difficult to confirm.

February 11 Saint Benedict of Aniane

Country: Visigoth Spain **Date:** 75-821

Family: Father: Aigulf Count of Maguelone of the Visigoths   Mother: Unknown
Spouse: Unknown   Siblings: Unknown

Ancestors: Egicca (Egica) King of the Visigoths

Branches of the Tree: Egicca (Egica) King of the Visigoths was Saint Benedict's Great Grandfather. This line from Portugal eventually married the Castile line at Rodrigo, and leads to Fernando I King of Castile.

Biography: Saint Benedict of Aniane is related to the Frankish monasticism revival that took place in the eighth and ninth

SAINTS DAILY
Kings, Queens, Popes, Princes, Princesses, Emperors, Hermits, Bishops

DAILY SAINTS WHOSE ANCESTRY IS KNOWN

centuries. Before becoming a monk he was the cupbearer of Pepin III and Charlemagne. He was the son of a noble Visigoth family. About 770-773 he entered St. Seine near Dijon as a monk. He became a hermit on his family estate, and lived on the banks of the Aniane. He was joined by other solitaries. Saint Benedict of Aniane is credited as compiling the rules of monastism that were available in his time. He compiled the rules in Codex regularum and composed Concordia regularum in order to demonstrate the known monastic rules as the universality of the Rule of Saint Benedict of Nursia. Also possibly compiled the supplement to the Gregorian sacramentary that may have been from Saint Alcuin of York. When King Louis I the Pious requested it he convoked and led the synod of Aachen in 817. Although not totally successful this synod determined that all monasteries in the Kingdom of Louis I should follow the Rule of Saint Benedict of Nursia.

February 12   Saint Humberline

Country: *Date:* 1135

Family: Parents: Father- Tescelin Of Sorus   Mother- Blessed Aleth   Husband: Guy de Marcy
        Children: Erad II Count of Brienne   Siblings: Saint Bernard of Clairvaux

Ancestry: Ancestry past parentage is not known.

Descendents: King Edward IV Plantagenet is a descendent. Also Edward Stafford 3rd Duke of Buckingham and John I Brienne King of Jerusalem.

Biography: Married and socially popular, Saint Humberline visited her brother and underwent a personal conversion. She was younger sister of St. Bernard of Clairvaux and Benedictine abbess. Receiving permission from her husband, Guy de Marcy, she entered the Benedictines at Jully-les-Nonnais. She became

SAINTS DAILY
Kings, Queens, Popes, Princes, Princesses, Emperors, Hermits, Bishops

DAILY SAINTS WHOSE ANCESTRY IS KNOWN

abbess after her sister-in-law Elizabeth. Saint Humberline died in her brother's arms.

February 14   Blessed Conrad of Bavaria
Feastday: Feb 14   Date: b. c. 1105 d. c.1154

Family: Father: Heinrich IX. der Schwarze von Bayern
         Mother: Wulfhild Billung
Spouse: Unknown   Siblings: Judith von Bayern

Country: Germany

Ancestors: The Flanders people going to Baldwin IV, and the

Branches of the Tree: Friedrich I. Barbarossa Kaiser des heiligen is very near in this branch of the tree.

Biography: Son of Duke Henry the Black, he studied at Cologne. He joined Saint Bernard at Clairvaux. He journed to Palestine to live as a hermit with Saint Bernard's permission, however ill health caused him to come home with the unsettled conditions. He died on the way back on March 15.

February 16   Saint Gilbert of Sepringham
Country: Britain   **Date:** b. 1083 d. 1189

Family: Father: Jocelin Fitz Lambert   Mother: Unknown
Spouse: Unknown   Siblings: Unknown

Ancestors: Only Father is known.

Branches of the Tree: Richard De Crevequer married his daughter Maud. This line continues including descendents such as the Neville line, the Taylor line, the Tyes line and the Wentworth line.

SAINTS DAILY
 Kings, Queens, Popes, Princes, Princesses, Emperors, Hermits, Bishops

DAILY SAINTS WHOSE ANCESTRY IS KNOWN

Biography: Saint Gilbert was born at Sempringham, England. He was the son of a wealthy Norman Knight, Jocelin. He was sent to France to study. Upon his return to England his father gave him the benefices of Sempringham and Tirington. He was ordained by Bishop Robert Bloet of Lincoln, of whom he was a clerk in his house. He returned to Sempringham when his father died in 1131 as Lord. In the same year he advised for a group of seven young women who he decided should be founded into an order. After several new foundations were established, Saint Gilbert went to Citeaux in 1148 to ask the Cistercians to take over the Community. This group continued as the Gilbertine Order after attaining the approval of Pope Eugene III. Saint Gilbert was the Master General. This was the only English religious order from the medieval period, having twenty six monasteries which continued until King Henry VIII suppressed monasteries in England. In 1165 he was imprisoned on a false charge of aiding Thomas of Canterbury during the latter's exile. Saint Gilbert was declared innocent of the charge. He was known for imposing a strict rule on his Order. When he was ninety some of his lay brothers revolted, but Pope Alexander III sided with Saint Gilbert. Late in life Saint Gilbert became blind and so resigned his office because of blindness and he died at Sempringham. In 1202 he was canonized. Feast Day February 16.

February 17   *Saint Loman*
Country: Ireland   **Date:** 450

Family: Father: Unknown   Mother: Tigris
Spouse: Unknown   Siblings: Unknown

Ancestors: Saint Loman's mother is Tigris, a sister of Saint Patrick Patron of Ireland. Saint Joseph of Arimathea is an Ancestor, as is Bran the Blessed King of Britain around 10 AD. Bran the Blessed ancestors include Camber and Tros, sons of Dardanus, who is the son of Zerah son of the Isralite Judah.

SAINTS DAILY
Kings, Queens, Popes, Princes, Princesses, Emperors, Hermits, Bishops

DAILY SAINTS WHOSE ANCESTRY IS KNOWN

Dardanus mother is also listed as Electra wife of Tarah, son of Ephriam who is the son of Joseph the Israelite. Saint Patrick is then descended from both Joseph and Judah, thru Dardanus and from David the King of Israel and Judah thru his son Nathan and the line leading to Matthat, father of Saint Joseph of Arimathea.

Branches of the Tree: The line of ancestry of Saint Patrick is sixteen generations from his ancestor Joseph of Arimathea, and fifteen generations from Bran the Blessed, whose ancestors are from the Israelites.

Biography: Another tradition dates Loman to the seventh century, denying his relationship to St. Patrick. Saint Loman was the Bishop of Trim, in Meath, Ireland. The sister of St. Patrick was Tigris and Saint Loman was her son. He converted a local chieftain when he accompanied St. Patrick to Ireland.

February 18   Saint Simon the Apostle
Country: Israel

Family: Father: unknown   Mother: Mary Alphaews   Spouse: Unknown   Siblings: Saint Judas the apostle, Saint Joseph Barsabas the apostle, Saint James the Lesser apostle

Ancestors:. Saint Joseph of Arimathea is an ancestor. A little know fact of the biblical character of Joseph of Arimathea is that he is the son of Mathat, who is in the line of Nathan that is listed in the New Testament book of Luke. His ancestors then must be King David of Israel and Judah, and so the Israelites Joseph, Levi, Zebulon, and Judah. Anna married Saint Joseph of Arimathea, and her ancestry is an unbroken male line to Levi the Israelite. Saint Joseph of Arimathea's mother may have been the daughter of Eleazor, who was of the Davidic line of Solomon. Eleazor was the Grandfather of Joseph who married the Virgin Mary and this line is listed in the Gospel of Mathew. The Israelite Benjamin was an ancestor of King Davids wife Maacah (Sauls daughter) whose line married in the line from Solomon

SAINTS DAILY
Kings, Queens, Popes, Princes, Princesses, Emperors, Hermits, Bishops

DAILY SAINTS WHOSE ANCESTRY IS KNOWN

joined by the marriage of Reheboam to Maacah. Therefore Saint Joseph of Arimathea has five Israelites as ancestors.

Branches of the Tree : This is a branch of the tree that has Saint Joseph of Arimathea in it. He is the Father of Cleopas who is the Father of Mary Alphaws. He is three generations the ancestor of Saint Simeon. This line also is close to Anna Arimathea who is the daughter of Joseph of Arimathea.

Biography: Some say that Saint Cleophas (the brother of Saint Joseph who raised the Lord) was the father of Simon and his brothers, and that Mary his mother was the sister of the Mother of the Lord. At any rate he was the kinsman of the lord, and one of the twelve disiples. He replaced James as Bishop of Jerusalem in about 62, after James was killed by the Jews.

February 18   *Saint Simeon*
Date: 1st Century (107)   **Feastday:** Feb 18

Family:
Parents: Father: Cleophas   Mother: Sister to Virgin Mary
Spouse: Unknown
Siblings: unknown

Ancestry: Of the house of David because Cleophas was the brother to Saint Joseph.

Branch of the Tree: Vicinity of Saint Joseph.

Biography: Saint Simeon would have been the first cousin to the Lord, due to his Father being the uncle of the Lord. Successor to James as Bishop of Jerusalem after Saint James was Martyred. Warned of the destruction of Jerusalem in 66 he led a group of Christians to Pella until it was safe. Arrested by Roman Govenor Atticus under Emperor Trajan he was tortured and crucified when he was over one hundred years old. Saint Simeon escaped the order to destroy all of Jewish Origin under Emperors

SAINTS DAILY
Kings, Queens, Popes, Princes, Princesses, Emperors, Hermits, Bishops

DAILY SAINTS WHOSE ANCESTRY IS KNOWN

Vespasian and Domitian. He may have been Simeon the Zealot an apostle.

February 18   *Saint Anglibert*
Country: France   *Date:* 740-814

Family: Parents: Unknown   Wife: Bertha of Holy Roman Empire
Children: Arsinde de Ponthieu; Nithard "The Chronicler" Abbot of St. Riquier

Ancestry: Saint Anglibert married Bertha, daughter of Charlemange. His ancestry is not known.

Descendents: Sainted descendents include Saint Cunigunda, Saint David I King of Scotland, Saint Fernando III King of Spain, Saint Henry II King of Germany, Saint Leopold III, Saint Louis IX, Saint Margaret of Scotland, and Saint Raymond. Royal descendents include King Edward III Plantagenet of England, King of Naples Charles II, King of France Philip IV, and King of Scotland William the Lion. Also Casimir King of Poland , Alphonso Enriquez I King of Portugal and Henry IV Holy Roman Emperor of Germany.

Biography: Saint Anglibert studied under the great English scholar, Alcuin. He was raised in the court of Emperor Charlemagne, and was Benedictine abbot and advisor to Charlemagne. Receiving minor orders, Angilbert accompanied King Pepin to Italy in 782. After this he returned to the court and he became known as "Homer" because of his literary and language skills. He also served as an envoy of the court to the pope. Angilbert either rebuilt or restored the abbey and endowed it with two hundred books as he in 790, was named the abbot of Saint-Riquier in Picardy, France. In the year 800, Charlemagne came to visit him. Angilbert also fathered two children, having had an affair with Bertha, Charlemagne's daughter. In the year 800, Charlemagne came to visit him. Angilbert did penance for

SAINTS DAILY
Kings, Queens, Popes, Princes, Princesses, Emperors, Hermits, Bishops

DAILY SAINTS WHOSE ANCESTRY IS KNOWN

this relationship, and Bertha entered a convent. Nithard, a noted historian of the era and Angilbert's son, wrote of the penance's and austerities undertaken. Angilbert died on February 18, 814. Some years after his burial, his body was found to be incorrupt.

February 21 Blessed Pepin Of Landen

Country: France   *Date:* d 639

Family: Parents: Unknown   Wife: Itte   Children: St Beggue, of Austrasia

Ancestry: Ancestry is not known. .

Descendents: Sainted descendents include Saint Adele of Blois, Saint Adelaide of Italy, Saint Louis IX of France, Saint Fernando III of Spain, Saint Cunigunda of Luxemborg, Saint Leopold III of Austria, Saint Henry II of Germany, Saint Lazlo King of Hungary, Saint Raymond Berenger IV. and Saint David and Saint Margaret of Scotland. Royal descendents include King Edward III Plantagenet of England, King of Naples Charles II, King of France Philip IV, and King of Scotland William the Lion. Also Casimir King of Poland, Alphonso Enriquez I King of Portugal, and Henry IV Holy Roman Emperor of Germany.

Biography: The husband of Blessed Ita, he was a close ally of Bishop Arnulf of Metz with whom he overthrew Queen Brunhilda of Austrasia. Frankish mayor of the palace, duke of Brabant, and the chief political figure during the reigns of the Frankish kings Clotaire II, Dagobert I, and Sigebert II he was soon appointed mayor of the palace for his role. He was exiled from the court and went into retirement near Aquitaine following an incident in which he reprimanded King Dagobert I for his adulterous life. Pepin once more became the chief figure of the kingdom until his death when he was called to serve as tutor to Dagobert's three year old son. Pepin earned a reputation for defending the interests of the Church, working to have only truly worthy bishops appointed to Frankish sees, and promoting the

SAINTS DAILY
Kings, Queens, Popes, Princes, Princesses, Emperors, Hermits, Bishops

DAILY SAINTS WHOSE ANCESTRY IS KNOWN

spread of Christianity. He is listed as a saint in some old martyrologies while never canonized. He was an ancestor of Charlemagne; his grandson, Pepin of Heristal, founded the Carolingian dynasty.

February 21   Saint Robert Southwell

Country: England   **Date:** c 1561 d. 1593

Family: Father: Richard Southwell   Mother: Bridget Copley
Spouse: Unknown   Siblings: Unknown

Ancestors: Ancestors include the noble lines of the De Vere, Wentworth, and also Saint Gilbert of Sepringham.

Branches of the Tree : This branch of the tree shows Richard De Crevequer married Saint Gilbert of Sepringham's daughter Maud. This line continues including descendents such as the Neville line, the Taylor line, the Tyes line and the Wentworth line.

Biography: Saint Robert Southwell was born in Norfolk and became a Martyr of England. He entered the Jesuits in Rome, From 1584 until 1592 he served as a missionary in London. Saint Robert Southwell was an ordained Priest. He was arrested and remained in jail for three years before being martyred at Tyburn. He is one of the Fory Martyrs of England and Wales, canonized in 1970.

February 23   Saint Milburga Of Thanet

Country: Great Britain   **Date:** 715

Family: Father: Merewald of Mercia   Mother: Saint Ermenburga

SAINTS DAILY
Kings, Queens, Popes, Princes, Princesses, Emperors, Hermits, Bishops

DAILY SAINTS WHOSE ANCESTRY IS KNOWN

Spouse: Unknown   Siblings: Mildred of Thanet Saint; Mildgytha Saint;

Ancestors: The line of the King of Mercia Penda who is the grandfather goes to Woden and Frigg.

Biography: Saint Milburga was a Benedictine abbess who received the veil from St. Theodore of Canterbury. She was the daughter of Merewald King of Mercia and sister of Sts. Mildred of Thanet and Saint Mildgytha. She was also daughter of Saint Ermenburga who founded a monastery. Saint Milburga was abbess of Wenlock Abbey in Salop, Shropshire, England. Her father King of Mercia Merewald and her uncle, King Wulfhere, provided funds for the abbey. It is said she had remarkable abilities, like power over birds, and levitation.

February 23   *Saint Jurmin*
Country: England   **Date:** 8th Century

Family: Father: Anna King of East Anglia
         Mother: Hereswitha Saint
Spouse: Unknown   Siblings: Sexburga Princess Of East Anglia Saint; Etheldreda Saint; Erconwald Saint; Withburga Saint

Ancestors: Saint Ethelburga mother is Saint Hereswitha. Further back ancestry is not known. Woden and Frigg are Ancestors. Saint Cyllin is an Ancestor. Ancestors that were the Kings of Siluria. Generations previous to this they were the Kings of Britain. The line then goes back to Zerah, whose father is Judah. This line also marries Anna Arimathea who is the daughter of Joseph of Arimathea. A little know fact of the biblical character of Joseph of Arimathea is that he is the son of Mathat, who is in the line of Nathan that is listed in the New Testament book of Luke. So Saint Cyllin is descended from the Davidic line of Nathan and so from Judah thru Perez, and also as previously mentioned thru Judah's son Zerah.

SAINTS DAILY
Kings, Queens, Popes, Princes, Princesses, Emperors, Hermits, Bishops

81

DAILY SAINTS WHOSE ANCESTRY IS KNOWN

Branches of the Tree: Kings of East Anglia

Biography: Saint Jurmin was from a family of Saints, his mother and four siblings all attaining the title Saint. He was the Prince of East Anglia, England. He was the son of King Anna. Saint Jurmin is honored as a confessor. Enshrined at Bury St. Edmunds are his relics.

February 25   *Saint Aldetrudis*
Country: Belgium   *Date:* before 670

Family: Parents: Father- Vincent Madelgaire de Hainault Saint Mother- Waldetrudis de Loomis Saint Husband: Waudbert VI de Lommois (Comte de Lommois) Children: Waudbert VII de Lommois (Comte de Lommois)

Ancestry: Only one generation is known and is listed above.

Descendents: Descendents include Saint Adelaide of Italy, Saint Anglibert, Saint Lazlo of Hungary, Saint Irene, Saint Leopold III, Saint Louis IX, Saint Hedwig, Saint Isabel of Aragon, and Saint Nithard the Cronicler. Royal Descendents include King of Naples Charles II, King of France Louis VIII, Alphonso IV of Portugal, and King Edward III Plantagenet of England.

Biography: The daughter of Sts. Vincent Maldegurus and Waldeturdis was also a neice of St. Aldegundis. She was a Benedictine abbess, the abbess of her aunt's convent.

February 25 Saint King Ethelbert
Country: Kent England   *Date:* 560-616

SAINTS DAILY
Kings, Queens, Popes, Princes, Princesses, Emperors, Hermits, Bishops

DAILY SAINTS WHOSE ANCESTRY IS KNOWN

Family: Parents: Father- Eormenric Kent King Kent Mother- Unknown
Wife: Bertha of the Franks   Children: Eadbald Kent King Kent

Ancestry: Saint Ethelbert of Kent ancestry traces back to Zerah thru the Kings of Troy. His wife Saint Bertha also is traced back to the lines of the Frankish Kings to Zerah whose father is Judah. Saint Bertha's ancestor is Saint Clotilde who converted the Frankish King Clovis to Christianity. Also included is Joseph of Arimathea. Also King David of Judah and Israel is an ancestor thru Nathan his son.

Descendents: Sainted descendants include Saint Adele of Blois, Saint Louis IX of France, Saint Fernando III of Spain, Saint Cunigunda of Luxemborg, Saint Leopold III of Austria, Saint Henry II of Germany, Saint Edgar the peaceful King of England and Saint David and Saint Margaret of Scotland. Royal descendents include King Edward III Plantagenet of England, King of Naples Charles II, King of France Philip IV, and King of Scotland William the Lion. Also Casimir King of Poland, Alphonso Enriquez I King of Portugal and Henry IV Holy Roman Emperor of Germany were descendents.

Biography: Converted by Saint Augustine, Ethelbert was King of Kent. He married a Christian daughter of King Charibert of Paris, Bertha, and fought the West Saxons in 568. Baptized in 597, Ethelbert brought a large part of Kent's population into the faith. He brought the King of the East Saxons and The King of the East Angles into the Church, but he did not enforce conversions. For fifty-six years, Ethelbert ruled, and founded the abbeys of Christ Church, Sts. Peter and Paul in Canterbury, and St. Andrew's in Rochester. Ethelbert is listed as Aedilbert by St. Bede.

February 25   *Saint Bertha of Paris*

Country: France   *Date:* 548-580

SAINTS DAILY
Kings, Queens, Popes, Princes, Princesses, Emperors, Hermits, Bishops

83

DAILY SAINTS WHOSE ANCESTRY IS KNOWN

Family: Parents: Father- Unknown Mother- Unknown
Husband: Saint Ethelbert of Kent
Children: Eadbald Kent King Kent

Ancestry: Saint Ethelbert of Kent ancestry traces back to Zerah thru the Kings of Troy. His wife Saint Bertha also is traced back to the lines of the Frankish Kings to Zerah whose father is Judah. Saint Bertha's ancestor is Saint Clotilde who converted the Frankish King Clovis to Christianity. Also included is Joseph of Arimathea. Also King David of Judah and Israel is an ancestor thru Nathan his son.

Descendents: Sainted descendants include Saint Adele of Blois, Saint Louis IX of France, Saint Fernando III of Spain, Saint Cunigunda of Luxemborg, Saint Leopold III of Austria, Saint Henry II of Germany, Saint Edgar the peaceful King of England and Saint David and Saint Margaret of Scotland. Royal descendents include King Edward III Plantagenet of England, King of Naples Charles II, King of France Philip IV, and King of Scotland William the Lion. Also Casimir King of Poland , Alphonso Enriquez I King of Portugal and Henry IV Holy Roman Emperor of Germany.

Biography: Wife of Saint Ethelbert of Kent she was the first Christian queen of England, a Frankish Princess. She brought her chaplain Luidhard to the pagan king Saint Ethelbert. Saint Ethelbert welcomed Saint Augustine to Kent in 596. She has been venerated since her death, but no feast day has been given to Bertha.

February 26 Saint Isabel of France

Country: France   **Date:** 1270

Family: Father: Louis VIII of France   Mother: Blanca Alphonsa Princess Castile

SAINTS DAILY
Kings, Queens, Popes, Princes, Princesses, Emperors, Hermits, Bishops

DAILY SAINTS WHOSE ANCESTRY IS KNOWN

Spouse: Unknown   Siblings: Louis IX Saint King of France

Ancestors: Saint Isabel's ancestors include Saint Fernando and so Muhammad, Ishmael and Abraham. Also Charlemagne and so Zerah. Also Joseph of Arimathea and Saint Helena of Rome. Also King David of Judah and Israel is an ancestor thru Nathan his son. King Solomon of Israel and Judah is also an ancestor. Sainted Ancestry includes more saints than any other saint. These are Saint Ethelbert, Saint Arnulf, Saint Itta, Saint Sigebert, Saint Dagobert, Saint Beggue, Saint Liuthwin, Saint Bathildis, Saint Sexburga, Blessed Pepin, Saint Clodulf, Saint Olga, Saint Matilda, Saint Elgiva, Saint Edgar, Saint Henry II, Saint Cunigunda, Saint Stephen, Saint Margaret, and Saint David. Bran the Blessed is an Ancestor, as is his wife Anna of Arimathea. Saint Joseph of Arimathea and so the Line of Nathan Son of David King of Israel and Judah. King David's ancestors include the Israelites, Zebulon, Levi, Joseph, and Judah. Also Anna of Arimathea, daughter to Joseph of Aramathea married Bran the Blessed whose line goes to Tros and so to Epraim son of Joseph the Israelite. Also the line from Anna of Arimathea's mother goes thru Simon the Just thru many High Priests to Judah the Israelite.

Branches of the Tree: Louis the IX is in this branch, the King of France, Saint Isabel's brother.

Biography: Saint Isabel of France was Sister of Saint Louis and daughter of King Louis VIII of France and Blanche of Castile. She refused offers of marriage from several noble suitors. She founded the Fransican Monastery of the Humility of the Blessed Virgin Mary at Longchamps in Paris. She lived there but refused to become abbess and was never a nun. She continued her life of virginity consecrated to God. She died there on February 23, and her cult was approved in 1521.

SAINTS DAILY
Kings, Queens, Popes, Princes, Princesses, Emperors, Hermits, Bishops

DAILY SAINTS WHOSE ANCESTRY IS KNOWN

February 27 Saint Leander of Seville
Country: Cartagena Spain   **Date:** 534-600

Family: Father: Severinum , Count Of Cartagena
          Mother: Theodora
Spouse: None   Siblings: Theodosia; Fulgentius Saint; Florentina Saint; Isadore Saint

Ancestors: Not much Ancestry is Known

Biography: Saint Leander was a Bishop. He was born at Cartagena Spain of Severianus and Theodora. He was from a family of Saints, his brothers being Saint Isidore and Fulgentius were both Bishops and his sister Florentina. He became the bishop of the See after being a monk at Seville. He was instrumental in converting the sons of the Arian Visigothic King Leovigild Hermenegild and Reccared. This action made the King angry, and he was exiled to Constantinople. It was in Constantinople that Saint Leander met the future Pope Gregory the Great. It was the suggestion of Saint Leander that inspired Gregory to write the Moralia, a famous commentary of the Book of Job. He returned home under King Reccard, and began work of reforming the Arians of Spain. He presided on the third local Council of Toledo which decreed the consubstantiality of the three Persons of the Trinity and brought moral reforms. He brought the Visigoths and the Suevi back to the true faith. This obtained the gratitude of Gregory the Great. Saint Leander also composed a Rule for nuns and introduced the Nicene Creed at Mass. Saint Leander died around 600 and his brother succeeded to the See of Seville. Saint Leander is honored as a Doctor of the Church by the Spanish Church.

February 28 Blessed Hedwig of Poland
Country: Poland   **Date:** b. 1371 1399

SAINTS DAILY
 Kings, Queens, Popes, Princes, Princesses, Emperors, Hermits, Bishops

DAILY SAINTS WHOSE ANCESTRY IS KNOWN

Family: Father: Louis I d Anjou King of Hungary and Poland Mother: Elisabeth Kontromanich Spouse: Unknown Siblings:

Biography: Blessed Hedwig of Poland was the Queen. She married Jagiello of Lithuania only after his conversion of becoming a Christian. She was the daughter of King Louis I of Hungary. She then actively promoted Christianity in Lithuania.

SAINTS DAILY
Kings, Queens, Popes, Princes, Princesses, Emperors, Hermits, Bishops

DAILY SAINTS WHOSE ANCESTRY IS KNOWN

Saints of March

FEAST DAY	SAINT	COUNTRY	BORN	DIED
1-Mar	Saint Dewi	England		600
2-Mar	Saint Charles the Good	Denmark	1081	1127
3-Mar	Saint Cunigunda of Luxemburg	Luxemberg	978	1033
3-Mar	Saint Non Saint	Wales		6th
3-Mar	Saint Anselm of Nonantola			803
3-Mar	Saint Winaloe	France		6th
4-Mar	Blessed Humbert III	France	1136	1189
4-Mar	Saint Casimir	France	1458	1484
5-Mar	Saint Piran	England	480	6th
6-Mar	Saint Chrodegang of Metz	France	712	766
6-Mar	Saint Kyneburga	England		c 680
6-Mar	Saint Kyneswide	England		c 680
6-Mar	Saint Agnes of Bohemia	Armenia	1205	1282
7-Mar	Saint Enodoch	Wales		6th
11-Mar	Saint Custennin ap Cadwy	Dumnonia	520	
11-Mar	Saint Constantine II of Scotland	Scotland	836	877
14-Mar	Saint Mathilda of Germany	Germany	892	967/68

SAINTS DAILY
Kings, Queens, Popes, Princes, Princesses, Emperors, Hermits, Bishops

88

DAILY SAINTS WHOSE ANCESTRY IS KNOWN

15-Mar	Saint Raymond Fitero	Aragon	1113	1162
16-Mar	Saint Dentlin	England		7th
16-Mar	Saint Eusebia	France		c 680
16-Mar	Saint Abban	Ireland		620
17-Mar	Saint Ceneu	Britain	374	
17-Mar	Saint Joseph of Arimathea	Israel		
17-Mar	Saint Paternus Pasrut	Scotland	305	
17-Mar	Saint Helen of the Host	Wales	330	
17-Mar	Saint Gertrude of Nivelles	France		659
17-Mar	Saint Gertrude	France	632	7th
17-Mar	Saint Patrick Saccatus	Ireland	385	461
18-Mar	Saint Edward "the martyr"	England		c 978
20-Mar	Saint Tetricus Bishop	France		572
21-Mar	Saint Enda	Ireland		c 530
22-Mar	Saint Darerca	Ireland	310	5th
24-Mar	Saint Catherine of Sweden	Sweden	1331	1381
26-Mar	Saint Margaret Clitherow	England	1556	1586
29-Mar	Saint Gwladys	Wales		5th
29-Mar	Saint Gwynllyw Farfog	Wales	466	523

TABLE FOUR SAINTS OF MARCH

SAINTS DAILY
Kings, Queens, Popes, Princes, Princesses, Emperors, Hermits, Bishops

89

DAILY SAINTS WHOSE ANCESTRY IS KNOWN

March 1 *Saint Dewi*
Country: Britain   **Date:** c. 600

Family: Father: Sant   Mother: Saint Non
Spouse: None   Siblings: Unknown

Ancestors: Saint Cyllus is an ancestor. Saint Helen of the Host is an Ancestor, Also Saint Brychan is an ancestor. Saint Constantine The Great is an Ancestor, as is Helen of the True Cross (Saint Helenus). Bran the Blessed is an Ancestor, as is his wife Anna of Arimathea. Saint Joseph of Arimathea and so the Line of Nathan Son of David King of Israel and Judah. King David's ancestors include the Israelites, Zebulon, Levi, Joseph, and Judah. Also Anna of Arimathea, daughter to Joseph of Aramathea married Bran the Blessed whose line goes to Tros and so to Epraim son of Joseph the Israelite. Also the line from Anna of Arimathea's mother goes thru Simon the Just thru many High Priests to Judah the Israelite.

Branches of the Tree: Saint Non is the granddaughter of Saint Brychan.

Biography: The son of King Sant of South Wales and Saint Non. Saint David was ordained to priesthood and studied under Saint Belinda's. He founded a number of monasteries and he was involved in missionary work. One monastery in southwestern Wales at Menevia of was noted for extreme asceticism. Monks at his monastery and Saint David drank only water never wanting beer also monks put in a full day of heavy manual labor. Saint David and his monks also were expected to do some intense study. There was a synod at Brevi in Cardiganshir about the year 550. Saint David was elected as primary of the Cambrian church. This was due largely to his contributions at the synod at Brevi. Saint David visited the holy land where he was reportedly consecrated Archbishop by the patriarch of Jerusalem. Pelagianism was near its end and Saint David is said to have

SAINTS DAILY
Kings, Queens, Popes, Princes, Princesses, Emperors, Hermits, Bishops

DAILY SAINTS WHOSE ANCESTRY IS KNOWN

invoked a council that ended its last vestiges. About the year 589 Saint David died at his monastery in Menevia. Pope Callista II approved his cult about 1120 A.D. Saint David is forever revered the patriot of Wales. There is no doubt Saint David was granted substantial qualities and quantities of spiritual leadership. Many monasteries leveraged as results of his leadership is good example. It is his monastic piety that sets an example for everyone. His feast day is March 1

March 2 Saint Charles the Good

Country: Denmark   **Date:** 1081-1127

Family: Father: Canute IV Svendsson King Of Denmark Saint   Mother: Adele Flandern   Spouse: Unknown   Siblings: Carl,"The Dane" Knutsson Prince Of Denmark; Cecilia Knudsdatter Princess Of Denmark; Ingegard Knutsdatter Princess Of Denmark

Ancestors: Ancestors include Odin, Kings of Denmark.

Branches of the Tree This is the branch of the tree near the kings of Denmark and Saint Canute.

Biography: Saint Canute, King of Denmark and father of Blessed Charles the Good, was slain. This happened in 1086 at St. Alban's Church, Odence. Charles was taken by his mother to the court of Robert, Count of Flanders, who was his mother's father. Saint Charles was five years old. Robert and Saint Charles went on a crusade to the Holy Land after he became a Knight. He also fought against the English on his return. He distinguished himself in the Holy Land crusade. Baldwin, Robert's son became Count of Flanders when Robert died. Baldwin designated Charles as the heir. Charles marriage to the daughter of the Count of Clermont was then arranged. Charles became known for his wise and beneficent ways and was recognized by the people for his personal holiness. In 1119 Baldwin died and Charles ruled his people with compassion. He

SAINTS DAILY
Kings, Queens, Popes, Princes, Princesses, Emperors, Hermits, Bishops

DAILY SAINTS WHOSE ANCESTRY IS KNOWN

employed diligence and wisdom and enforced truces. Black marketers horded food and were exploiting the people so Charles fought against them. In 1127 in the Church of St. Donatian they killed him. Saint Charles the Good feast day is March 2nd.

March 3 Saint Cunigunda of Luxemburg

Country: Luxemborg   Patron of Lithuania   *Date:* 978- c 1024

Family: Parents: Father- Sigefrid I Count of Luxemburg Mother- Hedwig of Hungary
Husband: Saint Henry II of Germany   Children: Agatha von Braunschweig

Ancestry: Saint Cunigunda married Saint Henry II of Germany. Her ancestor is Stephen Saint of Hungary. Her line also joins with the Frankish Kings and so is traceable to Zerah. Also included is Joseph of Arimathea. Also King David of Judah and Israel is an ancestor thru Nathan his son. King Solomon of Israel and Judah is also an ancestor. Sainted Ancestors include Saint Ethelbert, Saint Itta, Saint Arnulf, Saint Sigebert, Saint Dagobert, Saint Beggue, Saint Liuthwin, Saint Beggue, Saint Sexburga, Blessed Pepin, Saint Clodulf, and Saint Stephen.

Descendents: Descendents include Saint David and Margaret of Scotland, Saint Louis IX of France, and Saint Fernando III of Spain. Royal Descendents include King Edward Plantagenet III of England, King Philip IV of France, King of Naples Charles II, and William I of Scotland.

Biography: Sigfrid, first Count of Luxemburg was the father of Saint Cunegundes. She was married to Saint Henry Duke of Bavaria after a pious education. Saint Henry, upon the death of Emperor Otto III was chosen King of the Holy Roman Empire. As wife of Saint Henry Saint Cunegundes was crowned at Paderborn in 1002. She became Empress in 1014 when she went with her husband to Rome and received together with him the

SAINTS DAILY
Kings, Queens, Popes, Princes, Princesses, Emperors, Hermits, Bishops

DAILY SAINTS WHOSE ANCESTRY IS KNOWN

imperial crown from Pope Benedict VIII hands. With her husbands consent she had made a vow of virginity before marriage. And she lived in continence. She was accused of scandalous conduct, but she walked over pieces of flaming irons without injury proving her innocence as granted by Divine Providence. She was very charitable and when her husband Henry II died in 1024 she had given away nearly all her wealth. She closed herself with a poor habit in 1025 on the anniversary of Saint Henry's death and on the dedication of a monastery which she had built for Benedictine nuns at Kaffungen. She adopted the veil which she received from the hands of the Bishop and entered the same monastery. The last fifteen years of her life was spent in prayer, reading and manual labor. In 1040 she died and her body was carried to Bamberg where it was laid near that of her husband, Saint Henry.

March 3 *Saint Non*

Country: Wales Great Britain **Date:** 6th Century

Family: Father: Cynyr Ceinfarfog The Fair   Mother: Sefin Verch Brychan Brycheiniog
Spouse: Unknown   Siblings: Saint Gwen

Ancestors: Saint Brychan is an Ancestor, of which only a few generations are known on fathers side. Saint Helen of the Host is known as Mothers Ancestor.

Branches of the Tree: This branch is the Saint Brychan Branch. Saint Non is the mother of Saint Dewi (David) and Saint Brychan is the ancestor of King Edward IV Plantagenet.

Biography: Saint Non's relices were enchrined in Cornwall. They were moved after the Reformation. Saint Non is also called Nonnita or Nonna. She is the mother of Saint David who is also called Saint Dewi of Wales. Sant was her husband who was a local chieftain, if they were married. Possibly she was seduced

SAINTS DAILY
 Kings, Queens, Popes, Princes, Princesses, Emperors, Hermits, Bishops

DAILY SAINTS WHOSE ANCESTRY IS KNOWN

by Sant. The union had a son, who was Saint David of Wales. Saint Non died in Brittany, Possibly in Cornwall.

March 3   *Saint Winwaloe*

Country: Brittany France   **Date:** 6th Century

Family: Father: Saint Fracan   Mother: Saint Gwen   Spouse: Unknown   Siblings: Saint Wethoc, Saint Iocab, Chreirbia

Ancestors: James the son of Saint Joseph is an Ancestor, so is Conan.

Branches of the Tree: This is the branch that leads to Saint Judicael

Descendents:

Biography: Son of Fragan and Gwen on account of his beauty he was named Winwaloe or "He that is Fair". He was consecrated to God from his birth because he was their third son. He was a monk who made great progress and founded a monastery on an island, after three years moved it to the mainland because of the storms. There are dedications to him in Cornwall, at Gunwalloe, and Landewednack.

March 3   *Saint Anselm of Nonantola*

Date: d. 803   **Feastday:** March 3

Family:
Parents: Father: Unknown Mother: Unknown Spouse: None
Siblings: Gisaltruda De Nanantola Children: None

SAINTS DAILY
Kings, Queens, Popes, Princes, Princesses, Emperors, Hermits, Bishops

94

DAILY SAINTS WHOSE ANCESTRY IS KNOWN

Ancestry: None of his ancestors are known

Branch of the Tree: The relationship of Saint Anselm of Nonantola to his sister is how he relates to the Kings of the Lombards.

Biography: Saint Anselm of Nonantola was the brother in law to King Aistulf and had a hereditary title. He left this and formed a monastery at Tanano Italy. Two years later he formed the Nonantola Monastery in Italy. He was invested in the Benedictines by Pope Stephen II and made many charitable institutions. However when Aistulf lost power the charities had to stop without a patron. Desiderius banished Anselm in 756 and he went to Rome to Monte Cassino. When Charlemange defeated Desiderius he returned. He is patron of the region.

March 4   Blessed Humbert III

Country: France   *Date:* 1136-1189

Family: Parents: Father- Amadeo III Count of Savoy
Mother- Maud Countess of Albon
Wife: Beatrix De Vienne   Children: Thomas I Count of Savoy

Ancestry: Blessed Humbert III ancestors include Alfred the Great and the Kings of Wessex.

Descendents: Descendents include John Beaufort Duke of Somerset and Edmund Prince of England.

Biography: He was born at Avigliana, became Count of Savoy when quite young on the death of his father, and educated by Bishop Amadeus of Lausanne. Humbert was the son of Count Amadeus III of Savoy and Matilda of Vienna. Humbert ruled wisely and engaged in several wars to defend his principality. Late in life, he returned to the Cistercian Abbey of Hautecombe, where he probably died. A conflicting legend says that he

SAINTS DAILY
Kings, Queens, Popes, Princes, Princesses, Emperors, Hermits, Bishops

DAILY SAINTS WHOSE ANCESTRY IS KNOWN

emerged to lead his troops against invading German troops and died at Chambery. His cult was approved in 1831.

March 4 *Saint Casimir*

Country: England   **Date:** 03 Oct 1458- 04 Mar 1482/83   **Patron:** Lithuania; Poland; Youth of Lithuania

Family: Father: Casimir IV Jagellon   Mother: Elisabeth von Habsburg
Spouse: Unknown   Siblings: Unknown

Ancestors: About 18 generations are known with Geza I King of Hungary Saint included.

Branches of the Tree : This branch of the tree comes to King Casimir IV of Poland and so is part of the European Royalty.

Biography: Saint Casimir is the patron Saint of Poland and Lithuania. He was the third child of King Casimir IV and Elizabeth of Austria. Saint Casimir was born in 1458 or 1460 on October 3. At an early age he showed signs of holiness and was trained in spirituality. He refused to lead an army against King Matthias I Corminus of Hungary in 1471 when Casimir IV his father ordered him. Saint Casimir thought the mission unjust and refused to try to seize the Hungarian throne. As punishment he was confined to the castle of Dzoki and there he was ordered to marry. He refused this as well in opposition to his Father's orders. From 1479 to 1483 he served as regent of the nation when his father was away. Saint Casimir died of consumption on March 4 while visiting Grodno, Lithuania. In Lithuania at Vilnius his tomb became famed for miracles, and he was canonized in 1522 by Pope Adrian VI. Casimir is also patron of the Knights of Saint John and is invocked against enemies of Poland and the faith.

SAINTS DAILY
Kings, Queens, Popes, Princes, Princesses, Emperors, Hermits, Bishops

DAILY SAINTS WHOSE ANCESTRY IS KNOWN

March 5 *Saint Piran*

Country: English Wales **Date:** 480- 6th Century

Family: Father: Dywel (Prince Of Dumnonia)
Mother: Unknown
Spouse: Unknown   Siblings: Unknown

Ancestors: Conan Meriadoc, King of Brittany and Dumnonia and Saint Ursula are ancestors, then only a few generations are known

Branches of the Tree: Saloman King of the Bretons is near in this branch of the tree.

Biography: Saint Piran was also called Perran. He became a hermit in Cornwall near Padstow. Tin miners take Saint Piran as their patron. His feast day is March 5th.

March 6 *Saint Chrodegang of Metz*

Feastday: March 6   **Date**: b. 712 d. 766

Family: Father: Sigrammus   Mother: Landrada
Spouse: Unknown   Siblings: Saint Opportuna

Country: Franks

Ancestors: Chrodobertus I is an ancestor on his mothers side.

Branches of the Tree: Pepin Mayor of the Palace is a relative. This is the branch around Charlemagne.

Biography:Born near Leige at Hesbaye Brabant, Saint Chrodegang became the secretary to Charles Martel. He became Bishop of Metz about 742. Ambassador to Pope Stephen III for Pepin he was involved in the crowning of Pepin as King of the Franks. He was also involved with defending the Pope against the Lombards. He wrote a code of rules for the canons of his see

SAINTS DAILY
Kings, Queens, Popes, Princes, Princesses, Emperors, Hermits, Bishops

97

DAILY SAINTS WHOSE ANCESTRY IS KNOWN

and was responsible for the canon regular movement. He founded churches and monasteries and introduced the Gregorian Chant to his see. His choir school he founded in Metz became famous all over Europe.

March 6   *Saint Kyneburga*
Date: 680

Family: Father: King Penda of Mercia   Mother: Princess Cynewise of Northumbria
Spouse: Unknown   Siblings: Princess Wilburga of Mercia; Edburga of Bicester Saint; Kyneswide Saint; King Wulfhere Of Mercia; Merewald of Mercia

Country: Great Britain

Ancestors:
The line of the King of Mercia Penda goes to Woden and Frigg.

Biography:
Saint Kyneburga relics are in Saint Peterborough Abbey in England. Her relative was Tibba in all likelihood. Saint Kyneburga founded an abbey at Castor Northamptonshire. Her sister Kyneswide joined her there. She was from a sainted family with two sisters who became saints.

March 6   *Saint Kyneswide*
Country: Great Britain   **Date:** 680

Family: Father: King Penda of Mercia   Mother: Princess Cynewise of Northumbria
Spouse: Unknown   Siblings: Princess Wilburga of Mercia; Kyneburga Saint; Edburga of Bicester Saint; King Wulfhere Of Mercia; Merewald of Mercia

SAINTS DAILY
Kings, Queens, Popes, Princes, Princesses, Emperors, Hermits, Bishops

DAILY SAINTS WHOSE ANCESTRY IS KNOWN

Ancestors: The line of the King of Mercia Penda goes to Woden and Frigg.

Biography: Saint Kyneswide joined her sister in the abbey Saint Kyneburga founded in Castor Northamptonshire. Both hers and her sisters relics are in Saint Peterborough Abbey in England. She was the daughter princess of King Penda of Mercia and Princess Cynewise of Northumbria.

March 6   *Saint Agnes of Bohemia*

Feastday: March 6   Date: b.1205 d. 1282

Family: Father: Vratislav (Uratislas) Bohemia Duke Of Mother: Drahomira Von Stoder
Spouse: Unknown   Siblings: Boleslav I The Cruel King Of Bohemia; Saint Wenceslaus

Country: Armenia

Ancestors: Saint Ludmilla is an ancestors

Branches of the Tree: Bohemia is in this branch of the Tree in the vicinity of Saint Ludmilla.

Biography: Saint Agnes was related to Saint Elizabeth of Hungary. Her brother was Saint Wenceslaus. She was promised three times in marriage although educated by cisterian nuns. A suitor died, she was left for another, and finally got Pope Gergory IX to intervene. She built a hospital, established clinics, and became a Poor Clare after starting a convent for five nuns sent by Clare. She was fifty years in the cloister.

March 7   *Saint Enodoch*

d.c. 520   Feastday March 7

Family:

SAINTS DAILY
Kings, Queens, Popes, Princes, Princesses, Emperors, Hermits, Bishops

DAILY SAINTS WHOSE ANCESTRY IS KNOWN

Parents: Father-Saint Brychan Mother- Unknown
Husband: Unknown
Children: Unknown

Biography Welsh saint of the line of the chieftain Brychan of Brecknock, also called Wenedoc. Enodoch is believed by some historians to have been a woman, called Qendydd.:

March 11 *Saint Custennin*

Country: Great Britain   *Date:* b. 520 – d. 589

Family: Parents: Father- Cadwy ap Gereint, King of Dumnonia Mother- Unknown
Wife:Unknown   Children: NN ferch Custennin

Ancestry: Ancestors include Saint Joseph of Arimathea and so Nathan son of David. Also Saint Helen of the Cross is an ancestor. King of Britain and Romans including Mark Antony and Julia of Rome. Also Saint Cyllin so Zerah thru the Kings of Siluria and Tros King of Troy.

Descendents: Arthwys King of Morganwy, Edmund Duke of Somerset, Edward Stafford 3rd Duke of Buckingham, Richard Fitzalan Earl of Arundel, and Charles Howard Earl of Nottingham.

Biography: St. Constantine of Cornwall,   King of Dumnonia   (c. AD 520-576)
(Welsh-Custennin, Latin-Constantinus, English-Constantine)
Literary tradition indicates AD 537, after the Battle of Camlann from which, some sources say, he was the only survivor when Constantine probably succeeded his father, Cado, as King of Dumnonia. He was also, apparently left the High-Kingship of Britain, at this time, by his cousin, King Arthur. He was rebuked for disguising himself as a Bishop in order to sacrilegiously murder his two nephews in the sanctity of a church. According to

SAINTS DAILY
Kings, Queens, Popes, Princes, Princesses, Emperors, Hermits, Bishops

100

DAILY SAINTS WHOSE ANCESTRY IS KNOWN

Geoffrey of Monmouth, these were, in fact, the treacherous sons of the evil usurper, Mordred, who were killed in Winchester & London. Despite such positions of honor, Constantine was described as the "unclean whelp of the lioness of Dumnonia" by his contemporary, St. Gildas. However, it appears that, as an old man, this King's character was greatly changed through grief brought about by the death of his loving wife. One day, while out hunting a deer, his prey took shelter in St. Petroc's cell. So impressed was the King by the saint's power that he and his body guard immediately converted to Christianity. Constantine gave Petroc an ivory hunting horn in commemoration of the event and this was long revered along with the Saint's other relics at Bodmin. He moved amongst his people, founding churches at the two Constantines, near Padstow and Falmouth, and at Illogan; also at Milton Abbot and Dunsford in Devon. The King became co-founder of this famous Cornish monastery and, soon afterward, abdicated the throne in favour of his son, Bledric in order to take up the religious life himself. Later, he traveled across the Bristol Channel to join St. Dewi (David) at Mynyw (St. Davids), where he resided as a monk for many years. Near Pembroke he founded the church at Cosheston, but eventually settled as a hermit in Costyneston (Cosmeston) near Cardiff. He may have died there, though there are persistent stories that he traveled still further north and preached to the people of Galloway before being martyred in Kintyre on 9th March AD 576. The traditions of St. Constantine of Cornwall & St. Constantine of Strathclyde are, however, much confused.

March 11 Saint Constantine II of Scotland

Country: Scotland **Date:** 836-877

Family: Parents: Kenneth I MacAlpin King of Scotland b. 810 Mother- Unknown
Wife: Unknown   Children: Donald II King of Scotland

SAINTS DAILY
Kings, Queens, Popes, Princes, Princesses, Emperors, Hermits, Bishops

DAILY SAINTS WHOSE ANCESTRY IS KNOWN

Ancestry: Ancestors go back quite a few generations to Domegart King of Scotland.

Descendents: Saint David of Scotland, and Saint Louis IX are descendents of Saint Constantine. Also King Henry I of England, King Phillip IV King of France, King Malcolm II of Scotland, Charles II King of Naples, Edward III and Edward IV Plantagenet of England, Matilda Empress of Germany, and King John of England.

Biography: Saint Constantine was the King of Cornwall. The King of Brittany had a daughter. Constantine married her and when she died Saint Constantine left his throne to his son and joined the monastery at Rahan, Ireland at St. Mochuda. He performed menial tasks at the monastery, then studied for the priesthood and was ordained. Under St. Columba he went as a missionary to Scotland and then under St. Kentigern, preached in Galloway, and in Govan became Abbot of a monastery. On his way to Kintyre in old age, he was attacked by pirates who cut off his right arm, and he bled to death. Because of this he is regarded as Scotland's first martyr. His feast day is March 11th

March 13   *Saint Nicephorus*
Date: b.759

Family:
Parents: Father: Constantine V Emperor   Mother: Eudocia
Spouse: None Children: None Siblings: Prince Kristophos, Nicephorus Saint, Eudoxius, Anthusa, Anthimus

Ancestry: Two Emperors for ancestors, know much else is known.

Branch of the Tree: Byzantine Emperors, and Saint Niketas is very near in this branch

SAINTS DAILY
Kings, Queens, Popes, Princes, Princesses, Emperors, Hermits, Bishops

DAILY SAINTS WHOSE ANCESTRY IS KNOWN

Biography: Saint Nicephorus was the son of the secretary of Emperor Constantine V, raised as an opponent of the Iconoclasts in the imperial capital and remembered always the torture that his father experienced for opposing the Iconoclast emperor. Saint Nicephorus became known for his intellect and his eloquence. He founded a monastery near the Black Sea, and was chosen to the office of patriarch of Constantinople in 806, after Saint Tarasius. He was known for his intellect and eloquence. Saint Nicephorus forgave a priest who married Emperor Constantine VI to Theodota even though Constantine's wife Mary still lived and so was opposed for a time by Saint Theodore Studites. Saint Nicephorus the patriatrch also challenged the policies concerning Icononclast of Emperor Leo V the Armenian and so was deposed by a synod of Iconoclast bishops. He was nearly assiassinated on several occasions, and was then exiled to the monastery he had founded on the Black Sea. He died there at the monastery on June 2 or March 13 829. He had brought various reforms to his large diocese and inspired the lay people. He was also the author of anti Iconoclast writings and two historical works, a Chronographia and Brevianim.

March 14 Saint Mathilda of Germany

Country: Germany   Patron of parents of large families
   Date: 892-967/68

Family: Parents: Father- Theodoric Count of Ringleheim
Mother- Ludmilla Ragnhildis, Countess of Ringleheim
      Husband: Heinrich I, Emperor of Germany
Children: Hedwige (Hartwige) Princess of Germans; Otto I "The Great" Holy Roman Empire; Gerberge, Princess of Germans

Ancestry: Saint Mathilda ancestors include the kings of Saxony and Rigelheim.

SAINTS DAILY
Kings, Queens, Popes, Princes, Princesses, Emperors, Hermits, Bishops

DAILY SAINTS WHOSE ANCESTRY IS KNOWN

Decendents: Decendents include Saint Adele of Blois, Saint David and Margaret of Scotland, Saint Louis IX of France, Saint Ferdinand III of Spain, and Saint Lazlo King of Hungary. Royal descendents include King Edward III Plantagenet of England, King of France Philip IV, Also Boleslaw III King of Poland, and Henrick III Holy Roman Emperor.

Biography: Also known as Mechtildis and Maud Saint Matilda was the daughter of Count Dietrich of Westphalia and Reinhild of Denmark. The Abbess of Eufurt Convent raised her as she was her grandmother. In the year 909 Matilda married Henry the Fowler, son of Duke Otto of Saxony. In the year 912 he succeeded his father as Duke and in 919 succeeded to the German throne from King Conrad I. Matilda was noted for her charitable works and her piety. In 936 she was widowed and supported her son Henry's claim to his father's throne. Otto (the Great) was elected, and Saint Matilda persuaded him to name Henry Duke of Bavaria after he had led an unsuccessful revolt. Saint Matilda was very charitable, and she was severely criticized by both Otto and Henry for her extravagance along these lines. Her inheritance was resigned to her sons, and so she could retire to her country home but Otto's wife Edith interceded and called her back to court. Otto put down Henry when he revolted again with great cruelty. In 953 Henry again revolted and Matilda censored Henry. She also censored him for his ruthlessness in suppressing a revolt by his own subjects; at this time Saint Matilda prophesized his imminent death. When Henry died in 955, Saint Matilda devoted herself to building a monastery and three convents. Saint Matilda was left in charge of the kingdom when Otto went to Rome in 962 to be crowned Emperor (this event is often regarded as the beginning of the Holy Roman Empire.). She spent most of her life during her declining years at the convent at Nordhausen she had built. Saint Matilda died at the monastery at Quedlinburg on March 14 and was buried there with Henry. Her feast day is March 14th.

SAINTS DAILY
Kings, Queens, Popes, Princes, Princesses, Emperors, Hermits, Bishops

DAILY SAINTS WHOSE ANCESTRY IS KNOWN

March 15 *Saint Raymond of Fitero*

Country: Aragon   **Date:** 1113-1162

Family: Parents: Father- Raymond III the Great Count of Berengar Mother- Dolca Countess of Provence   Wife: Ramirez, Petronilla Queen of Aragon   Children: Alphonso II the Chaste King of Aragon

Ancestry: Saint Raymond has Helena of Rome for an Ancestor. Also Joseph of Arimathea. Also Charlemange. Also King David of Judah and Israel is an ancestor thru Nathan his son. King Solomon of Israel and Judah is also an ancestor.

Descendents: His son King of Aragon Alphonso, and King Henry III of England are descendents.

Biography: Cistercian abbot and founder of the Order of Calatrava, also called Ramon Sierra. Born in Spain, in Aragon, he was a canon at Tarazona Cathedral and then at the Monastery Scala Dei he joined the Cistercians. Sent to Spain to serve as abbot and establish the Fitero Abbey in Navvre, the post brought him to the forefront of the Christian Spanish and the Moor struggle. Raymond convinced King Sancho III of Castile to aid his call for an army when the Moors were on the verge of attacking the Toledo outpost of Calatrava in 1158. A one time Knight, then a monk assisted Raymond, namely Diego Velasques, who with the enlisted aid of the archbishop of Toledo they created a vast host of Christian Soldiers. The Moors failed to attack, but the host was formed into the military order of the Knights of Calatrava. Members distinguished themselves as one of the most powerful causes of the Reconquist (reconquest of Spain against the Moors) and too the Benedictine rule. The cult of Raymond as a saint was approved in 1719.

SAINTS DAILY
Kings, Queens, Popes, Princes, Princesses, Emperors, Hermits, Bishops

DAILY SAINTS WHOSE ANCESTRY IS KNOWN

March 16   *Saint Dentlin*

Country: England   **Date:** 7th Century

Family: Father: Vincent Madelgaire de Hainault Saint
Mother: Waldetrudis de Loomis Saint
Spouse: Unknown   Siblings: Adeltrude de Hainault Saint; Landericus Saint; Madelberta Saint

Ancestors: Only one generation is known and is listed above.

Branches of the Tree: Saint Adeltrude Descendents are known.

Biography: Seven-year-old confessor, called also Dentilin or Denain. He was from a family of Saints, mother, father and three siblings are all Saints. He was the son of St. Vincent Madelgarus and St. Waldetrudis. There is a church in Cleves, in Germany, named after Saint Dentlin.

March 16   *Saint Eusebia*

Country: Franconia, Prussia   **Date:** 680

Family: Father: Adalbald I De Artois Saint   Mother: Saint Rictrudis
Spouse: Unknown   Siblings: Adalbald II De Artois, Clotsind Saint, Adalsind Saint, and Mauront Saint

Ancestors: None known

Branches of the Tree: This branch is the branch near Saint Gertrude of Hamage.

SAINTS DAILY
Kings, Queens, Popes, Princes, Princesses, Emperors, Hermits, Bishops

DAILY SAINTS WHOSE ANCESTRY IS KNOWN

Biography: Saint Eusebia was the Benedictine abbess sent as a child to see Saint Gertrude, her great Grandmother. Saint Gertrude was the abbess of Hamage Abbey in France. In 652 her father Saint Adalbald was murdered and she was sent to Hamage Abbey for safety. At the age of twelve she was elected Abbess. Her mother, Saint Rictrudis as then abbess of merchiennes, and she brought her and her community into her care. Later Eusebia and her nuns returned to Hamage Abbey.

March 16   *Saint Abban*
Country: Ireland   **Date:** 620

Family: Father: Cormac Ui Dunlainge, King Of Laigin & Leinster   Mother: Unknown
Spouse: None   Siblings: Saint Dar-Carthaind, Saint Ethne

Branches of the Tree: The King of Ireland Brian Boroimhe is in this branch of the tree. Saints in the branch of King Brian include Saint Flannan, Saint Breacan. A related branch of the tree of King Brian's wife Gormflaith Of Nass is the Saint Cumne, Saint Sodelb, Saint Ethne, Saint Dar-Carthaind, Saint Fedelm, Saint Coeman Santlethan and Saint Mugain, all in the branch of the tree of King Brian's wife Gormflaith Of Nass

Biography: Saint Abban was an Irish prince. He was the nephew of Saint Ibar and son of King Cormac of Leinster. In modern County Wexford and Ferns Saint Abban founded many churches. This was in the Old district of Ui Cennselaigh. The main monastery was in Adamstown, Ireland, called Magheranoidhe. Part of this monastery's fame is because of a different Abban, according to some records, the Abban of New Ross. Saint Abban served as abbot at Kill-Abban Avvey in

SAINTS DAILY
Kings, Queens, Popes, Princes, Princesses, Emperors, Hermits, Bishops

107

DAILY SAINTS WHOSE ANCESTRY IS KNOWN

Leinster until March 16, 1620. Adamstown was once called Abbanstown, and he is revered there.

March 17   Saint Ceneu (King of Northern Britain)

Country: Britain   *Date:* 374

Family: Parents: Father- Coel Hen ap Tegfan King of Northern Britain Mother- Ystradwal verch Cadfan (Gadeon) Wife: Unknown Children: Pabo ("Post Prydyn") ap Ceneu Saint

Ancestry: Thru the Kings of Britons back to Zerah son of Judah and so from Abraham.

Descendents: Judicael King of the Bretons Saint

Biography: SAINT CENEU AP COEL King of Northern Britain was born 404 and died 470. Ceneu upheld the old Christian ways while under intense pressure from invading pagans. This appears to be the reason for canonization. His Kingdom stretched from Coast to Coast Ceneu was obliged to accept the help of the Saxons, Octha and Ebissa, for most of his reign, in pushing back invading Picts from his kingdom because of High-King Vortigern's policy of employing Saxon mercenaries to defeat British enemies. It was not until after the Kentish rebellion that they were finally brought under control. Their interference was widely resented. Ceneu allowed the Saxons to settle in Deywr (Deira - East Yorkshire) because he was magnanimous in victory. He must have lived to an extreme old age because Ceneu appears in Geoffrey of Monmouth's History of the Kings of Britain as having attended the coronation of the great King Arthur. Ceneu's kingdom was divided between his two sons, Gwrast and Mor. Upon his death, Mor inherited the

SAINTS DAILY
Kings, Queens, Popes, Princes, Princesses, Emperors, Hermits, Bishops

108

DAILY SAINTS WHOSE ANCESTRY IS KNOWN

central kingdom around the old capital, Ebrauc (York), while Gwrast took the western lands stretching from the Salway to the Mersey.

March 17   *Saint Joseph of Arimathea*

Country: Israel   ***Date:*** 50
   Patron: Cemetary Keepers;
Coffin Bearers; Funeral Directors; Gravediggers; Pallbearers

Family: Parents: Father- Mathat   Mother- Daugter of Eleazor   Wife:Unknown
Children: Anna of Arimathea

Ancestry: From the line listed in the Gospel According to Luke Nathan son of David is an ancestor so also David, Judah, Jacob, Isaac, and Abraham.

Descendents: Saint Adele of Blois, Saint Cunigunda, Saint David I of Scotland, Saint Edgar the Peaceful, Saint Ethelbert, Saint Ethelreda, Saint Fernando III of Spain, Saint Leopold III, Saint Louis IX of France, Saint Olav, Saint Sexburga. King of Naples Charles II, King of England Edward I, King of France Phillip IV, and King of Scotland William the Lion are also descendents.

Biography: Saint Joseph of Arimathea was the councilor (Lk 23:50) who requested the body of Christ from Pontius Pilate, after the Crucifixion, and provided for a proper burial for Christ. Joseph was termed in the New Testament the "virtuous and righteous man" (Lk 23:50) An immensely popular figure in Christian lore, and the man "who was himself awaiting the kingdom of God" (Mk 15:43). Described as secretly a disciple of Jesus for fear of the Jews, [he] asked Pilate if he could remove the body of Jesus. And Pilate permitted it" (In 19:38). He also was a prominent figure in the legends surrounding the Holy Grail, appearing in Robert de Barron's early thirteenth-century romance Joseph d 'Arirnathea, William of Malmesbury's twelfth-

SAINTS DAILY
Kings, Queens, Popes, Princes, Princesses, Emperors, Hermits, Bishops

DAILY SAINTS WHOSE ANCESTRY IS KNOWN

century De Antiquitate Glastoniensis Ecclesiae, and Thomas Mallory's famed Morte D 'Arthur. William of almesbury's tale recounts Joseph's arrival in England with the Holy Grail and the building of the first church on the isle at Glastonbury; the passage on Joseph, however, was added in the thirteenth century. According to the apocryphal Gospel of Nicodemus, he helped establish the community of Lydda.

March 17   Saint Paternus Pasrut
Country: Scotland   *Date:* 305

Family: Parents: Father- Tegid (Tacitus) ap Cein (King of Gwynedd)   Mother- Unknown
Wife:Unknown   Children: Edern ("King of Aeturnus") ap Padarn

Ancestry: Ancestry goes back to Zarah son of Judah thru the Kings of Briton.

Descendents: Saint Cadwallyr and Saint Judicael are descendents. King of Gwynedd Rhodi Molwynog is a descendent and King of South Wales Cadell ap Rhodi Mawr is also a descendent. King Edward IV of England Plantagenet is a descendent as well.

Biography: Saint Paternus Pasrut was the son of the King of Gwynedd and had Edern the King of Aeturnus as a son.

March 17   Saint Helen of the Host
Country: Wales   *Date:* 330

Family: Parents: Father- Eudaf Hen (Octavian) (High King of Britain)   Mother- Unknown

SAINTS DAILY
Kings, Queens, Popes, Princes, Princesses, Emperors, Hermits, Bishops

DAILY SAINTS WHOSE ANCESTRY IS KNOWN

Husband: Magnus Maximus ("Macsen Wledig") Emperor
Children: Gratianna verch Macsen

Ancestry: Saint Cyllus is an ancestor. Little else is known.

Descendents: Saint Cadwalldr and Saint Tudlydd verch Brychan are descendents.
King Edward IV Plantagenet is also a descendent.

Biography: Saint Helen of the Host was born about 330 in Ewyas now Monmouth, Wales. Her father was a High King of Britain, Octavian, and Saint Helen married Magnus Maximus Emperor. The length of her life is not known.

March 17 *Saint Gertrude of Nivelles*
Country: Gaul   **Date:** 659

Family: Father: Pepin I Mayor of the Palace Blessed
Mother: Saint Itta (Iduberga) de Schelde
Spouse: Unknown   Siblings: Begga De Landen Saint

Ancestors: Only the father is known

Branches of the Tree: Saint Kentigern is in this branch of the Tree. This is the branch of the tree in the vicinity of King Arthur of the Round Table.

Biography: Saint Gertrude of Nivelles was the daughter of Blessed Pepin, and daughter of Saint Itta. She is also the sister of Saint Begga. She was a Benedictine abbess installed at Nivelles Abbey an Abbey her mother founded. The Irish Saint Foillian and Ultan became her friends. She was gifted with visions and was considered a mystic. Saint Gertrude of Nivelles is a patroness of travelers and gardeners.

SAINTS DAILY
Kings, Queens, Popes, Princes, Princesses, Emperors, Hermits, Bishops

DAILY SAINTS WHOSE ANCESTRY IS KNOWN

March 17 *Saint Gertrude*
Country: Franks **Date:** 626-659

Father: Pepin I Mayor of the Palace   Mother: Itta of Metz Saint
Spouse: Unknown   Siblings: Saint Begga

Ancestors: The franks and so Joseph the Israelite.

Branches of the Tree: This is the time and era of Charlemagne, and this is the Frankish branch of the tree a few generations before Charlemagne.

Biography: Saint Gertrude was the daughter of Blessed Itta of Metz and Blessed Pepin of Landen. Itta founded Nivelles Abbey. She installed her daughter Saint Gertrude there as abbess in the year 639. As abbess she was gifted with visions and was a mystic. Two Irish Saints Ultan and Foillian became her friends. Saint Gertrude is recognized as patroness of travelers and gardeners.

March 17 *Saint Patrick*
Country: Ireland **Date:** b. 387 d.461
Patron: Ireland

Family: Father: Calpinn (Calpurnius) Mother: Conchessa
Spouse: Unknown   Siblings: Darerca

Ancestors: Saint Joseph of Arimathea is an Ancestor, as is Bran the Blessed King of Britain around 10 AD. Bran the Blessed ancestors include Camber and Tros, sons of Dardanus, who is the son of Zerah son of the Isralite Judah. Dardanus mother is also listed as Electra wife of Tarah, son of Ephriam who is the son of Joseph the Israelite. Saint Patrick is then descended from both Joseph and Judah, thru Dardanus and from

SAINTS DAILY
 Kings, Queens, Popes, Princes, Princesses, Emperors, Hermits, Bishops

DAILY SAINTS WHOSE ANCESTRY IS KNOWN

David the King of Israel and Judah thru his son Nathan and the line leading to Matthat, father of Saint Joseph of Arimathea.

Branches of the Tree: The line of ancestry of Saint Patrick is sixteen generations from his ancestor Joseph of Arimathea, and fifteen generations from Bran the Blessed, whose ancestors are from the Israelites.

Biography: One of the world's most popular Saints, with a feast day celebrated with many parties in festivities Saint Patrick of Ireland is a major saint. Saint Patrick is considered the apostle of Ireland. He was born in the year 387 in Scotland at Kilpatrick near Dumbarton. St. Patrick's parents were Calpurnius and the Conchessa lived in Britain and were Romans in charge of the British colonies when St. Patrick was 14 he was captured to during a rating party. He ended up in Ireland and was a slave and had to tend and herd sheep. At this time Ireland was a land of Druids and Pagans. Saint Patrick learned the language and practices of the people who held him captive. During his captivity and throughout his life he turned to God in prayer. Saint Patrick wrote "The love of God and his fear grew in me more and more, as did the faith, and my soul was roused, so that, in a single day, I have said as many as a hundred prayers and in the night, nearly the same." "I prayed in the woods and on the mountain, even before dawn. I felt no hurt from the snow or ice or rain." Finally when St. Patrick was about 20 he escaped from Ireland after having received adrenal from God. He went to the coast and found some sailors who took them back to Britain and was reunited with his family. Later he had another dream. The people of Ireland were calling up to him to return. St. Patrick had begun his studies for the priesthood. Saint Germanic the Bishop of Auxerre ordained Saint Patrick. Later he was sent to take the Gospel to Ireland and by this time had been ordained a Bishop. He arrived at Salne in Ireland on March 25, 433. He met a chieftain of one of the tribes, who tried to kill Patrick according to one legend. Saint Patrick converted Dacha (the chieftain) after his arm froze and was unable to move his arm until he became

SAINTS DAILY
Kings, Queens, Popes, Princes, Princesses, Emperors, Hermits, Bishops

DAILY SAINTS WHOSE ANCESTRY IS KNOWN

friendly to Patrick. Saint Patrick converted many Irish after he began preaching the Gospel. St. Patrick converted thousands due to his preaching. The entire kingdom was converted to Christianity when hearing Patrick's message. These kingdom's included the King's and their families. By this time Patrick had many disciples; among them Beningnus, Auxilius, Iserninus, and Fiaac, (all later canonized as well). St. Patrick's Day is celebrated in Ireland. Many miracles are attributed to St. Patrick's and he broached his confessions where he wrote about his love for God. After years of traveling, hardship, and poverty he died on March 17 461.

March 18   Saint Edward the Martyr
Country: England   **Date:** c. 978

Family: Father: Edgar "the Peaceable" King of England Saint   Mother: Elfrida
Spouse: Unknown   Siblings: Aethelred II "The Unready"; Edith of Wilton Saint

Ancestors: Saint Edgar's ancestors (father of Saint Edward) include his mother Saint Elgiva, four generations previous Saint Alfred. Also included is Joseph of Arimathea. Also King David of Judah and Israel is an ancestor thru Nathan his son.   King Solomon of Israel and Judah is also an ancestor.

Branches of the Tree: This is the branch of the tree of the English Kings.

Biography: Saint Edward the Martyr was the eldest son of King Edgar of England and his first wife. Queen Ethelfleda died shortly after her son's birth. Saint Dunstan baptized Saint Edward. In 975 he became King and this is when he was baptized. His stepmother was against his gaining the throne. Queen Elfrida wished the throne for her son Ethelred. Only three years later while hunting he was murdered supposedly by Queen Elfrida supporters, on March 18, near Corfe Dastle. There is a

SAINTS DAILY
Kings, Queens, Popes, Princes, Princesses, Emperors, Hermits, Bishops

DAILY SAINTS WHOSE ANCESTRY IS KNOWN

twelfth century historian William of Malmesbury that states he was murdered by Elfrida. Saint Elfrida in her remorse for her crime was responsible for the monasteries of Amesbury and Wherwell, in Wherwell she died. His cultus was very large, although he was one who suffered an unjust death. There were many miracles reported at his tomb at Shaftesbury. The Diocese of Plymouth still observes his feast day of March 18.

March 20   Saint Tetricus Bishop of Langres

Country: France   **Date:** 572

Family: Father: Gregory Bishop of Langres Saint
        Mother: Unknown
Spouse: Unknown   Siblings: Georgia

Ancestors: None known.

Branches of the Tree: Georgia is the Grandfather of Saint Gregory Bishop of Tours and sibling to Saint Tetricus Bishop of Langres. Georgia married Leocardia, who had a different husband Mundéric des Francs Ripuaires. He is the father of Gondolfus who is a saint in his own right. Saint Gondolfus has descendents such as Saint Ladislaus of Hungary, Saint Louis IX of France, Saint Leopold III of Austria, Saint Leutwinus, Saint Margaret, Saint William of Toulouse, Saint Ansigisel, Saint Hedwig, Saint Clotilde, Saint Fernando III of Spain, Saint Ida, Saint Irene of Hungary, Saint Isabelle of Aragon, and Saint Nithard the Chronicler are all Descendents also King of England Edward III Plantagenet, King of Naples Charles II, King of France Louis VIII are also Descendents.

Biography: Bishop of Langres, France. He was the uncle of St. Gregory of Tours and the son of St. Gregory, bishop of Langres. Tetricus succeeded to the see upon his father's passing, a custom in that era.

SAINTS DAILY
Kings, Queens, Popes, Princes, Princesses, Emperors, Hermits, Bishops

DAILY SAINTS WHOSE ANCESTRY IS KNOWN

March 21   *Saint Enda*
Country: Ireland   **Date:** c. 530

Family: Father: Ainmire De Ireland   Mother: Brigid
Spouse: Unknown   Siblings: Unknown

Ancestors: Fergus De Meath; Tuathal Teachtmar King of Ireland.

Branches of the Tree: Fergus De Meath who was Saint Enda Great Grandfather had a son Dermot who was a King of Ireland.

Biography: Saint Enda was the brother of Saint Fanchea. He was noted for his military feats but was convinced by Saint Fanchea to renounce his warring activities and marry. His fiancée was found dead, so he decided to become a monk. He went on a pilgrimage to Rome. He was ordained in Rome, returned to Ireland, and built churches at Drogheda. He built the monastery of Killeaney on the island of Aran that he secured from his brother-in-law King Oengus of Munster. Ten other foundations on the island developed. With Saint Finnian of Clonard, Enda is considered the founder of monasticism in Ireland. March 21 is his feast day.

March 22   *Saint Darerca*
Country: Ireland   **Date:** 5th Century

Family: Father: Calpinn (Calpurnius)   Mother: Unknown
Spouse: Conan (Cynan) Meriadoc (King of Dumnonia)
       Siblings: Saint Patrick

Ancestors: Saint Joseph of Arimathea is an Ancestor, as is Bran the Blessed King of Britain around 10 AD. Bran the Blessed ancestors include Camber and Tros, sons of Dardanus,

SAINTS DAILY
Kings, Queens, Popes, Princes, Princesses, Emperors, Hermits, Bishops

DAILY SAINTS WHOSE ANCESTRY IS KNOWN

who is the son of Zerah son of the Isralite Judah. Dardanus mother is also listed as Electra wife of Tarah, son of Ephriam who is the son of Joseph the Israelite. Saint Patrick is then descended from both Joseph and Judah, thru Dardanus and from David the King of Israel and Judah thru his son Nathan and the line leading to Matthat, father of Saint Joseph of Arimathea.

Branches of the Tree: The line of ancestry of Saint Patrick is sixteen generations from his ancestor Joseph of Arimathea, and fifteen generations from Bran the Blessed, whose ancestors are from the Israelites.

Biography: Saint Darerca was the sister of St. Patrick. Saint Darerca had fifteen sons. Ten of her sons became bishops throughout Ireland.

March 24 Saint Catherine of Sweden

Country: Sweden **Date:** c.1330-1381 **Patron:** Protection against Abortion; Protection against Miscarriage

Family: Father: Ulf Godmarsson Mother: Birgitta Spouse: Unknown Siblings: Bridget Saint; Cecilia Ulfsdotter; Charles Ulfsdotter, Martha Ulfsdotter

Ancestors: Svend II Ulfsson (Estridssen) King Of Denmark;

Branches of the Tree: This branch goes up many generations before it joins with the Kings of Denmark who are the royal link.

Biography: Saint Catherine of Sweden was the daughter of Saint Bridget. Saint Catherine went to Rome in 1348 after her mother had gone there after the death of Catherine's father. Catherine had taken a vow of continence with her husband who died a short time after she had been in Rome. For twenty-five years Saint Bridget and Saint Catherine made pilgrimages to various places, including Jerusalem. When they were not on pilgrimage they spent their days in prayer and meditation. They

SAINTS DAILY
Kings, Queens, Popes, Princes, Princesses, Emperors, Hermits, Bishops

DAILY SAINTS WHOSE ANCESTRY IS KNOWN

also worked with the poor and did some religious instruction. This seemingly quiet life was not without perils and adventures. Many young lords sought to seduce the Swedish princess, but God's providence kept Saint Catherine safe. Saint Bridget died after the trip to Jerusalem, and Saint Catherine took her mother's body back to Sweden. Saint Bridget was buried at Vadstena in the convent of the Order of the Holy Savior. Catherine became superior of the order and died on March 24, 1381. She was mourned like her mother was by the whole of Sweden.

March 26 Saint Margaret Clitherow

Country: England   **Date:** b. 1585 d. 10 Sep 1641   Patron: Business Women

Family: Father: Alexander Barlowe   Mother: Mary Brereton
Spouse: Unknown   Siblings: Unknown

Ancestors: Ancestors include the De Quincy line, King of Man and Isle Olaf II Godredson, and Thorfinn the Black Sigurdson.

Branches of the Tree: This is a very noble branch of the tree that goes back many generations, with the Gascoigne and the Percy and the De Quincy line.

Biography: Saint Margaret Clitherow was born in Middleton, England in 1555 of parents who were protestant. In 1571 a butcher and grazier John Clitherow became her husband, and they had two children. She was in England and joined the Catholic Church and she harbored fugitive priests, so she was arrested and imprisoned by hostile authorities. It was attempted to make her deny her faith, but she held firm. On March 25 1586 her execution by being pressed to death was begun. A door was put on top of her as she was stretched out on the ground. The door had weights put on it. She died within fifteen minutes. When she learned she was going to be condemned she said to a

SAINTS DAILY
 Kings, Queens, Popes, Princes, Princesses, Emperors, Hermits, Bishops

DAILY SAINTS WHOSE ANCESTRY IS KNOWN

friend " The sheriff's have said that I am going to die this coming Friday, and I feel the weakness of my flesh which is troubled at this news, but my spirit rejoices greatly. For the love of God, pray for me and ask all good people to do likewise."

March 29 Saint Gwynllyw Farfog (King of Gwynllwg)

Country: English Wales   **Date:** 6th Century

Family: Father: Glywys Cernyw ap Solor Saint
         Mother: Gwawl verch Ceredig
Spouse: Gwladys verch Brychan Saint   Siblings: Pedrog (Abbot of Lanwethinoc) Saint
Offspring: Saint Cadoc

Ancestors: Saint Brychan is an Ancestor, of which only a few generations are known on fathers side. Saint Helen of the Host is known as Brychan's Mother's Ancestor.

Branches of the Tree: This is the branch of the tree in the vicinity of Saint Brychan

Biography: This saint was the brother of Pedrog who was Abbot of Lanwethinoc, and the son in law of Saint Brychan who had 24 Sainted offspring. His Father Glywys Cernyw ap Solar was also a Saint. His wife as a daughter of Saint Brychan was a Saint, and the only family relationship that was not a saint was his mother Gwawl verch Ceredig, who must have also been very holy. According to tradition Gundelaus (latin for Gwynllyw) captured his soon to be wife by kidnapping and stole her from the house of Saint Brychan. They led a life of banditry and outlawness until their first son Saint Cadoc convinced them to adopt a releigious life together at Newprot, Monmouthshire. Later he had them separate and live as hermits, with Gwladys eventually living at Oencarnau, Bassaleg. The anglicized version of Gudleus is Woolo.

SAINTS DAILY
 Kings, Queens, Popes, Princes, Princesses, Emperors, Hermits, Bishops

DAILY SAINTS WHOSE ANCESTRY IS KNOWN

March 29 *Saint Gwladys*
Country: English Wales   **Date:** 6th Century

Feastday March 29

Family:
Parents: Father-Saint Brychan Mother- Prawst verch Tudwal
Husband: Saint Gwynllyw
Children: Saint Maches, Saint Cadoc, Saint Cadog Ddoeth

Biography:
Wife of Saint Gundleus (Gwynllyw). Saint Cadoc is her son. A romantic legend says the Gudleus kidnapped Gladys. The romance is part of the Arthurian legend.

- *Name:* Saint Gwladys verch Brychan
- *Sex:* F
- *Birth:* 0460
- *Burial:* Capel Wladus in Gelligaer
- *Note:*

Note: St. Gwladys (Born c.AD 460) (Latin-Claudia, English-Gladys) -Princess Gwladys was the eldest - and best attested – daughter of the saintly Irish immigrant, King Brychan of Brycheiniog (Wales). With her countless brothers and sisters, she was raised at the Royal & Christian Court at Garthmadrun (Talgarth), where she grew into a beautiful young woman. Before long she came to the notice of some of the most eligible bachelors around, particularly Brycheiniog's menacing neighbor, King Gwynllyw Farfog (the Bearded) of Gwynllwg.

Gwynllyw sent envoys to King Brychan requesting the hand of his daughter in marriage, but the holy man sent them away. Gwynllyw was a rough pagan warrior king, quite unsuitable for his delicate offspring. The King of Gwynllwg, however, was not so easily put off and decided he would take his prize by force. With three hundred men to help him, he made a daring raid on Brycheiniog and made off with Princess Gwladys. Brychan

SAINTS DAILY
Kings, Queens, Popes, Princes, Princesses, Emperors, Hermits, Bishops

DAILY SAINTS WHOSE ANCESTRY IS KNOWN

pursued him as far as Fochriw where the two were accosted by their High-King, Arthur. Struck by the lady's beauty, Arthur was, at first, tempted to take her for himself; but his fellows persuaded him to support Gwynllyw's cause and Brychan was eventually brought round.

Gwladys reigned with her husband as a pious and wise monarch, tempering his, often rash, behavior. They became the parents of saints Cadog, Eigion, Cyfyw, Cynidr, Maches & Glywys. Cadog - if not all the children - was raised as a Christian by St.Tathyw at Caerwent, probably at his mother's insistence, and later converted his father to Christianity. As a widow, Queen Gwladys became a hermit in Pencarnau and, latterly, at the Capel Wladus in Gelligaer. Here, she was buried and a Celtic cross slab found there is thought to be her memorial. It can now be seen in Gelligaer parish church. Since her death, she has been revered as a Saint. Her feast day is the same as her husband, 29th March.

SAINTS DAILY
Kings, Queens, Popes, Princes, Princesses, Emperors, Hermits, Bishops

DAILY SAINTS WHOSE ANCESTRY IS KNOWN

Saints of April

FEAST DAY	SAINT	COUNTRY	BORN	DIED
4-Apr	Blessed Aleth		1069	
4-Apr	Saint Isadore	Spain	c 500	c 600
5-Apr	Saint Derfel Gadarn	England		6th
5-Apr	Saint Ethelburga	Northumbria		647
6-Apr	Saint Brychan King of Brycheiniog	Wales	419	
9-Apr	Saint Madrun ferch Gwerthefyr	Gwent	440	
9-Apr	Saint Waldetrudis	France		640
9-Apr	Saint Hugo Bishop of Rouen	France		730
9-Apr	Saint Mary Cleopas	Israel		1st
13-Apr	Saint Ida of Loraine or Boulogne	Boulogne	1040	1113
13-Apr	Saint Hermengild	Spain		585
17-Apr	Saint Landericus	England		c. 660
19-Apr	Saint Geraud	France		c 1000
19-Apr	Saint Pope Leo IX ,	France	1002	11th
21- Apr	Saint Beuno	England		?
22-Apr	Saint Opportuna	France		770
27-Apr	Saint Floribert	France		746
27-Apr	Saint Enoder	Wales		6th
29-Apr	Saint Endellion	Wales		6th
30-Apr	Blessed Hildegard	France	754	783

SAINTS DAILY
Kings, Queens, Popes, Princes, Princesses, Emperors, Hermits, Bishops

122

DAILY SAINTS WHOSE ANCESTRY IS KNOWN

TABLE FIVE SAINTS OF APRIL

April 4   *Blessed Aleth*
Country: *Date:* b 1069

Family: Parents: Father- Bernard II de Montbard Mother- Humberge De Roucy
Husband: Tecolin   Children: Saint Humberline and Saint Bernard of Clairvaux

Ancestry: Ancestry past parentage is not known.

Descendents: King Edward IV Plantagenet is a descendent. Also Edward Stafford 3rd Duke of Buckingham and John I Brienne King of Jerusalem.

Biography:
Married to Tecolin she had several children. She is the mother of Saint Bernard of Clairvaux. She was also a widow. Her relics are enshrined in Clairvaux. Also the mother of Saint Humberline.

April 4   *Saint Isadore*
Country: Spain   **Date:** 636

Family: Father: Severinum , Count Of Cartagena
       Mother: Theodora
Spouse: None Siblings: Saint Fulgentius; Saint Leander; Saint Florentina.

Country: Cartagena Spain

Ancestors: Not much Ancestry is Known

SAINTS DAILY
Kings, Queens, Popes, Princes, Princesses, Emperors, Hermits, Bishops

DAILY SAINTS WHOSE ANCESTRY IS KNOWN

Biography: Saint Isadore had two brothers Saint Leander and Saint Fulgentius and one saintly sister Florentina also a Saint. Both Leander and Fulgentius or bishops and the whole family or leaders and had strong minds. Saint Florentina was also an Abbess.

Saint Isadore was educated by his brother the Saint. The Anders treatment of Saint Isadore shocked many people. Saint Leander used pedagogical theory involving force and punishment. From Isadore's later accomplishments he was intelligent and hard-working. One day Isadore ran away. He was frustrated by his inability to learn as fast as his brother wanted and he was hurt by his brother's treatment. Although he couldn't escape his brother he could not escape the feelings of failure and rejection finally the outside world attracted his attention when he noticed water dripping on the rock. These rocks were not harmed by the water it seems however there was a hole warn in the rock by the many drops. Saint Isador realized if you work hard his small efforts would eventually pay off. He decided he was capable of great learning. Finally when he returned his brother confined him to a cell to complete his studies believing he might run away again.
.
Isadore must have loved his brother because after Leander's death Saint Isadore completed many of the projects he had began including a missile and breviary.

Saint Isadore rose above his past accomplishments to become what was known as the greatest teacher in Spain. He promoted an establishment of a seminary in every diocese of Spain due to his love of learning he never limited his studies and did not want others to limit theirs. He also made sure all the branches of knowledge including the arts and medicine were taught in the seminary's. The Encyclopedia of knowledge the etymologies was a popular textbook for nine centuries books on grammar astronomy history and biography as well as theology were written by Saint Isadore. When finally the Arabs brought the study of Aristotle back to Europe however the subject had been

SAINTS DAILY
Kings, Queens, Popes, Princes, Princesses, Emperors, Hermits, Bishops

DAILY SAINTS WHOSE ANCESTRY IS KNOWN

thoroughly taught in Spain by Saint Isadore. Saint Isadore was Bishop of Seville from 37 years. He replaced Leander and made a model for representative government. Isadore remembered the dire needs of his brother he rejected autocratic decision making and organized cyanides to discuss government of the Spanish church. Saint Isadore is credited to have helped convert the barbarian Visigoth's Aryanism to Christianity. Saint Isadore lives until he was almost 80 years old. Crowds of poor flocked to his house as he was dying. One of his last acts was to give all his possessions to the poor. In 636 this doctor of the church had done more than his brother and ever hoped. The light of his learning held back the dark ages of barbarism from Spain. The genius of his heart which allowed him to see beyond rejection discouragements must have been greater than his outstanding mind.

April 5 *Saint Derfel Gadarn*

Feastday: April 5   **Date:** 6th

Family:
Parents: Father: Hoel II Fychan ('the Small') de Bretagne
Mother: Rimo verch Rhun
Spouse: None   Children: None   Siblings: Alain I de Bretagne (King of Bretagne)

Ancestry: Saint Derfel Gadarn was nine generations the grandson of Conan and Saint Ursula, so therefore a descendant of Saint James son of Saint Joseph (thru Conan). Also Saint Alma Pompee de Domonee was his Grandmother on his fathers side and on his fathers side is a descendent of Conan and Saint Dareca. Saint Cyllin is an Ancestor as is Saint Cyllin's sibling (from the ascent of Saint Dareca) and Saint Salomon is an Ancestor who was Conan's Grandson. Therefore David is an ancestor, and the five Israelites Benjamin, Joseph, Levi, Judah, and Zebulon are ancestors.

SAINTS DAILY
Kings, Queens, Popes, Princes, Princesses, Emperors, Hermits, Bishops

DAILY SAINTS WHOSE ANCESTRY IS KNOWN

Branches of the Tree: This is the Branch of the Tree in the vicinity on King Arthur, son of Uther Pendragon.

Biography: Saint Derfel Gadarn may have been in the last battle with King Arthur. The legend has him in the battle at Camlan where Arthur was killed. Possibly a monk at Bardsey. At Llanderfel, Merionethshire, Wales he may have been a solitary. A wooden statue of him was reported to survive until the burning of Blessed John Forest at Smithfiled in 1538 where it apparently was used as firewood.

April 5   *Saint Ethelburga*

Country: Northumbria   **Date:** d. 647

Family: Parents: Father- Unknown Mother- Unknown Husband: Saint Edwin of Northumbria Children: Princess Cynewise of Northumbria

Ancestors: Daughter of Saint Ethelbert of Kent.

Descendents: Sainted Descendents include Saint Adele Countess of Blois, Saint Alfred the Great, Saint Cunigunda of Luxembory, Saint David and Saint Margaret of Scotland, Saint Louis IX, Saint Edgar the Peaceful, Saint Ferdinand III of Spain, Saint Leopold III of Austria, and Saint Henry II King of Germany. Royal descendents include King Edward III Plantagenet of England, King of Naples Charles II, King of France Philip IV, and King of Scotland William the Lion. Also Casimir King of Poland , Alphonso Enriquez I King of Portugal and Phillip II King of Germany.

SAINTS DAILY
Kings, Queens, Popes, Princes, Princesses, Emperors, Hermits, Bishops

DAILY SAINTS WHOSE ANCESTRY IS KNOWN

Biography: Daughter of St. Ethelbert of Kent, also called Tate. Ethelburga converted King St. Edwin, and when he died, she founded a convent at Lyminge. Wife of King St. Edwin of Northumbria, England, St. Paulinus was her chaplain. Ethelburga served as abbess until her death.

April 6   Saint Brychan King of Brycheiniog
Country: Briton   *Date:* 419

Family: Parents: Father- Anlach mac Coronac   Mother- Marchell verch Tewdrig
Wife: Prawst verch Tudwal   Children: Tudlydd verch Brychan Saint, St. Dyfnan, St. Teath, St. Menefrida, St. Dingad, St. Merewenna, St. Endellion, St. Dogfan, St. Dwynwen, St. Austell, St. Tydfil, St. Gwen, St. Enodoch, St. Veep, St. Gladys, St. Mabyn, St. Enoder, St. Kevoca, St. Keyne, St. Nectan, and St. Almedha

Ancestry: Only a few generations are known on fathers side. Saint Helen of the Host is known as Mothers Ancestor.

Descendents: Saint Cadwalldyr, and Saint Tudlydd verch Brychan and all the rest of his Sainted Children. King Edward IV Plantagenet is also a descendent.

Biography: King of Wales, undocumented but popular saint. Brychan is credited with having twenty-four children, all saints.

April 9   Saint Waldetrudis
Country: France   *Date:* 688   *Patron:* Hainault Belgium; Mons Belgium

Family: Father: Saint Walbert   Mother: Saint Bertilla

SAINTS DAILY
 Kings, Queens, Popes, Princes, Princesses, Emperors, Hermits, Bishops

DAILY SAINTS WHOSE ANCESTRY IS KNOWN

Spouse: None   Siblings: Saint Aldegundis
    Children: Saint Landericus, Saint Madalberta, Saint Dentelin, and Saint Adeltrudis.

Ancestors: None known past parentage

Branches of the Tree: Branch of the tree that contains Saint Vincent Madelgaire de Hainault who would be the brother in law to Saint Aldegundis.

Biography: Saint Waldetrudis is from a large family of Saints. Her father, mother, and siblings became Saints. Other names she is known by are Waltrude or Waudru. She also married a Saint, Vincent of Madelgarius, and had four children also all Saints, Landericus, Madalberta, Dentelin, and Adeltrudis. She founded a convent at Chateaulieu, when her husband became a monk about 643 in Hautrnont France. The town of Mons, Belgium grew up around the monastery Saint Waldetrudis founded.

April 9   *Saint Madrun*
Country: Gwent   *Date:* b. c. 440

Family: Parents: Father- Vortimer Fendigaid, King of Gwerthefyriwg Mother- Unknown
Husband: Ynyr Gwent ap Dyfnwal, King of Gwent Children: Caradog Freichfras ap Ynyr, King of Gwent

Ancestry: Saint Helen of the Cross. King of Britain and Romans including Mark Antony and Julia of Rome. Also Joseph of Arimathea so David thru Nathan. Also Saint Cyllin so Zerah thru the Kings of Siluria and Tros King of Troy. Tros is a few generations away from Zerah the son of Judah.

Descendents: Rhys King of Morgannwg, Peibio King of Ergyng. Henry De Stafford Duke of Buckingham.

SAINTS DAILY
 Kings, Queens, Popes, Princes, Princesses, Emperors, Hermits, Bishops

DAILY SAINTS WHOSE ANCESTRY IS KNOWN

Biography: A Welsh or Cornish widow. No details of her life are extant, but some Welsh churches bear her name. Feast Day April 9.

April 9   Saint Hugo Bishop of Rouen
Country: France   **Date:** 730

Family: Father: Drogo of Champagne, Duke of Campagne
Mother: Anstrude
Spouse: Unknown   Siblings: Arnulf

Ancestors: Drogo of Champagne was the son of Pepin II and half brother to Charles Martel the Hammer. Charles Martel was the Grandfather of Charlemagne.

Branches of the Tree: This is the branch of the tree in the vicinity of Charlemagne.

Biography: Saint Hugo was the bishop of Rouen Paris and Bayeux France. He was the nephew of Charles Martel. In 722 he was named bishop of Rouen. He was the son of Duke Drogo of Burgundy. After he was named Bishop he moved to Paris and then later to Bayeux. At the same time he was Bishop he was abbot of Jumieges and Fontenelles. As Hugo got to the end of his life, he retired to Jumieges and died as a simple choir monk.

April 9   Saint Mary Cleopas
Country: Israel   **Date:** 1st

Family: Father: Joachim   Mother: Saint Joanne
Spouse: Clephas   Siblings: Saint Mary Salome; Escha   Children: James the Lesser Apostle; Joseph Barsabbas; Lillian; Johanne; Cyria; Salome; Miriam; Dinah; Jude Apostle Saint; Simeon 2nd Bishop of Jersualem

SAINTS DAILY
Kings, Queens, Popes, Princes, Princesses, Emperors, Hermits, Bishops

DAILY SAINTS WHOSE ANCESTRY IS KNOWN

Ancestors: Thru father Joachim Zerubbabel is an ancestor and thus the line of Solomon. Hebrew names of Sirach and Haggai appear in the line between Joachim and Zerubbabel; On the Mothers side Saint Joanne is the daughter of Bianca the daughter of Matthat and Rachel. Matthat ancestor was Nathan son of David and Rachel is daughter of Eleazor of the line of Solomon.

Branches of the Tree: This is the branch of the tree in the vicinity Saint Joseph and the Blessed Virgin Mary.

Biography: Saint Mary Cleopas is also known as Mary Alphaes. She is the mother of Apostles Jude and Saint James the lesser. She had a large family. She is on e of the three Mary's that were at the base of the Cross, with Mary the Virgin Mother of God and Saint Mary Magdalene.

April 13   Saint Ida of Loraine

Country: Boulogne   *Date:* c1040-1113

Family: Parents: Father- Godfrey (Godfroi), Duke of Upper and Lorraine Mother- Ida
Husband: Eustache II, Count of Boulogne   Children: Eustache III Count of Boulogne,
Godfrey Duke of Bouillon

Ancestry: Ancestry is not known. One source lists her as a descendent of Charlemange.

Descendents: King Edward III of England is a descendent.

Biography: Daughter to the Duke of Lorraine, married Eustace II count of Boulogne at the age of seventeen. She had numerous children, the most famous son Duke of Bouillon was Godfrey, and her daughter married Henry IV emperor of Germany. St. Anselm was her spiritual director the then abbot of Bec in Normandy. Humility and practiced mortification with charity in proportion to her considerable wealth characterized Saint Ida.

SAINTS DAILY
Kings, Queens, Popes, Princes, Princesses, Emperors, Hermits, Bishops

DAILY SAINTS WHOSE ANCESTRY IS KNOWN

She enjoyed making fine ornaments for altars. When her husband died, she consecrated all her disposable goods to found and endow religious establishments. She was always on good terms with her husband.

April 13   Saint Hermengild
Country: Spain   **Date:** 585

Family: Parents: Father-Leovigild The Visigoth Mother-Unknown   Wife: Unknown
Children: Athanagildo

Ancestry: Saint Hermengild prince of Spain, father was a Visigoth. Further ancestry is not known.

Descendents: Descendants include Saint Louis IX King of France and Ferdinand III King of Spain.

Biography: Son of Leovigild the Visigoth, King of Spain Saint Hermengild was a Prince and Martyr. Indegundis, his wife converted him from the Arian heresy, which brought about his disinheritance by Leovigild and his defeat at Seville Spain. Hermenegild was axed to death when he refused to accept Arianism. His feast is now confined to local calendars.

April 17 Saint Landericus
Country: England   **Date:** 7th Century

Family: Father: Vincent Madelgaire de Hainault Saint
         Mother: Waldetrudis de Loomis Saint   Spouse: Unknown   Siblings: Adeltrude de Hainault Saint; Madelberta Saint; Dentlin Saint

Ancestors: Only one generation is known and is listed above.

Branches of the Tree: Saint Adeltrude Descendents are known.

SAINTS DAILY
Kings, Queens, Popes, Princes, Princesses, Emperors, Hermits, Bishops

DAILY SAINTS WHOSE ANCESTRY IS KNOWN

Biography: Saint Landericus was a Benedictine bishop. He was from a large family of Saints, with three siblings who became Saints and both parents who were Saints. He was bishop of Meaux, in France. In 650 he resigned his see and moved to Belgium, in Soignes to become abbot there.

April 19 Saint Geraud
Country: France   **Date:** 978

Family: Father: Geraud Count of Bourges   Mother: Rothilde
Spouse: Unknown   Siblings: Tietberga (Tetrisca) \Bourges\ of

Ancestors: Not much ancestry is known, as the tree connects thru the siblings descent.

Branches of the Tree: Descends and connects to the Lusignan branch, at Hugh the fifth.

Biography: Saint Geraud was nobleman who became a hermit in Switzerland. There was a family of Saxon counts the Rhaetian family that he was born into. He became a recluse and gave his lands to Einsiedeln Monastery. This was in Switzerland and his sons were monks in the monastery. He went to the forest near Mitternach in the Waalgu and became a hermit.

April 19 Saint Pope Leo IX
Country: English Wales   **Date:** 21 Jun 1002

Family: Father: Hugo VI Count In Nordgau   Mother: Heilwig Von Dagsburg
Spouse: Unknown   Siblings: Gertrud Countess In Nordgau

SAINTS DAILY
Kings, Queens, Popes, Princes, Princesses, Emperors, Hermits, Bishops

132

DAILY SAINTS WHOSE ANCESTRY IS KNOWN

Ancestors: Only a few generations are known.

Branches of the Tree: Sibling Gertrud Countess In Nordgau is the mother of Agatha Von Brunswick who married King Edward the Exile of England

Biography: Saint Leo IX was Bruno, son of Count Hugh of Egisheim, and was born in 1002 in Alsace. In 1027 he became its archbishop after being educated in Toul. After he became pope he canonized Gerard of Toul. Bruno was elected in 1049, after being nominated by Emperor Henry III. He called for an abolition of simony and an end to clerical unchastity in synods that he held. Where ever he visited he held synods. He led a small troop against the Normans in 1053 and was captured. For nine months he was a prisoner in Benevento and he died a month after his return to Rome. Possible miscommunication but certainly disagreements led to the Great Schism between Constantinople and Rome in 1054.

April 21   *Saint Beuno*
Feastday: April 21   **Date**: ?

Family: Father: Tyfid ap Eiludd   Mother: Gwenlo Verch Bugi   Spouse: Siblings: Saint Beuno

Ancestors: Ancestors include Saint Brychan and so all of his ancestors as well.

Branches of the Tree: This is a few generations up on her mothers side Saint Brychan of Wales area.

Biography: Saint Beuno was Saint Winifred's brother. There is an untrustworthy legend that he was a monk in Wales. One of

SAINTS DAILY
Kings, Queens, Popes, Princes, Princesses, Emperors, Hermits, Bishops

DAILY SAINTS WHOSE ANCESTRY IS KNOWN

the miracles he performed was restoring Saint Winifred's head. It is said he founded his own community. Saint Beuno seems to have been an effective preacher who evangelizad much of North Wales. At Clynnog Fawr (Carnavonshire) he founded a monastery.

April 22 *Saint Opportuna*

Feastday: April 22   **Date**: c. 770

Family: Father: Sigrammus   Mother: Landrada
Spouse: Unknown   Siblings: Saint Chrodegang of Metz

Country: Franks

Ancestors: Chrodobertus I is an ancestor on his mothers side.

Branches of the Tree: Pepin Mayor of the Palace is a relative. This is the branch around Charlemagne.

Biography: Born near Hyesmes in Normandy she entered a convent at a young age. The convent for Saint Opportuna was near Almeneches, and she received the veil from her brother the Bishop of Seez Chrodengang. She was very pius and autere. Her brother was murdered, and his tragic end was so great a shock to her that she died shortly afterwards. Saint Opportuna's legend was very popular in France. She left behind a memory of a life of prayer, mortification, and obedience as well as humility.

April 21 *Saint Beuno*

Feastday: April 21   **Date**: ?

SAINTS DAILY
Kings, Queens, Popes, Princes, Princesses, Emperors, Hermits, Bishops

DAILY SAINTS WHOSE ANCESTRY IS KNOWN

Family: Father: Tyfid ap Eiludd   Mother: Gwenlo Verch Bugi   Spouse: Siblings: Saint Beuno

Ancestors: Ancestors include Saint Brychan and so all of his ancestors as well.

Branches of the Tree: This is a few generations up on her mothers side Saint Brychan of Wales area.

Biography: Saint Beuno was Saint Winifred's brother. There is an untrustworthy legend that he was a monk in Wales. One of the miracles he performed was restoring Saint Winifred's head. It is said he founded his own community. Saint Beuno seems to have been an effective preacher who evangelizad much of North Wales. At Clynnog Fawr (Carnavonshire) he founded a monastery.

April 27   *Saint Floribert*

Country: Franks   **Date:** 746

Father: Hubert "The Confessor" Bishop of Liege Saint
        Mother: Floribanne of Austrasia
Spouse: Unknown   Siblings: Unknown

Ancestors: The Frankish kings are ancestors so Joseph the Vizier of Egypt son of Israel and so Abraham and Noah.

Branches of the Tree: This is the time and era of Charlemagne, and this is the Frankish branch of the tree.

Biography: Saint Floribert became the Bishop of Liege, Belgium. He was the son of St. Hubert and Floribane. Floribane died giving him birth. He succeeded to be the bishop 727

SAINTS DAILY
Kings, Queens, Popes, Princes, Princesses, Emperors, Hermits, Bishops

DAILY SAINTS WHOSE ANCESTRY IS KNOWN

replacing his father. He was described as a man avid in correcting others.

April 27   Saint Enoder

d. Sixth   Feastday: April 27

Family:
Parents: Father- Unknown Mother-Unknown
Wife: Unknown
Children: Unknown

Biography:
Grandson of Welsh chieftain Brychan of Brecknock, also called Cnydr, Keneder, and Quidic. There is considerable dispute as to his identity, as he could be St. Enoder or Enodoc of Cornwall, England. Llangynidir of Powys wrote of him. Enoder was an abbot.

April 29   Saint Endellion

Date: d. Sixth   Feastday: April 29
Family:
Parents: Father-Saint Brychan   Mother- Rigrawst b. 450
Husband: Unknown
Children: Unknown

Biography:
Virgin recluse honored at St. Endellion, in Cornwall, England. She was the sister of St. Nectan of Hartland, and the daughter of Brychan of Brecknock. Two wells are named after her. She has a chapel dedicated to her at Tregony, where she may have lived. Roscarrock records the legend that she lived off the milk of one cow only, that strayed on the lord of Tregony's land who had it killed. Saint Endellion's godfather, caused the lord to be slain, but Saint Endellion miraculously revived him. Opposite her

SAINTS DAILY
Kings, Queens, Popes, Princes, Princesses, Emperors, Hermits, Bishops

DAILY SAINTS WHOSE ANCESTRY IS KNOWN

brother Saint Nectan's settlement at Harland at Lundy Island another chapel was dedicated to her.

April 30   Blessed Hildegard

Date: 754-783   *Feastday:* April 30

Family:
Parents: Father-Gerold I Duke of Swabia   Mother-Imma of Swabia
Husband: Blessed Charlemange
Children: Louis I King of France; Pepin I de Lombardy King of Italy; Charles the Younger Duc de Ingelheim

Ancestry:
Blessed Hildegard married Charlemange. Her ancestry goes back only one or two generations.

Descendents:
Her descendents are the same as those of Charlemange. Almost all nobles after the year 1200 can find some link to Hildegard and Charlemange. There are numerous societies dedicated to proving lineage to Charlemange.

Biography:
Wife of Charlemange. Her sons and daughters include Charles the younger, Pippin, Louis I, and Alpais, and also Bertha.

SAINTS DAILY
 Kings, Queens, Popes, Princes, Princesses, Emperors, Hermits, Bishops

DAILY SAINTS WHOSE ANCESTRY IS KNOWN

Saints of May

FEAST DAY	SAINT	COUNTRY	BORN	DIED
1-May	Saint Joseph	Israel		1st
1-May	Saint Asaph	Wales		6th
1-May	Saint Sigismund de Bourgogne	France		523
2-May	Saint Mafalda	Portugal	1204	1252
3-May	Saint James the Lesser	Israel		1st
5-May	Saint Mauront	France		701
5-May	Saint Pius V Pope	Italy		1572
6-May	Saint Elizabeth of Hungary	Hungary	1207	
6-May	Saint Agnes of Bohemia	Armenia	1205	1282
6-May	Saint Eadbert	Great Britain		698
7-May	Saint Liudhard	France		c 602
10-May	Blessed Beatrice D'Este	Italy	1206	1226
11-May	Saint Walbert	Belgium		c 678
12-May	Blessed Joan of Portugal	Portugal	1452	1490
12-May	Saint Domitilla	Italy		1st
12-May	Saint Rictrudis	France		c 688
13-May	Saint Erconwald	England		693
16-May	Saint Carranog	Wales		6th

SAINTS DAILY
Kings, Queens, Popes, Princes, Princesses, Emperors, Hermits, Bishops

138

DAILY SAINTS WHOSE ANCESTRY IS KNOWN

18-May	Saint Elgiva of Wessex	England	942	944
18-May	Saint Eric IX of Sweden	Sweden		1160
19-May	Saint Dunstan	England	900	988
19-May	Saint Prudentiana	Rome		1st
21-May	Saint Contantine the Great	Rome		337
23-May	Saint Euphrosyne of Polotsk	Russia		1173
24-May	Saint David of Scotland	Scotland	1085	1153
26-May	Saint Dyfan	Wales		6th
27-May	Saint Bruno Bishop of Wurzburg	France		1045
28-May	Blessed Margaret Pole	England	1471	1541
30-May	Saint Fernando of Spain	Spain	1199	1252
31-May	Saint Mechildis	Holland	1125	1160

TABLE SIX SAINTS OF MAY

May 1   *Saint Joseph*

Country: Italy (Rome)   **Date:** 1st Century
    Patron: The Universal Church; Cabdrivers; Carpenters; Church; Croation People; Doubters: Fathers; House Hunting; Joiners; Korea; Oblates of Saint Joseph; Travelers; Vietnam

Family: Father: Jacob   Mother: Unknown
Spouse: Unknown   Siblings: Unknown

Ancestors: Heir to the house of David.

SAINTS DAILY
Kings, Queens, Popes, Princes, Princesses, Emperors, Hermits, Bishops

139

DAILY SAINTS WHOSE ANCESTRY IS KNOWN

Branches of the Tree: Lines are found in the books of Mathew and Luke.

Biography: Saint Joseph is credited with providing for Jesus and Mary as Jesus grew up. By the time of most of the gospels, Joseph had past away and Mary was a Widow. Although his name is in the lineage's mentioned in the bible there are words attributed to his being the father of Jesus such as Joseph it was thought was the father of Jesus. In other words it does not completely say he was the father, possibly due to the conception of Jesus. There are other texts written the same time as the bible that mention he was a widower when he married Mary. Whatever the case at the time he was considered the heir to the house of David. There is a considerable amount of literature about Joseph found in other books as well.

May 1   *Saint Asaph*

d.c. 600   Feastday May 1

Family:
Parents: Father- Sawyl Penuchel Mother- Gwenasedd
Husband: none
Children: none

Ancestors: Rhein Red-Faced was the eldest son of King Brychan Brycheiniog and the grandfather of Saint Asa.

Biography:

Also called Asa first bishop of Asaph in Wales. (The place is named after him). He lived in a hermitage near Tenegel near Holywell. Saint Asaph is also described in a life of Saint Kentigern or Mungo. Asaph served Saint Kentigern while young. When asked to bring firewood to Saint Kentigern Asaph brought live coals in his apron, showing his sanctity. In 573 when Kentigern left the area, Asaph was consecrated a Bishop. He is

DAILY SAINTS WHOSE ANCESTRY IS KNOWN

relatives with Deiniol, Tysilo and others who are honored as Saints.

May 1   *Saint Sigismund ('the Holy') de Bourgogne*

Country: France   **Date:** d 523

Family: Father: Gondebaut (Gundobad) (King of the Burgundians) Mother: Unknown
Spouse: Theodegotho Princess   Siblings: Unknown

Ancestors: Ancestors include Faramund, and so the line of Joseph the Israelite. Also found is a line of Ancient Britain which goes to Priam, and so to Zerah son of Judah the Israelite.

Biography: One year before the death of his father Saint Sigismund was converted to Christianity. He succeeded to the throne of course replacing his father the Arian Vandal ruler of Burgundy Gondebaut. In a rage one year after he took the throne he had his son strangled for yelling at his stepmother. With remorse, thoroughly stricken he prayed for atonement and was generous to the Church. The sons of Clovis defeated him in battle to avenge Chilperic their grandfather, brother of Gondebaut. Gondebaut had attained the throne through his murder. After the battle Sigismund escaped and lived as a hermit near St. Maurice. He was executed after capture by King Clodomir at Orleans. Sigismund restored the monastery of St. Maurice at Agaunum and endowed it. The constant chant or laus perennis was associated with Sigismund and the monastery of St. Maurice.

SAINTS DAILY
Kings, Queens, Popes, Princes, Princesses, Emperors, Hermits, Bishops

DAILY SAINTS WHOSE ANCESTRY IS KNOWN

May 2 *Saint Mafalda*
Country: Portugal   **Date:** 1204-1252

Family: Father: Sancho De Portugal I   Mother: Dulce Aldonza De Aragon
Spouse: Alfonso IX Fernandez King Of Castile And Leon
          Siblings: Affonso De Portugal II; Sanchia Saint; Teresa Saint

Ancestors: Kings of Castile and Burgundy and Portugal.

Branches of the Tree: Saint Isabel of Aragon is in this branch of the tree.

Biography: She was married at age eleven to King Henry I of Castile, and when the marriage was annulled because of the close family ties she became a Benedictine nun at Arouca convent. She was responsible for the convent adopting the Cistercian rule, and she devoted a large amount of her father's income to charitable works. She built a hostel for travelers. She also built a home for widows. She restored Oporto Cathedral, and lived a life of great austerity. Her cult was approved in 1793.

May 3   *Saint James the Lesser*
Country: Israel   **Patron:** Dying

Family: Father: unknown   Mother: Mary Alphaews
Spouse: Unknown   Siblings: Saint Judas the apostle, Saint Simon the apostle, Saint Joseph Barabas the apostle

Ancestors: Saint Joseph of Arimathea is an ancestor. A little know fact of the biblical character of Joseph of Arimathea is that he is the son of Mathat, who is in the line of Nathan that is listed in the New Testament book of Luke. His ancestors then must be King David of Israel and Judah, and so the Israelites Joseph, Levi, Zebulon, and Judah. Anna married Saint Joseph of

SAINTS DAILY
Kings, Queens, Popes, Princes, Princesses, Emperors, Hermits, Bishops

DAILY SAINTS WHOSE ANCESTRY IS KNOWN

Arimathea, and her ancestry is an unbroken male line to Levi the Israelite. Saint Joseph of Arimathea's mother may have been the daughter of Eleazor, who was of the Davidic line of Solomon. Eleazor was the Grandfather of Joseph who married the Virgin Mary and this line is listed in the Gospel of Mathew. The Israelite Benjamin was an ancestor of King David's wife Maacah (Sauls daughter) whose line married in the line from Solomon joined by the marriage of Reheboam to Maacah. Therefore Saint Joseph of Arimathea has five Israelites as ancestors.

Branches of the Tree : This is a branch of the tree that has Saint Joseph of Arimathea in it. He is the Father of Cleopas who is the Father of Mary Alphaws. He is three generations the ancestor of Saint James. This line also marries Anna Arimathea who is the daughter of Joseph of Arimathea.

Biography: Saint James the lesser was an apostle of the lord. He was one of the twelve disciples. He wrote the epistle of James. His mother was Mary and his grandfather was Cleopas, who was the son of Saint Joseph of Arimathea.

May 5   *Saint Mauront*

Country: Franconia, Prussia   **Date:** 701

Family: Father: Adalbald I De Artois Saint   Mother: Saint Rictrudis
Spouse: Unknown   Siblings: Adalbald II De Artois, Eusebia Saint, Clotsind Saint, and Adalsind Saint

Ancestors: None known

Branches of the Tree: This branch is the branch near Saint Gertrude of Hamage.

SAINTS DAILY
Kings, Queens, Popes, Princes, Princesses, Emperors, Hermits, Bishops

143

DAILY SAINTS WHOSE ANCESTRY IS KNOWN

Biography: Saint Mauront founded the abbey of Breuil after he entered Marchiennes Monastery. This abbey was founded on his personal property. He was from a family of Saints, with three siblings and both parents achieving Sainthood. His sister was an abbess at Marchiennes. Saint Mauront served King Clovis II of the Franks.

May 5   *Saint Pius V Pope*
Date: d. May 1 1572   **Feastday**: May 5

Family:
Parents: Father: Ghislieri Mother: Unknown Spouse: None
Siblings: Gardina Ghislieri

Country: Italy

Ancestors: Not Known

Branch of the Tree: His Brothers Descendents married the Gibertis, the Bonelli, the Gallio and the Borremeo. His brothers descendents are related to the descendents of Saint Charles Borromeo's Sister.

Biography: Michele Ghisleri was born in 1504. In 1556 was he was Bishop of Sutri. He was elected Pope in 1566 pm January 7. He worked closely with Saint Charles Borromeo. He excommunicated Elizabeth I of England and declared Mary Stuart, Queen of Scots as the rightful heiress to the English Throne. He prayed while the Spanish Fleet, the Papal Fleet and Venice's Fleet fought the Turks Fleet off in the Mediteranean and the victory was granted to him. He made October 7 the feast of Our Lady Of Victory, later changed to Our Lady of the Rosary. Pope Pius V carried out the reforms of the Council of Trent. Some scholars say he founded the counter reformation. He founded the Congregation of the Index to monitor writing. His relics are in Santa Maria Maggiore.

SAINTS DAILY
Kings, Queens, Popes, Princes, Princesses, Emperors, Hermits, Bishops

DAILY SAINTS WHOSE ANCESTRY IS KNOWN

May 6   Saint Elizabeth of Hungary

Country: Hungary   Patron of services, Bakers, tertiarties, widows, and young brides; Catholic Charities   ***Date:*** 1207

Family: Parents: Father- Andrew II King of Hungary Mother- Gertrude of Meran
Husband- Saint Louis IV of Thuringia   Children: Sophia of Thuringia

Ancestry: Saint Elizabeth ancestry is not known.

Descendents: Descendents include King Edward III of England and King Edward IV of England.   Also Isabelle Princess of France who married King Phillipe the IV of France is a descendent. Edward Stafford 3rd Duke of Buckingham.

Biography: At the age of four she was sent for education to the court of the Landgrave of Thuringia, to whose infant son she was betrothed. St. Elizabeth was born in Hungary in 1207, the daughter of Alexander II, King of Hungary. As she grew in age, her piety also increased by leaps and bounds. In 1221, she married Louis of Thuringia and in spite of her position at court began to lead an austerely simple life, devoted herself to works of charity, and practiced penance.

Her husband highly esteemed her virtue and was himself much inclined to religion. He encouraged her in her exemplary life. Louis was killed while fighting with the Crusaders. They had had three children when this tragedy struck After his death, Elizabeth made arrangements for the care of her children, left the court, and in 1228, renounced the world, becoming a tertiary of St. Francis. She built the Franciscan hospital at Marburg and devoted herself to the care of the sick until her death at the age of 24 in 1231.

SAINTS DAILY
Kings, Queens, Popes, Princes, Princesses, Emperors, Hermits, Bishops

DAILY SAINTS WHOSE ANCESTRY IS KNOWN

St. Elizabeth is the patron saint of bakers, countesses, death of children, falsely accused, the homeless, nursing services, tertiaries, widows, and young brides. Her symbols are alms, flowers, bread, the poor, and a pitcher.

SAINTS DAILY
Kings, Queens, Popes, Princes, Princesses, Emperors, Hermits, Bishops

DAILY SAINTS WHOSE ANCESTRY IS KNOWN

May 6   *Saint Agnes of Bohemia*

Date: b.1205   d. 1282

Family: Father: Vratislav (Uratislas) Bohemia Duke Of   Mother: Drahomira Von Stoder
Spouse: Unknown   Siblings: Boleslav I The Cruel King Of Bohemia; Saint Wenceslaus

Country: Armenia

Ancestors: Saint Ludmilla is an ancestors

Branches of the Tree: Bohemia is in this branch of the Tree in the vicinity of Saint Ludmilla.

Biography: Saint Agnes was related to Saint Elizabeth of Hungary. Her brother was Saint Wenceslaus. She was promised three times in marriage although educated by cisterian nuns. A suitor died, she was left for another, and finally got Pope Gergory IX to intervene. She built a hospital, established clinics, and became a Poor Clare after starting a convent for five nuns sent by Clare. She was fifty years in the cloister.

May 6   *Saint Eadbert*

Date: b.   d. 698

Family: Father: Eata   Mother: Unknown
Spouse: Unknown   Siblings: Unknown

Ancestors: Not much is known. Ancestors include Cuthwine and Bearnoch of Bercia

Branches of the Tree: In the area of the Northumbrians in Great Britain.

SAINTS DAILY
Kings, Queens, Popes, Princes, Princesses, Emperors, Hermits, Bishops

DAILY SAINTS WHOSE ANCESTRY IS KNOWN

Biography: Also call Edbert Saint Eadbert was the successor to Saint Cuthbert. Saint Bede praised him for his learning and knowledge of the Scriptures. In Durham England Saint Eadbert's relics are enshrined. He was an Abbot Bishop.

May 7 *Saint Liudhard*
Country: France   **Date:** 600

Family: Father: Charibert I Franks
     Mother: Ingoberge
Spouse: Unknown   Siblings: Bertha

Ancestors:. Charibert is of the line of Joseph the Vizier of Egypt son of Israel, Isaac, and Abraham.

Branches of the Tree This is the early branch of the tree of the Franks.

Biography: Saint Liudhard was also called Lip hard and Leotard. Queen Bertha, who was daughter to King Charibert of France, was his sister, and he was Bishop and Chaplain to her. Queen Bertha went to England to marry King Ethelbert of Kent, and Saint Liudhard also went to England. King Ethelbert converted, was baptized by Saint Augustine, and Saint Liudhard had played an important part of the conversion process. Saint Liudhard was buried at Canterbury.

May 8 Saint Desire or Desideratus
Country: France   **Date:** c 512 – d 554

Family: Father: Gondobald   Mother: Unknown
Spouse: Unknown   Siblings: Desiderius; Deodatus

SAINTS DAILY
 Kings, Queens, Popes, Princes, Princesses, Emperors, Hermits, Bishops

DAILY SAINTS WHOSE ANCESTRY IS KNOWN

Ancestors:. Argotta of the Franks is an ancestor as is Pharamond. Saint Constantine and Saint Helen of the Cross thus the Davidic ancestry. The Franks ancestors were the line to Joseph the Israelite and so also the Greek from Priam back to Zerah son of Judah the Israelite.

Descendents: Saint Dominic, Saint Edburga, Saint Edward Ambrose Barlow, Saint Emeric, Saint Ferdinand III, Saint Henry II, Saint Hugh, Saint Isabel of France, Saint Isabella of Aragon, Saint Hedwig of Poland, Saint Joan De Valois, Saint John Southworth, Saint Leger, Saint Leutwinus, Saint Lothaire, Saint Louis IX, Saint Louis of Anjou, Saint Louis of Toulous, Saint Mafalda, Saint Margaret of Scotland, Saint Margaret De Lorraine, Saint Norbert Bon Xanten, Saint Raymond Berengar IV, Saint Rusticus, Saint Sanchia, Saint Teresa, Saint Thibaud Archbishop of Vienna, Saint Thomas D'Aquino, Saint Thomas De Cantelou, Saint Waltheof, Saint William Archbishop of York, Saint William D'Autun, Saint Wiltrude Duchess of Bavaria. Royalty Descendents include King Henry I of France, King Charles I of Naples, King of Italy Bernard, King of France Robert I, King of England Henry I, King of England William the Conqueror, King of England Edward I, Prince of Kiev Svyatopolk II, King of Castile, Alfonso VII.
.

Biography: Saint Desideratus was brother or Desiderius and Deodatus. He is also known as Desire. He was a courtier at the court of King Clotaire, was active in combating heresy and simonry and was made bishop of Bourgues in 541. There were several councils he attended. These councils battled Nestorianism and Eutychianism. Was known for his peace making abilities and to have performed miracles.

May 10 Blessed Beatrice D'Este
Country: Italy   **Date:** 1206-1226

SAINTS DAILY
Kings, Queens, Popes, Princes, Princesses, Emperors, Hermits, Bishops

DAILY SAINTS WHOSE ANCESTRY IS KNOWN

Family: Father: Count Azzo VII of Este   Mother: Princess Giovanna of Este
Spouse: Unknown   Siblings: Count Rinaldo of Este; Princess Cubitosa of Este; Princess Constanza of Este; Count Contardo of Este; Princess Alisia of Este

Biography: Marquis Azzo was the father of Blessed Beatrice D'Este. When she was six she was orphaned. After resisting her family who wanted her to marry she joined the Benedictine 's at Solarola, Italy while only fifteen. She moved to Gemmola, where she died held in great veneration for the holiness. Her cult was approved in 1763.

May 11 *Saint Walbert*
Country: Belgium   *Date:* d 678

Family: Parents: FatherUnknown   Mother- Unknown
Wife: St. Bertilia   Children: Saint Waldetrudis and Saint Alegundis

Ancestry: Unknown

Descendents: Descendents include Saint Adelaide of Italy, Saint Anglibert, Saint Lazlo of Hungary, Saint Irene, Saint Leopold III, Saint Louis IX, Saint Hedwig, Saint Isabel of Aragon, and Saint Nithard the Cronicler.   Royal Descendents include King of Naples Charles II, King of France Louis VIII, Alphonso IV of Portugal, and King Edward III Plantagenet of England.

Biography: He was the father of Saints Waldetrudis and Alegundis and husband of St. Bertilia.
Saint Walbert was Duke of Lorraine, France, and count of Hainault, Belgium, also called Vaubert.

SAINTS DAILY
Kings, Queens, Popes, Princes, Princesses, Emperors, Hermits, Bishops

DAILY SAINTS WHOSE ANCESTRY IS KNOWN

May 12   *Blessed Joan of Portugal*

Feastday: May 12   Date: 1452-1490

Family: Father: Alfonso V "The Africian" PORTUGAL
Mother: Isabel of COIMBRA
Spouse: Unknown   Siblings: unknown

Country: Portugal

Ancestors: Kings of Portugal and Spain are Ancestors.

Branches of the Tree: This is the branch of the tree of the Portugese Kings..

Biography: She was born in 1452 and became heir to the throne because of the illness of her brother and death of her mother. She was refused permission by her father to enter the religious life. In the war against the Moors she was regent. In 1471 when the Moors were defeated her father approved her request to go into the religious life. She entered the Benedictine convent of Odivellas in 1472 and later transferred to the Dominican convent at Aveiro. She was unable to take vows until 1485 because of her families objections. She lived as a simple nun at Aveiro and devoted her charities to redeeming captives. She died at Aveiro and her cult was approved in 1693.

May 12   *Saint Domitilla*

Date: 1st Century   Feastday: May 12

Family:
Parents: Father: Q. Petillius Cerealis Consul Mother: Flavia Domitilla Spouse: Titus Flavius Clemens Saint Children: T Flavius Titianus Praefect Egypt Siblings: None

Ancestry: Not more than parentage is known. Her mother was the sister to Emperor Domitian.

SAINTS DAILY
Kings, Queens, Popes, Princes, Princesses, Emperors, Hermits, Bishops

151

DAILY SAINTS WHOSE ANCESTRY IS KNOWN

Descendents: Saint Margaret of Scotland, Saint Louis IX, Saint Raymond Berenger, Saint John Southwell, Saint Hedwig, Saint Edward the Confessor, Saint Leutwinus, and at least 54 other saints in the file Saints in the Tree are Descendents.

Biography: In the year 96 Saint Domitilla's husband was martyred and she was banished to the island of Pandatania in the Tyrrhenian Sea for her faith. Her husband was a roman consul.

May 12   *Saint Rictrudis*

Country: Franconia, Prussia   **Date:** 688

Family: Father: Unknown   Mother: Unknown
Spouse: Adalbald I De Artois Saint   Siblings: Unknown
Children: Saint Eusebia, Saint Clotsind, Saint Adalsind, and Saint Mauront

Ancestors: None known

Branches of the Tree: This branch is the branch near Saint Gertrude of Hamage.

Biography: Saint Rictrudis was a member of a noble family from Gascony France. The family objected however she wed Saint Adalbald who was a Frankish Nobleman. They had four children, all of which became Saints. Saint Adalbald was murdered by relatives in Gascony. Instead of remarriage, Saint Rictrudis became a nun at Marchiennes, in Flanders, Belgium. She founded this monastery and two of her children, Saint Clotsind and Saint Adalsind joined her there. Later Mauraont became a monk, and Saint Rictrudis was abbess for forty years until her death.

SAINTS DAILY
Kings, Queens, Popes, Princes, Princesses, Emperors, Hermits, Bishops

DAILY SAINTS WHOSE ANCESTRY IS KNOWN

May 13   *Saint Erconwald*
Country: England   *Date:* d. c. 686

Family: Father: Anna King of East Anglia   Mother: Hereswitha Saint
Spouse: Unknown   Siblings: Sexburga Princess Of East Anglia Saint; Etheldreda Saint Erconwald Saint Withburga Saint

Ancestors: Saint Ethelburga mother is Saint Hereswitha. Further back ancestry is not known. Woden and Frigg are Ancestors. Saint Cyllin is an Ancestor. Ancestors include the Kings of Siluria. Generations previous to this they were the Kings of Britain. The line then goes back to Zerah, whose father is Judah. This line also marries Anna Arimathea who is the daughter of Joseph of Arimathea. A little know fact of the biblical character of Joseph of Arimathea is that he is the son of Mathat, who is in the line of Nathan that is listed in the New Testament book of Luke. So Saint Cyllin is descended from the Davidic line of Nathan and so from Judah thru Perez, and also as previously mentioned thru Judah's son Zerah.

Branches of the Tree: Kings of East Anglia.

Biography: Saint Erconwald is the offspring of Anna King of East Anglia and Hereswitha Saint. Her mother Hereswitha is not the only Saint in the Family however. Saints Sexburga, Etheldreda and Erconwald and Withburga are all sainted siblings. He went to the kingdom of the East Saxons and founded a monastery there. He became the abbot of the monastery at Chertsey, Surrey. About 675 he became bishop of London, which he ruled until his death.

May 16   *Saint Carannog*
Feastday: May 16   Date: Sixth Century

Family: Father: Coryn   Mother: Unknown

SAINTS DAILY
Kings, Queens, Popes, Princes, Princesses, Emperors, Hermits, Bishops

DAILY SAINTS WHOSE ANCESTRY IS KNOWN

Spouse: Unknown　　　　　　　　　　Siblings:
Unknown

Country: Wales

Ancestors: Saint Mereri is the daughter of Saint Brychan who is an ancestor of Saint Carannog. Saint Helen of the Host is known as Saint Brychan's Mothers Ancestor.

Branches of the Tree: This is the branch of the tree of the Wales Kings.

Biography: Welsh abbot also called Carantac. Founded a monastery.at Cernach. He also spent some time in Ireland. He is associated with Crantock in Cornwall, and Carhampton in Somerset, England. A Welsh prince was an aide to Saint Patrick and this Carannog may have been that aide. (called Carantac). He founded a church at Llangrannog Wales.

May 18　　　　*Saint Elgiva*

Country: England　　　　　　　　　**Date:** c 944

Family:　　Parents: Unknown　　　Husband: Edmund I "the Magnificent" King of England
Children: Edgar "the Peaceable" King of England Saint

Ancestry:　　Saint Elgiva ancestors are not known and she married Edmund King of England.

Descendents: Descendents include Saint Edgar the Peaceable of England, Saint Louis IX of France, Saint Fernando of Spain, and Saints Margaret and David of Scotland. Royal descendents include King Edward III Plantagenet of England, King of Naples Charles II, King of France Philip IV, and Matilda Empress of Germany and Queen of England.

Biography:　　Wife of Edmund the First King of England, she was Queen and mother of Kings Dewy of the Saxons, and Edgar,

SAINTS DAILY
Kings, Queens, Popes, Princes, Princesses, Emperors, Hermits, Bishops

DAILY SAINTS WHOSE ANCESTRY IS KNOWN

King of England. She became a Benedictine nun at Shaftesbury after she gave up public life.

May 18   Saint Eric IX of Sweden

Country: Sweden   *Date:* d. 1160
        Patron: Sweden

Family: Parents: Father- Jedvard Thordsson   Mother- Cecilia Svendsdotter
Wife: Christine Bjornsdatter Sweden b. c 1125   Children: Margaret EricDtr Of Sweden, Knut Eriksson, Philip Eriksson Sweden, Catherina (Katerina) Eriksdotter Sweden

Ancestry: Ancestry past one or two generations not known.

Descendents: Thomas Boleyn, Constance Dudley, Stephen Hopkins.

Biography: Eric IX of Sweden wrote the Code of Uppland. This was also called King Eric's Law. He was a Martyr. He was crowned in 1150 and spread the faith thoughout Sweden. The pagan Finns were campaigned against, and King Eric asked Bishop Henry of Uppsala to remain as a missionary in Finland. Bishop Henry was an Englishman and was persuaded to do just that. Prince Magnus of Denmark had many allies however and King Eric was slain by Swedish nobles, associated with Prince Magnus. Saint Eric was beheaded near Uppsala as Prince Magnus entered the region with an army. Although never officially canonized Saint Eric the IX is the patron of Sweden.

May 19   Saint Prudentiana

Date: 1st Century

Family: Father: Rufus Pudens Saint   Mother: Gladys (Claudia) Britain

SAINTS DAILY
Kings, Queens, Popes, Princes, Princesses, Emperors, Hermits, Bishops

DAILY SAINTS WHOSE ANCESTRY IS KNOWN

Spouse: Unknown   Siblings: Timotheus; Novatus Saint; Praxedes Saint

Country: Italy (Rome)

Ancestors: Bran the Blessed is an Ancestor, as is his wife Anna of Arimathea as is Saint Joseph of Arimathea and so the Line of Nathan Son of David King of Israel and Judah. King David's ancestors include the Israelites, Zebulon, Levi, Joseph, and Judah. Also Anna of Arimathea, daughter to Joseph of Aramathea married Bran the Blessed whose line goes to Tros and so to Ephraim son of Joseph the Israelite. Also the line from Anna of Arimathea's mother goes thru Simon the Just thru many High Priests to Judah the Israelite.

Branches of the Tree: Go up three generations to Bran the Blessed and Anna of Arimathea. The Apostle Paul is very near in this branch of the tree.

Biography: Also known as Potentiana, a tradition states she was a Roman virgin and daughter of St. Pudens. Another tradition says she was the daughter of the Roman senator named in St. Paul's Second Letter to Timothy. It was this daughter the tradition says who aided the burials of Christians, gave away her wealth to the poor, and died at the age of sixteen. The cult of Pudentiana was suppressed in 1969 as her name is not found in any of the ancient martyrologies. Therefore owing to the unreliability of her origins, her veneration is confined to her basilica in Rome.

May 19   Saint Dunstan Archbishop of Canterbury

Country: Britain   *Date:* b. 900 d. 988
              Patron: Gunsmiths

SAINTS DAILY
 Kings, Queens, Popes, Princes, Princesses, Emperors, Hermits, Bishops

DAILY SAINTS WHOSE ANCESTRY IS KNOWN

Family: Parents: Father- Heorstan   Mother- Unknown
Wife: Unknown   Children: Unknown

Ancestry: King Ethelred of England is his Great Grandfather.

Branches of the Tree: Branch near King Ethelred and Mercia.

Biography: Saint Dunstan became Archbishop of Canterbury. He started as an Abbot of Galstonbury. He is one of the great figures of English History. He studied at the monastery at Glastonbury, and was born in the region of Galstonbury. His Uncle Athelm was Archbishop of Canterbury and he served the Archbishop. He left service after receiving appointment to the Court of King Athelstan . He was accused of black magic and withcraft by his enemies at court. He fled to Bishop of Winchester, Aelfheah, and became a monk and hermit at Glasonbury. In 939 King Edmund I Ironsid recalled Saint Dunstan to the royal court. He received appointment as Abbot of Glastonbury at this time. He acted as advisor of King Edmund I and his brother King Edrd and reformed the monastery at Glastonbury and instituted the Benedictine rule. He was expelled by King Edwy the Fair and Saint Dunstan wandered across the Continent observing monastic institutions, favorably at the abbey of Blandinium. King Edgar the Peaceful asked his return to the Isles and he became Bishop of Worcester, and then Bishop of London.. In 959 he became archbishop of Canterbury. Saint Dunstan worked with King Edgar to bring reforms to the entire English Church. Saint Dunstan was considered a prominent leader in the country. King Edward the Martyr rose to the throne largely thru Saint Dunstan's influence in 975. The Regularis Concordia, a compilation on the monastic life was written by Saint Dunstan after he retired to Canterbury to teach at the Cathedral School.

SAINTS DAILY
Kings, Queens, Popes, Princes, Princesses, Emperors, Hermits, Bishops

DAILY SAINTS WHOSE ANCESTRY IS KNOWN

May 21 Saint Constantine the Great

Country: Rome   **Date:** 337

Family: Parents: Father- Flavius Valerius Constanius I Chlorus   Mother- Helen Flavia Julia Helena Elen Britannica Saint   Wife: Fausta Children: Constantius II Flavius Julius Constantius Rome

Ancestry: Also King David of Judah and Israel is an ancestor thru Nathan his son.

Descendents: Descendents include Saint Margaret of Scotland, Saint Adele of Blois, Saint Olav of Norway, Saint Leopold III of Austria and Saint Louis IX of France.

Biography: Junior Emperor and emperor called the "Thirteenth Apostle" in the East. Constantine was raised on the court of co-Emperor Diocletian. He was the son of Constantius I Chlorus, junior emperor and St. Helena. When his father died in 306, Constantine was declared junior emperor of York, England, by the local legions. By defeating his main rivals at the battle of the Milvian Bridge in 312 he earned a place as a ruler of the Empire. The military standards that held the banners his armies carried into battle to vanquish their pagan enemies, according to legend, he adopted the insignia of Christ, the chi-rho, and placed it upon his labarum -. His purple banners were inscribed with the Latin for "In this sign conquer." He exerted his considerable influence upon his colleague Licinius to secure the declaration of Christianity to be a free religion. Constantine then shared rule of the Empire with Licinius who was a pagan. Constantine marched to the East and routed his opponent at the battle of Adrianople when, however, Licinius launched a persecution of the Christians. Constantine was the most dominating figure of his lifetime, towering over his contemporaries, including Pope Sylvester I. He gave extensive grants of land and property to the Church, presided over the Council of Nicaea, undertook a long-sighted program of Christianization for the whole of the Roman

SAINTS DAILY
Kings, Queens, Popes, Princes, Princesses, Emperors, Hermits, Bishops

DAILY SAINTS WHOSE ANCESTRY IS KNOWN

Empire and founded the Christian city of Constantinople to serve as his new capital. While he was baptized a Christian only on his deathbed, Constantine nevertheless was a genuinely important figure in Christian history and was revered as a saint, especially in the Eastern Church.

May 23   *Saint Euphrosyne*
Of Polotsk

Feastday: May 23   Date: d.1173

Family: Father: Svyatoslav Yurij Vseslavich Polotsk
MotherUnknown
Spouse: Unknown   Siblings: Vasilko I Polotsk

Country: Russia

Ancestors: Saint Vladimir is five generations her ancestor. Saint Olga is then seven generations her ancestor.

Branches of the Tree: This branch of the tree is near the Russian Czars.

Biography: At age 12 the daughter of Svyatoslav Polotsk Saint Euphrosyne became a nun. Later she became a recluse in a cell at Holy Wisdom Cathedral, copying manuscripts. Her earnings from the manuscripts she gave to the poor. At Seltse she founded a convent. She traveled to Constantinople and the Holy Land where she died at Jerusalem in 1173.

May 24   *Saint David of*
Scotland

Country: Scotland   *Date:* 1085-1153

SAINTS DAILY
Kings, Queens, Popes, Princes, Princesses, Emperors, Hermits, Bishops

159

DAILY SAINTS WHOSE ANCESTRY IS KNOWN

Family: Parents: Father- Malcolm III, Canmore, King of Scotland Mother- Saint Margaret Atheling Queen of Scotland   Wife: Matilda (Maud) Huntington   Children: Henry Prince of Scotland

Ancestry: Ancestry includes of course his mother Saint Margaret of Scotland, and so include Charlemange, Joseph of Arimathea, and Saint Helena of Rome. Also King David of Judah and Israel is an ancestor thru Nathan his son as ancestors of Saint Joseph of Arimathea. . King Solomon of Israel and Judah is also an ancestor. Sainted Ancestry includes Saint Ethelbert, Saint Arnulf, Saint Itta, Saint Sigebert, Saint Dagobert, Saint Beggue, Saint Liuthwin, Saint Bathildis, Saint Sexburga, Saint Clodulf, Blessed Pepin, Saint Matilda, Saint Elgiva, Saint Edgar, Saint Henry II, Saint Cunigunda, Saint Stephen, and his mother Saint Margaret.

Descendents: Descendents include King of Scotland William the Lion, and Henry II DeBohun Surety Magna Carta.

Biography: Saint David is the son of Saint Margaret of Scotland and King Malcolm III. He was educated at the Anglo Norman Court, and married Matilda daughter of Waldef the Anglo Saxon patriot earl of Northampton and Huntingdon. His niece married Henry I king of England. In 1135 after King Stephen became king instead of his Niece (who was the successor to the English Throne in David's eyes,) he captured nearly all the border castles. In 1136 he further claimed Northumberland and invaded the north of England in 1138, helped by miscellaneous allies from Norway, Denmark, Germany, and especially the Picts of Galloway, who murdered women, and other barbaric acts, which were long remembered. David's Army was defeated at the battle of the Standard (near Northallerton) but David got favorable terms, Northumberland and Cumberland were ceded, and David had a court at Carlisle.

David improved Scotland, with a feudal system of land tenure replacing the Celtic tribal one, and an Anglo-Norman

SAINTS DAILY
Kings, Queens, Popes, Princes, Princesses, Emperors, Hermits, Bishops

judicial system. He developed towns such as Edinburgh, Berwick, and Perth with many nations trade by his merchants. Rome was frequently contacted and the relationship was close. Bishoprics of Brechin, Dunblane, Caithness, Ross and Aberdeen were founded as well as many Churches and Monasteries.

After numerous prayers he died on May 24 1153.

May 26   Saint Dyfan verch Brychan

Date: d. Fifth Century

Family:
Parents: Father-Saint Brychan   Mother- Rigrawst b: 0450

Children: Unknown

Biography:
Founder at Anglesey, Wales.

May 27   Saint Bruno Bishop Of Wurzburg

Country: France   **Date:** 1045

Family: Father: Conrad III Duke Of Franconia And Carinthia   Mother: Maud of Swabia
Spouse: Unknown   Siblings: Unknown

Ancestors:.   Ancestors include Heinrich Emperor, Duke of Lorraine and Dukes of Bavaria

Biography: Saint Bruno was Bishop of Würzburg, Germany. While dining with Emperor Henry III he was killed in an accident. He had became a bishop in 1033. Saint Bruno started many parishes in Wurzburg, of which he used personal wealth to start. While dining at Bosenberg with Emperor Henry III on the

SAINTS DAILY
 Kings, Queens, Popes, Princes, Princesses, Emperors, Hermits, Bishops

DAILY SAINTS WHOSE ANCESTRY IS KNOWN

Danube, a galley gave way and he was killed. Saint Bruno was revered as a scholar and author and was the son of Duke Conrad of Carinthia and Baroness Matilda.

May 28   Blessed Margaret Pole
Country: England   **Date:** 1471-1541

Family: Father: Duke George Plantagenet   Mother: Lady Isabel de Neville
Spouse: Unknown   Siblings: Unknown

Ancestors: Ancestors include Saint Fernando and so Muhamed, Ishmael and Abraham. Also Charlemagne and so Zerah. Also Joseph of Arimathea and Saint Helena of Rome are ancestors. Also King David of Judah and Israel is an ancestor thru Nathan his son. King Solomon of Israel and Judah is also an ancestor. Sainted Ancestry includes more saints than any other saint. These are Saint Ethelbert, Saint Arnulf, Saint Itta, Saint Sigebert, Saint Dagobert, Saint Beggue, Saint Liuthwin, Saint Bathildis, Saint Sexburga, Blessed Pepin, Saint Clodulf, Saint Olga, Saint Matilda, Saint Elgiva, Saint Edgar, Saint Henry II, Saint Cunigunda, Saint Stephen, Saint Margaret, and Saint David.

Branches of the Tree: This branch of the tree is very near Edward IV Plantagenet.

Biography: Blessed Margaret Pole was the niece of Edward IV and Richard III. She was born Margaret Plantagenet and married Sir Reginald Pole about 1491 and bore five sons, including Reginald Cardinal Pole. Margaret became widowed, was was named countess of Salisbury. Blessed Margaret was appointed governess to Princess Mary, the daughter of Queen Catherine of Aragon, Spain and Henry VIII. She was opposed to Henry's marriage to Anne Boleyn, was called "the holiest woman in England" and was exiled by Henry from court. Cardinal Pole, Blessed Margaret's son denied Henry's Act of Supremace, and the king imprisoned Margaret in the Tower of London for two

SAINTS DAILY
Kings, Queens, Popes, Princes, Princesses, Emperors, Hermits, Bishops

DAILY SAINTS WHOSE ANCESTRY IS KNOWN

years. On May 28 she was beheaded. In 1538 her other two sons were executed. She was seventy years old when she was executed and she was never given a legal trial. Blessed Margaret was beatified in 1886.

May 30   Saint Fernando of Spain

Country: Spain   *Date:* 1199-1252   *Patron:* Engineers; Persons in Authority; Spanish Army; Govenors; Magistrates; Poor; Prisoners; Rulers; Seville Spain

Family: Parents: Father- Alfonso IX of Leon, King of Leon   Mother- Berengaria Alfonsez Princess of Castile   Wife: Joana De Dammartin Children: Eleanor Princess of Castile

Ancestry: Saint Fernando ancestors include Charlemange, Helena of Rome, and Joseph of Arimathea. Also the prophet Muhamed is an ancestor of Saint Fernando. Muhamed is a descendent of Ishmael the eldest son of Abraham. Also King David of Judah and Israel is an ancestor thru Nathan his son. King Solomon of Israel and Judah is also an ancestor. Sainted Ancestors include Saint Ethelbert, Saint Itta, Saint Arnulf, Saint Sigebert, Saint Dagobert, Saint Beggue, Saint Liuthwin, Saint Beggue, Saint Sexburga, Blessed Pepin, Saint Clodulf, Saint Matilda, Saint Elgiva, Saint Edgar, Saint Henry II, Saint Cunigunda, Saint Stephen, and Saint Margaret.

Descendents: Descendents include Edward I Longshanks King of England, King Edward IV Plantagenet of England.

Biography: He was declared king of Castile at age eighteen. Ferdinand III of Castile was the son of Alfonso IX, King of Leon, and Berengaria, daughter of Alfonso III, King of Castile (Spain). Ferdinand was born near Salamanca; his mother advised and assisted him during his young reign and was proclaimed king of Palencia, Valladolid, and Burgos. He married Princess Beatrice, daughter of Philip of Suabia, King of Germany and they had seven sons and three daughters. His father (the king of Leon)

SAINTS DAILY
Kings, Queens, Popes, Princes, Princesses, Emperors, Hermits, Bishops

163

turned against him and tried to take over his rule. The two reconciled later, and fought successfully against the Moors. He was extremely devoted to the Blessed Virgin and in 1225, he held back Islamic invaders; prayed and fasted to prepare for the war. Between 1234-36, Ferdinand conquered the city of Cordoba from the Moors. He overtook Seville shortly after Queen Beatrice died in 1236. He founded the University of Salamanca and the Cathedral of Burgos and married Joan of Ponthieu after the death of Beatrice. He died on May 30th after a prolonged illness, and buried in the habit of his secular Franciscan Order. His remains are preserved in the Cathedral of Seville and was canonized by Pope Clement X in 1671. Ferdinand was a great administrator and a man of deep faith. Ferdinand rebuilt the Cathedral of Burgos and changed the mosque in Seville into a Cathedral. He founded hospitals and bishoprics, monasteries, churches, and cathedrals during his reign. He also compiled and reformed a code of laws which were used until the modern era. He was a just ruler, frequently pardoning former offenders to his throne. His feast day is May 30th.

May 31   *Saint Mechildis*

Country: Holland   **Date:** 1160

Family: Father: Berthold IV Andechs Count Of
       Mother: Sophia Of Istria
Spouse: Unknown   Siblings: Berthold V von Diessen (Count of Andechs)

Ancestors: Ancestors are not known

Branches of the Tree: This branch contains Stephen of Hungary and Margaret of Hungary

Biography: Saint Mechildis was a miracle worker. She was a Benedictine abbess. At age five her parents, Berthold IV Count of Andechs and Sophia, put her in a monastery they founded on

SAINTS DAILY
Kings, Queens, Popes, Princes, Princesses, Emperors, Hermits, Bishops

DAILY SAINTS WHOSE ANCESTRY IS KNOWN

their estate at Diessen Bavaria. She became a nun and later an abbess. The bishop of Augsburg placed her in charge of Edelstetten Abbey in 1153. She died at Diessen on May 31 and was revered for her mystical gifts and miracles.

SAINTS DAILY
Kings, Queens, Popes, Princes, Princesses, Emperors, Hermits, Bishops

DAILY SAINTS WHOSE ANCESTRY IS KNOWN

Saints of June

FEAST DAY	SAINT	COUNTRY	BORN	DIED
1-Jun	Saint Gracia	Cordoba	1071	
1-Jun	Saint Wistan	Prince	835	892
1-Jun	Saint Mary	Spain		1180
1-Jun	Saint Bernard	Spain		1180
3-Jun	Saint Clotilde of the Franks	Franks	475	545
5-Jun	Blessed Ferdinand	Portugal	1402	1443
8-Jun	Saint Edgar the Peaceful	England	943	975
8-Jun	Saint Clodulphe Bishop	Metz	615	690
8-Jun	Saint William of York	England	c 1100	1154
9-Jun	Saint Columba	Ireland	c. 521	c 579
12-Jun	Blessed Jolenta	Hungary		1299
14-Jun	Saint Dogmael	Wales		6th
15-Jun	Saint Trillo	Wales		6th
15-Jun	Saint Edburga of Winchester	England		960
17-Jun	Saint Sanchia of Portugal	Portugal	1182	1229
17-Jun	Saint Nectan	Wales	468	510
17-Jun	Saint Teresa	Portugal	1181	13th

SAINTS DAILY
Kings, Queens, Popes, Princes, Princesses, Emperors, Hermits, Bishops

166

DAILY SAINTS WHOSE ANCESTRY IS KNOWN

20-Jun	Saint Novatus	Rome		137
20-Jun	Saint Florentina	Spain		c 636
22-Jun	Saint Pulcheria	Italy	399	453
22-Jun	Saint Pontius Meropius Anicius Paulinus	Italy	354	431
22-Jun	Saint Thomas More	England	1477	1534
22-Jun	Saint Flavius Clemens	Italy		c. 96
23-Jun	Saint Etheldreda	England		679
27-Jun	Saint Lazlo of Hungary (d 1095)	Hungary		1095
28-Jun	Saint John Southworth	England	1592	1654
28-Jun	Saint Austell	Wales		6th
29-Jun	Saint Paul	Israel		c 67
30-Jun	Saint Eurgen of Llan Ilid	BRITAIN		6th
30-Jun	Saint Clotsind	France		714

TABLE SEVEN SAINTS OF JUNE

June 1   *Saint Gracia*

Country: Cordoba   *Date: c. 1180*

Family: Parents: Father- Abul-Kasim Muhammad Be Abbad Mother- Slave-Itamid
Husband: Alfonso IV Jimenez   Children: Theresa Jimenez

Ancestry: The line of Muhamed the Prophet is discovered in her ancestry. This line goes thru to Ishmael brother of Isaac both

SAINTS DAILY
Kings, Queens, Popes, Princes, Princesses, Emperors, Hermits, Bishops

DAILY SAINTS WHOSE ANCESTRY IS KNOWN

sons of Abraham. Therefore Saint Gracia is a descendent of Abraham.

Descendents: Saint Fernando is a descendent of Saint Gracia. Descendents include Edward I Longshanks King of England, King Edward IV Plantagenet of England.

Biography: These Children of Almanzor, the Muslim Capital of Lerida, in Catalonia, were originally named Achmed, Zorainda, and Zaida. Moorish converts and martyrs, the patron saints of Alcira in Valencia Spain. Achmed (Bernard) became a Cistercian monk at Poblet, near Tarragona after he converted. He attempted to bring his brother Almanzor, into the faith and succeeded into converting his two sisters. Almanzor had them arrested and executed by beheading. Feastday, June 1.

June 1   *Saint Wistan*

Country: England   ***Date:*** b. 835 d. 892

Family: Parents: Father- Prince Wigmund   Mother- Princess Elfleda
Wife: Unknown   Son: AEthelred II of Mercia

Ancestry: Woden and Frigg are listed as ancestors from Princess Elfleda

Descendents: King Edward IV Plantagenet; Duke Richard III Plantagenet

Biography: Wistan was a martyr of England. Wistan was the grandson of the King of Mercia Wiglaf. Wistan opposed the ruler's plan to marry his mother. Therefore his Godfather murdered him, a man by the name of Bertulph. Wistan's remains were translated to Evesham Cathedral. originaly buried at Repton.

SAINTS DAILY
 Kings, Queens, Popes, Princes, Princesses, Emperors, Hermits, Bishops

DAILY SAINTS WHOSE ANCESTRY IS KNOWN

June 1   *Saint Mary*
Country: Spain   **Date:** d. c. 1180

Family: Father: Caliph of Lerida   Mother: Spouse: Unknown   Siblings: Gracia Zayda Princess Of Sevilla Saint; Bernard Saint

Ancestors: This line will lead all the way thru Muhammad the Prophet to Ismael the eldest son of Abraham thru the wife Hagar.

Branches of the Tree: .Descendents include the Spanish Royalty including Saint Fernando.

Biography: Saint Mary was named Zoraida, and was converted to Christianity and became a Cistercian monk at Poblet near Tarragona, taking the name Bernard. She was the sister to Zayda both offspring of the Moslem caliph of Lerida in Catalonia. Saint Bernard attempted to convert his brother Almanzor and when he found them out he turned them in to the authorities and had them beheaded.

June 1   *Saint Bernard*
Country: Spain   **Date:** d. c. 1180

Family: Father: Caliph of Lerida   Mother: Spouse: Unknown   Siblings: Gracia Zayda Princess Of Sevilla Saint

Ancestors:. This line will lead all the way thru Muhammad the Prophet to Ismael the eldest son of Abraham thru the wife Hagar.

Branches of the Tree : Descendents include the Spanish Royalty including Saint Fernando.

SAINTS DAILY
Kings, Queens, Popes, Princes, Princesses, Emperors, Hermits, Bishops

DAILY SAINTS WHOSE ANCESTRY IS KNOWN

Biography: Saint Bernard was named Achmed, and was converted to Christianity and became a Cistercian monk at Poblet near Tarragona, taking the name Bernard. He was the brother to Zayda both offspring of the Moslem caliph of Lerida in Catalonia. His other sister Zoraida was also converted and took the name Mary. He attempted to convert his brother Almanzor and when he found them out he turned them in to the authorities and had them beheaded.

June 3   *Saint Clotilde*
Country: France   *Date:* 475-545

Family: Parents: Father- Gondebaud Burgundy King Burgundy   Mother- Unknown
Husband: Clovis Franks Chief Salian Franks b 467 Children: Clotaire I Franks King Franks

Ancestry: Saint Clotilde ancestry can be traced only about one generation. Further Ancestry is not known.

Descendents: Descendents include Saint Adelaide of Italy Empress, Saint Adele Countess of Blois, Saint Arnolf Bishop of Metz, Blessed Charlemange, Saint Cunigunda of Luxemborg, Saint David and Saint Margaret of Scotland, Saint Edgar of England, Saint Ferdinand III of Spain, Saint Louis IX of France, Saint Raymond Berenger Count, Saint Henry II King of Germany, Saint Lazlo King of Hungary, and Saint Leopold III of Austria.

Biography: King Clovis and his wife St. Clotilde started the dynasty of the Franks, called the Merovingian dynasty. Clotilde converted King Clovis to Christianity in 496 and they were married in 492 or 493. Clotilde retired to Tours when Clovis died. Great sorrow was caused by her son's quarrels. St. Martin of Tours tomb is where Clotilde died. She was buried in Sainte-Genevieve in Paris, a church that Clovis and Clotilde founded. Medieval art has a popular theme of St. Clotilde at prayer.

SAINTS DAILY
Kings, Queens, Popes, Princes, Princesses, Emperors, Hermits, Bishops

DAILY SAINTS WHOSE ANCESTRY IS KNOWN

June 5   *Blessed Fernando*

Country: Portugal   **Date:** 1402-1443

Family: Father: King John Of Portugal
        Mother: Phillippa Lancaster
Spouse: Unknown   Siblings: Unknown

Ancestors: King Edward III Plantagenet is an ancestor thru Phillippa of Lancaster who is the daughter of Duke John of Gaunt.

Branches of the Tree: This is the branch of the tree of the English Kings.

Biography: Blessed Fernando was the son of Phillippa Lancaster who was the daughter of John of Gaunt. He was the son of King John of Portugal. Born on September 29 at Santarem he led a princely life of piety unusual for the age. He was grandmaster of the Knights of Aviz (originally the New Militia to Fight the Moors), but he refused a cardinate from Pope Eugene IV. With his brother he led an army against the Moors at Tangiers, Africa. He brother was Henry the navigator and it ended in disaster with his expedition defeated. Henry escaped but Blessed Fernando was mistreated when hid brother Edward refused to ransom him with the strong hold of Ceuta. He was in prison six years until he died there at Fez on June 5, and his body was hung from the prison walls. Surnamed the Constant he is the hero of one of the most popular tragedies, El Principe Constantia, of the famous Spanish dramastist Pedro Calderon. His cult was approved in 1470.

June 8   *Saint Edgar the Peaceful King of England*

Country: England   *Date:* 943-c 975

SAINTS DAILY
Kings, Queens, Popes, Princes, Princesses, Emperors, Hermits, Bishops

DAILY SAINTS WHOSE ANCESTRY IS KNOWN

Family: Parents: Father-Edmund I "the Magnificent" King of England Mother- Saint Elgiva
Wife: Elfrida   Children: Aethelred II "The Unready" King of England

Ancestry: Saint Edgar's ancestors include his mother Saint Elgiva, four generations previous Saint Alfred. Also included is Joseph of Arimathea. Also King David of Judah and Israel is an ancestor thru Nathan his son. King Solomon of Israel and Judah is also an ancestor.

Descendents: Descendents include Saint Louis IX of France, Saint Fernando of Spain, and Saints Margaret and David of Scotland. Royal descendents include King Edward III of England, King Philip IV of France, Empress of Germany and Queen of England Matilda, and King of Naples Charles II.

Biography: Patron of St. Dunstan, and English King, Saint Dunstan served as Saint Edgar's counselor. He is venerated at Glastonbury as England underwent a religious revival in his reign. He had a daughter, St. Edith of Wilton, who was borne by one or two religious woman that he had an affair with.

June 8   *Saint Clodulph*
Country: France   *Date:* 615-690

*Family*Parents: Father- Saint Arnuf Bishop Of Metz   Mother- Dode (Ode) De Heristal
Wife: Unknown   Children: Kunza of Metz

Ancestry: Saint Cloduoph's ancestor is Saint Arnulf of Metz. Also King David of Judah and Israel is an ancestor thru Joseph of Arimathea and David's son Nathan.

Descendents: Sainted descendants include Saint Adele of Blois, Saint Adelaide of Italy, Saint Louis IX of France, Saint Fernando III of Spain, Saint Cunigunda of Luxemborg, Saint Leopold III of

SAINTS DAILY
Kings, Queens, Popes, Princes, Princesses, Emperors, Hermits, Bishops

DAILY SAINTS WHOSE ANCESTRY IS KNOWN

Austria, Saint Henry II of Germany, Saint Lazlo King of Hungary, Saint Raymond Berenger IV. and Saint David and Saint Margaret of Scotland. Royal descendents include King Edward III Plantagenet of England, King of Naples Charles II, King of France Philip IV, and King of Scotland William the Lion. Also Casimir King of Poland, Alphonso Enriquez I King of Portugal and Henry IV Holy Roman Emperor of Germany.

Biography: He is also known as Cloud or Clou. He married Goda, who became a nun when he was ordained. Bishop of Metz, France, the son of St. Arnulf, born circa 605. In 657, he was named bishop of Metz.

June 8   Saint William of York
Country: Franconia, Prussia   **Date:**

Family: Father: Herbert the Chamberlain   Mother: Emma Of Blois
Spouse: Unknown   Siblings: Herbert Fitz Herbert

Ancestors: Saint Adele Countess of Blois.

Branches of the Tree: This branch of the tree is very near William the Conqueror whose daughter was Saint Adele Countess of Blois.

Biography: Saint William of York was a Bishop. He was the son of Count Herbert treasurer to Henry I. Emma his mother was the half-sister to King William. Young William became treasurer of the church of York at an early age. In 1140 he was elected Archbishop. Saint William's opponents challenged the election accusing him of simony and unchastity. The pope in Rome cleared him, however the next Pope, the Cistercian Eugene III suspended William. In 1147 he was deposed. Saint William next went to Winchester where he became a monk. His accusers died and also the Pope Eugene III died. The next Pope Anastastius IV restored William his See and he was once again Archbishop.

SAINTS DAILY
 Kings, Queens, Popes, Princes, Princesses, Emperors, Hermits, Bishops

DAILY SAINTS WHOSE ANCESTRY IS KNOWN

One month later he died. The year was 1154. There are some who claim he was poisoned by the archdeacon of York. There is no record of any resolution in the case however. Saint William was canonized in 1227 by Pope Honorius III.

June 9   Saint Columba (Crimthann O'Donnell)

Country: Ireland   **Date:** 521

Family: Father: Fedhlimidh (Phelim)   Mother: Eithne
Spouse: Unknown   Siblings: Unknown

Ancestors: Fergus is and ancestor, as are the monarch's of Ireland.

Branches of the Tree: This is the branch of the tree of the Irish Kings.

Biography: Saint Columba was born in Donegal Ireland of royal descent. Saint Finnian instructed him at Moville and then at Clonard under another Saint Finnian he received instruction. Before he was twenty five he was ordained and spent the next fifteen years preaching and setting up foundations at Derry, Durrow, and Kells. Possibly because of a family feud which resulted in 3000 dead, (he thought he was responsible) and he left Ireland at 42. He landed on the island of Iona off the coast of Scotland. He built a monastery here that became famous. With Saints Canice and Comgall he evangelized the Pics, and he also developed a monastic rule. Saint Columba's rule was followed until the introduction of Saint Benedict's rule. Saint Columba is also known as Colm, Columcille, and Colum. He died at Iona. His feast day is June 9

June 12 Blessed Jolenta of Hungary

Country: Hungary   **Date:**d. 1299

SAINTS DAILY
Kings, Queens, Popes, Princes, Princesses, Emperors, Hermits, Bishops

174

DAILY SAINTS WHOSE ANCESTRY IS KNOWN

Family: Father: Bela IV (King of Hungary)
Mother: Marie Lascarina
Spouse: Duke Boleslaus of Kalisz   Siblings: Stephen V (King of Hungary); Saint Margaret; Blessed Cunegunda

Ancestors: Ancestors include thru Turkey to Armenia Saint Isaac Pahlav and Saint Gregory the Enlightened.

Branches of the Tree: This branch contains Stephen of Hungary and Margaret of Hungary.

Biography: Blessed Jolenta of Hungary was the daughter of King Bela IV. She was raised by her older sister Blessed Cunegunda who was wife of Boleslaus V of Poland. Jolenta married Duke Boleslaus of Kalisz and he died in 1279, so Blessed Jolenta and one of her daughters and Cunegunda went to the Poor Clares Convent. Blessed Cunegunda had founded this convent at Sandeck. Blessed Jolenta became superior of the convent at Gnesen, which she had founded and this is where she eventually died. Her cult was approved in 1827 and she is known as Helen of Poland in Poland.

June 14   *Saint Dogmael*
Country: Wales   **Date:** Sixth Century

Family: Father: Ithel ap Ceredig   Mother: Unknown
Spouse: Unknown   Siblings: Unknown

Ancestors: Saint Brychan is Saint Dogmael's Great Grandfather. Only a few generations are known on Saint Brychan's fathers side. Saint Helen of the Host is known as Saint Brychan's Mothers Ancestor.

Branches of the Tree: This is the branch of the tree of the Wales Kings.

SAINTS DAILY
Kings, Queens, Popes, Princes, Princesses, Emperors, Hermits, Bishops

175

DAILY SAINTS WHOSE ANCESTRY IS KNOWN

Biography: Saint Dogmael was of the house of Cunedda. He became a Welsh monk. Saint Dogmael was the son of Ithel ab Ceredig ab Cunedda Wledig. He stayed for a time in Pemborkeshire Wales were he was known for his preaching. He then went to Brittany in France. Saint Dogmael has several churches named after him.

June 15 Saint Edburga of Winchester
Country: Great Britain   *Date:* 960

Family: Father: Edward I "The Elder"
      Mother: Edgiva
Spouse: Unknown   Siblings: Eadgifu

Ancestors: Ancestors of the line of the Kings of England have been debated. David the King of Israel and Judah is an Ancestor thru Nathan. Lines of Zerah brother to Perez and son of Judah the Israelite have been documented. Saint Margaret of Scotland is an ancestor. Saint Margaret ancestors include Charlemagne, Joseph of Arimathea, and Saint Helena of Rome. Also King David of Judah and Israel is an ancestor thru Nathan his son. King Solomon of Israel and Judah is also an ancestor.

Branches of the Tree: Saint Adeltrude Descendents are known.

Biography: Saint Edburga of Winchester the daughter of King Edward the Elder and Edgiva who was a granddaughter of Alfred the great. She was a Benedictine abbess who became and not at Winchester Abbey and was known for miracles. Her shrine is a Pershore, in Worchestershire, England.

June 15   Saint Trillo
Country: Great Britain   *Date:*6th

Family: Father: Ithel Hael   Mother: Unknown

SAINTS DAILY
 Kings, Queens, Popes, Princes, Princesses, Emperors, Hermits, Bishops

176

DAILY SAINTS WHOSE ANCESTRY IS KNOWN

Spouse: Unknown Siblings: Tegid ap Ithel Saint; Gredyw ap Ithel Saint; Llechid ap Ithel Saint

Ancestors:

Branches of the Tree: This is the branch near Saint Judicael and Hoel II and Budig II

Biography: Patron Saint of two sites in Gweneyyd Wales. Also called Drel or Drillo. Welsh.

June 17   Saint Teresa

Feastday: June 17   Date: d. 1250

Family: Father: Sancho De Portugal I   Mother: Dulce Aldonza De Aragon
Spouse: Alfonso IX Fernandez King Of Castile And Leon
    Siblings: Affonso De Portugal II; Mafalda Saint; Sanchia Saint

Country: Portugal

Ancestors: Kings of Castile and Burgundy and Portugal.

Branches of the Tree: Saint Isabel of Aragon is in this branch of the tree.

Biography: Saint Teresa was the eldest daughter of King Sancho I of Portugal and sister of SS. Mafalda and Sanchia. Her marriage to her dousing King Alfonso IX of Leon was declared invalid because of consanguinity. She returned to Portugal and founded a Benedictine monastery on her estate at Lorvao. Her monastery accommodated three hundred nuns who followed the Cistercian Rule. In 1231 Alfonso's second wife and widow Berengaria requested she settle a dispute among their children over the succession of the throne of Leon. Her cult and that of

SAINTS DAILY
Kings, Queens, Popes, Princes, Princesses, Emperors, Hermits, Bishops

DAILY SAINTS WHOSE ANCESTRY IS KNOWN

her sister Sanchia was approved by Pope Clement XI in 1705. June 17 is her feast day.

June 17　　Saint Sanchia

Country: Portugal　　　　　　　　**Date:** 1182-1229

Family:　　Father: Sancho De Portugal I　　Mother: Dulce Aldonza De Aragon
Spouse:　Alfonso IX Fernandez King Of Castile And Leon
　　　Siblings: Affonso De Portugal II; Mafalda Saint; Teresa Saint

Ancestors: Kings of Castile and Burgundy and Portugal.

Branches of the Tree: Saint Isabel of Aragon is in this branch of the tree.

Biography: Her father was King Sancho De Portugal. She is sister to Saints Mafalda and Teresa. She retired to her father's Estates at Alenquer when he died in 1211. In Portugal the foundations of the first Franciscan and Dominican orders were aided by Saint Sanchia. At Celles she founded a convent with the Augustinian rule. Saint Sanchia later changed it into a Cistercian abbey in 1223 and she became a nun there. Her cult and that of her sister Teresa were approved in 1705.

June 17　　　　　Saint Nectan

Date: Fifth Century b. 468 d. 510

Family:
Parents: Father-Saint Brychan　Mother- Rigrawst b: 0450
Wife: Unknown
Children: Unknown

Biography:

SAINTS DAILY
Kings, Queens, Popes, Princes, Princesses, Emperors, Hermits, Bishops

178

DAILY SAINTS WHOSE ANCESTRY IS KNOWN

Also called Nighton or Nectaran. He was a hermit in Devonshire England founding churches there and at Cornwall. Patron saint of Hartland, Devonshire, very venerated in the Middle Ages. He was beheaded by robbers. Only in some traditions is he a relative of the chieftain Brychan.

Note: St. Nectan is one of the most celebrated saints in the West of England, although details from his life-story are rather sparse. He is chief amongst the Cornish list of children of King Brychan Brycheiniog, usually said to have been the eldest.

Nectan sailed south from Wales and landed on the Corno-Devon border at Hartland Point. He found a beautiful valley there, at Stoke St. Nectan near Hartland, with a never-failing spring. He built a little church and a hermitage, forty paces away and lived there many years. He tended to the needs of the poor throughout Devon, Cornwall and even Brittany, where churches dedicated to him may be found. He once helped a swineherd find his lost pigs and, in return, was given two cows who provided his daily comestible needs. Most of Nectan's siblings followed him from Wales and were instrumental in evangelizing the south-west. They saw Nectan as their leader and gathered every New Year's Eve at Hartland to talk with him.

Eventually, Nectan's two cows were stolen by bandits. He tracked them to New Stoke, took them back and tried to convert his persecutors to Christianity. For all his hard work, they struck off his head! Legend says Nectan picked up the severed object and returned, with it, to his chapel at Stoke. This occurred on 17th June AD 510. His body was translated to a more fitting shrine in the 1030s and later looked after by the Austin Canons who built an Abbey nearby.

Little historical credit is given to the Cornish lists of the children of Brychan and many scholars believe they only indicate that the named persons originated in South Wales. Nechtan's name is

SAINTS DAILY
Kings, Queens, Popes, Princes, Princesses, Emperors, Hermits, Bishops

DAILY SAINTS WHOSE ANCESTRY IS KNOWN

Pictish and some think he has been confused with Noethon ap Gildas who is known to have come from the North. Prof. Charles Thomas, meanwhile, believes that Nectanis, in fact, a corruption of the name Brychan itself: father and son being one and the same. He identifies Lundy Island as Brychan's mysterious burial place, Ynys Brychan, from where his body was removed to Stoke in the 7th century.

The medieval cult was considerable in the West Country. Lyfing, Bishop of Crediton 1021-46, who had at first refused to translate Nectan's body approved of it and provided treasures for the church at Harland including bells, lead for the roof, and a sculptured reliquary. Saint Nectan's staff was decorated with gold, silver, and jewels; and the church was also endowed with manors to strengthen it against pirates from the Viking settlements in Ireland. Saint Nectan's Church benefactors included King Harthacnut, Earl Godwin, and his wife. Early 12th century saw the Austin Canons restored the church and shrine at Hartland which remained in their care until the Reformation. There are five churches in Devon and Cornwall dedicated to Saint Nectan and possibly two Breton place names may be connected with him. According to William Worcester Nectan was the most important of the Children of Brychan in Devon and Cornwall. His feast was kept at Launceston, Exeter, Wells, and elsewhere. Saint Nectan died on June 17, and this is one of the days his feast day may be celebrated on. Also 18 May (given by Roscarrock) and Gotha text gives 4 December. The fair in his honour at St. Winnoc was on 14 February, his feast day according to Wilson's Martyrology (1640).

SAINTS DAILY
Kings, Queens, Popes, Princes, Princesses, Emperors, Hermits, Bishops

DAILY SAINTS WHOSE ANCESTRY IS KNOWN

June 20   *Saint Novatus*

Country: Italy (Rome)   **Date:** 1st Century

Family: Father: Rufus Pudens Saint   Mother: Gladys (Claudia) Britain
Spouse: Unknown   Siblings: Timotheus; Prudentiana Saint; Praxedes Saint

Ancestors: Bran the Blessed is an Ancestor, as is his wife Anna of Arimathea. Saint Joseph of Arimathea and so the Line of Nathan Son of David King of Israel and Judah is an ancestor. King David's ancestors include the Israelites, Zebulon, Levi, Joseph, and Judah. Also Anna of Arimathea, daughter to Joseph of Aramathea married Bran the Blessed whose line goes to Tros and so to Epraim son of Joseph the Israelite. Also the line from Anna of Arimathea's mother goes thru Simon the Just thru many High Priests to Judah the Israelite.

Branches of the Tree: Go up three generations to Bran the Blessed and Anna of Arimathea. The Apostle Paul is very near in this branch of the tree.

Biography: Very little is known of Saint Novatus. He is listed as a saint and is the son of Rufus Pudens and Claudia. His siblings are listed above and are Saint Prudentiana, Saint Praxedes, and Timotheus.

June 20   *Saint Florentina*

Country: Cartagena Spain   **Date:** 636

Family: Father: Severinum, Count Of Cartagena
       Mother: Theodora
Spouse: None   Siblings: Theodosia; Leander of Seville Saint; Fulgentius Saint; Isadore Saint

SAINTS DAILY
Kings, Queens, Popes, Princes, Princesses, Emperors, Hermits, Bishops

DAILY SAINTS WHOSE ANCESTRY IS KNOWN

Ancestors: Not much Ancestry is known

Biography: Saint Florentina was raised by Leander, her brother. She was from a large family of Saints, four in all counting herself. Saint Leander founded a convent for her. She was born in Cartagena, Spain. She became abbess of her convent.

June 22   *Saint Pulcheria*
Feastday: June 22   Date: b. 19 Jan 399 d. 453

Family: Father: Arcadius Claudius Claudianus Emperor
                Mother: Eudoxia
Spouse: Marcian E. Roman emperor   Siblings: Theodosius   Children: Euphemia

Country: Italy

Ancestors: Very few generations known

Descendents: Saint Leodegar and Saint Leutwinus are descendents. Saint Margaret Queen of Scotland, Saint Bruno, Saint Adelaide of Italy, Saint Cunigunda, Saint Dominic, Saint Louis IX of France and Saint Raymond Berenger are all descendents. Blessed Charlemange Emperor is a Descendent.

Biography: Daughter of Emperor Claudius she was born on January 19 and her father died when she was nine in 408. Her younger brother Theodosius was declared Emperor and she was declared regent and Augustus in 414. She declared her virginity, ran the empire, and raised her little brother. Athenais became the wife of Theodusius in 421 and was baptized Eudocia. Now Eudocia was declared augustus. Eudocia supported Nestorius but Pulcheria did not and Saint Pulcheria got her brother to condemn Nestorius. Pulcheria was banished from the court due to intrigue inspired by Eudocia. However due to infidelity Eudocia was exiled to Jerusalem and Pulcheria was restored. Pulcheria supported the plea of Pope St. Leo the Breat when Theodosius

SAINTS DAILY
Kings, Queens, Popes, Princes, Princesses, Emperors, Hermits, Bishops

DAILY SAINTS WHOSE ANCESTRY IS KNOWN

sported Eutyches and monophusitism and supported the Robber Synod. In 450 Emperor Theodosius was killed in a fall from his horse while hunting and Saint Pulcheria became Empress. She married General Marcian who was aged on the condition of respecting her virginity and the two ruled. In 451 the council of Chalcedon was sponsored by the Empress and Emporer and Saint Pulcheria attended the third session. Pope Leo credited her with overcoming the Nestorian and Eutychian heresies. She also recalled all the Catholic Bishops that Theodosius had exiled and Pope Leo recognized her for this. She built many hospices, hospitals, churches. She encouraged the building of a university in Constantinople. She died in the University in July.

June 22   *Saint Thomas More*

Feastday: June 22   Date: b. 5 Feb 1477/78   d. 5 Jul 1535

Family: Father: John More   Mother: Agnes Graunger
Spouse: Jane Colt, Alice Middleton   Siblings: none

Country: England

Ancestors: Only Parentage is known

Branches of the Tree: Follow Descendents for three generations to the Scrope Line whose ancestors were the De Percy.

Biography: He wrote the book Utopia in 1516 and is a major saint. Saint Thomas More was the lord chancellor of England in 1529. He resigned in 1532 due to the opinions of King Henry VIII. He opposed King Henry VIII when he was told he had to recognize the King and go against the supremacy of the Pope. He was confined to the Tower of London for fifteen months with his close friend Saint John Fisher. On July 6 1535 he was beheaded.

SAINTS DAILY
Kings, Queens, Popes, Princes, Princesses, Emperors, Hermits, Bishops

DAILY SAINTS WHOSE ANCESTRY IS KNOWN

June 22 Saint Pontius Meropius Anicius Paulinus

Feastday: June 22   Date: b. 354 d. 431

Family: Father: Pontius Paulinus   Mother: Unknown
Spouse: Therasia De España   Siblings: none

Country: Italy

Ancestors: Very few generations known

Branches of the Tree: This is the branch of the tree around some Romans, near Avitus

Biography: Son of the Roman prefect of Gaul, Saint Paulinus was born near Bordeaux. He became a successful and prominent lawyer after studing rhetoric and poetry under Ausonius. He married a Spanish lady Therasia and quit his travels and retired to Aquitaine. He met Bishop Delphinus of Bordeaux who baptized him and his brother. In 390 he moved to Therasia's estate and when his only child died he gave property to the church and lived a devout life. In 393 he was ordained a priest. In 395 he moved near the tomb of Saint Felix, sold everything and gave it to the poor. He built a church at Fondi, a basilica near the tomb of Saint Felix, also a hospice for travelers at Nola, and housed many of the poor at his own home. In 409 he was elected Bishop of Nola. He corresponded with Saint Augustine and Saint Jerome and was friend to Saint Martin of Tours and Saint Ambrose. His writings still exist, at least some of them with 51 letters, and 32 poems still exist. He is ranked with Prudentius as the foremost Christian Latin poets of the patistic period.   A letter he wrote to Saint Augustine inspired Saint Augustine's reply "On the Care of the Dead".

SAINTS DAILY
Kings, Queens, Popes, Princes, Princesses, Emperors, Hermits, Bishops

DAILY SAINTS WHOSE ANCESTRY IS KNOWN

June 22   *Saint Flavius Clemens*

Date: 1st Century c. 96 **Feastday:** June 22

Family:
Parents: Father: unknown Mother: unknown Spouse: Flavia Domitilla Saint Children: T Flavius Titianus Praefect Egypt Siblings: Emperor Vespasian

Ancestry: Unknown

Descendents: Saint Margaret of Scotland, Saint Louis IX, Saint Raymond Berenger, Saint John Southwell, Saint Hedwig, Saint Edward the Confessor, Saint Leutwinus, and at least 54 other saints in the file Saints in the Tree are Descendents.

Biography: He was martyred as a Christian when the Emperor Domitian learned of his faith and he was beheaded. He was uncle to the successors of Vespasian Titus and Domitian.

June 23   *Saint Ethelreda*
"Saint Audrey"

Country: England   **Date:** d. 967

Family: Father: Anna King of East Anglia
        Mother: Hereswitha Saint
Spouse: Unknown   Siblings: Sexburga Princess Of East Anglia Saint; Ethelburga Saint

Ancestors: Saint Ethelreda mother is Saint Hereswitha. Further back ancestry is not known. Woden and Frigg are Ancestors. Saint Cyllin is an Ancestor. Ancestors include the Kings of Siluria. Generations previous to this they were the Kings of Britain. The line then goes back to Zerah, whose father is Judah. This line also marries Anna Arimathea who is the daughter of Joseph of Arimathea. A little know fact of the biblical character of Joseph of Arimathea is that he is the son of Mathat, who is in

SAINTS DAILY
Kings, Queens, Popes, Princes, Princesses, Emperors, Hermits, Bishops

the line of Nathan that is listed in the New Testament book of Luke. So Saint Cyllin is descended from the Davidic line of Nathan and so from Judah thru Perez, and also as previously mentioned thru Judah's son Zerah.

Branches of the Tree: Kings of East Anglia.

Biography: Saint Ethelreda was known as Audrey. She was an English princess around 640. She married and was widowed after three years, and the marriage may have never been consummated. There was a perpetual vow of virginity involved. She married again for reasons of state but her young husband made advances on her. She refused. So her husband attempted to bribe the local bishop, Saint Wilfrid of York, to release Audrey from her vows. Instead Saint Wilfrid helped Audrey escape, fleeing south with husband following. There was a promontory known as Colbert's Head where a heaven sent seven day high tide separated the husband and wife. Finally her husband left and remarried. Saint Ethelreda or Audrey took the veil and lived and austere life in the abbey she founded called the great abbey of Ely. She got a large tumor on her neck, and died. It is said the tumor was gratefully accepted as Divine retribution for all the necklaces she had worn in her early years. A festival, Saint Audrey's Fair was held throughout the middle ages at Ely on her feast day. The word tawdry, is said to be a corruption of Saint Audrey because of the shoddiness of the merchandise at the fair, especially the neckerchiefs.

June 27   *Saint Lazlo of Hungary*
Country: Hungary   **Date:** d c 1095

Family: Parents: Father- Bela I Adalbertus, King of Hungary   Mother- Richza (Ryksa Miciszlava) of Poland
   Wife: Adelheid of Rheinfels, Princess of Swabia
   Children: Xenia Piroska (Irene) Princess of Hungary

SAINTS DAILY
Kings, Queens, Popes, Princes, Princesses, Emperors, Hermits, Bishops

DAILY SAINTS WHOSE ANCESTRY IS KNOWN

Ancestry: Saint Lazlo of Hungary ancestry's include Charlemange and so Zerah. Also King David of Judah and Israel is an ancestor thru Nathan his son. Ancestors include Saint Arnulf, Saint Itta, Saint Sigebert, Saint Dagobert, Saint Beggue, Saint Liutwin, Blessed Pepin, and Saint Matilda.

Descendents: Descendents include King Edward III Plantagenet King of England and Phillippe IV King of France.

Biography: Younger brother of Geza I and son of Bela I he grew up in the court of Poland. When Andrew I was King of Hungary, Ladislaus recalled his brother Bela, but Andrew has a son Salomon which upset all plans. Intrigues, foreign interference, wars, troubles and much bloodshed followed. Lazlo himself bore arms to uphold the cause of Geza. In thirty years the throne passed to Andrew, Bela, Salomon, Geza, and in 1077 to Lazlo. Salomon now began to try to overthrow his cousin. Lazlo had to subjugate the Serbs, and Bulgars, drive back the Tattars and to war in Dalmatia and Croatia until united in 1089.

His reign was of the utmost beneficence. He followed what he judged to be the will of God and used his power only for the good of his people. Following St. Stephen who a century earlier had introduced Christianity into Hungary, he carried on the work. He was tall and large and showed great bravery on the battlefield. He was wise, virtuous and generous. When the West went on the first crusade, the English, the French, and the Spanish begged him to head the expedition. He accepted and then had to stem a revolt of the Bohemians before setting out. The Bohemian revolt resulted in his death at Neutra in Moravia June 30th 1095.

June 28   *Saint John Southworth*

Country: England   **Date:** 1592 d. 1654

Family: Father: Sir John Southworth   Mother: Mary Asheton
Spouse: Unknown   Siblings: Unknown

SAINTS DAILY
Kings, Queens, Popes, Princes, Princesses, Emperors, Hermits, Bishops

DAILY SAINTS WHOSE ANCESTRY IS KNOWN

Ancestors: Ancestors include Malcolm III of Scotland and also Saint Margaret of Scotland. Saint Margaret ancestors include Charlemagne, Joseph of Arimathea, and Saint Helena of Rome. Also King David of Judah and Israel is an ancestor thru Nathan his son. King Solomon of Israel and Judah is also an ancestor. Sainted Ancestry includes Saint Ethelbert, Saint Arnulf, Saint Itta, Saint Sigebert, Saint Dagobert, Saint Beggue, Saint Liuthwin, Saint Bathildis, Saint Sexburga, Saint Clodulf, Blessed Pepin, Saint Matilda, Saint Elgiva, Saint Edgar, Saint Henry II, Saint Cunigunda, and Saint Stephen. Charlemagne's ancestors include the line to Joseph the Israelite. King David is descended from Israelites Judah, Levi, Zebulon and Joseph.

Branches of the Tree : This branch of the tree is the Scottish branch, and is very near to King Edward III of England.

Biography: Saint John Southworth was one of the Fory Martyrs of England and Wales. He was born in Lancashire. In 1619 he became a priest. He was sent to England that same year and arrested. He was released because Queen Henrietta Maria interceded on his behalf. He began working with Saint Henry Morse, and subsequently worked during the plague of 1636. He was arrested again, he was martyred by being hanged, drawn, and quartered at Tyburn. His relics were discovered in 1927 in Westminster Cathedral in London. Pope Paul VI canonized him in 1970.

June 28 *Saint Austell*
Date: d. Sixth   Feastday: June 28

Family:
Parents: Father-Saint Brychan Mother- Unknown
Husband: Unknown
Children: Unknown

SAINTS DAILY
Kings, Queens, Popes, Princes, Princesses, Emperors, Hermits, Bishops

DAILY SAINTS WHOSE ANCESTRY IS KNOWN

Biography: Confessor and disciple of St. Newman of Cornwall, England. Modern scholars believe that Austell was a woman named Hoystill, a daughter of Brychan of Wales.

June 29   Saint Paul

Country: Israel   **Date:** 1st Century
Patron: Catholic Action; Cursillo Movement; Greece; Lay apostolate

Family: Father: Unknown   Mother: Priscilla
Spouse: Unknown   Siblings: Unknown

Ancestors: Priscilla is an ancestor, and Benjamin the Israelite is an ancestor.

Branches of the Tree: Priscilla married Rufus Pudens, although he may not be the father of Saint Paul. Saint Rufus's father was Pudens who married Gladys so from there go up three generations to Bran the Blessed and Anna of Arimathea. The Apostle Paul is very near in this branch of the tree.

Biography: Saint Paul is probably one of the major Saints of the bible. He has always been associated with the Gentiles. It is in the scriptures where St. Paul, the indefatigable Apostle of the Gentiles, was converted from Judaism on the road to Damascus. He was converted and then he remained some days in Damascus after his Baptism. Saint Paul then went to Arabia, possibly for a year or two to prepare himself for his future missionary activity. It is difficult to trace the travels of St. Paul in the early church. This is a summary of some of his travels. Having returned to Damascus, Saint Paul stayed there for a time, preaching in the synagogues that Jesus is the Christ, the Son of God. For this he incurred the dislike of the Jews and Saint Paul had to flee from the city. He then went to Jerusalem to see Peter and pay his homage to the head of the Church there in Jerusalem.

SAINTS DAILY
Kings, Queens, Popes, Princes, Princesses, Emperors, Hermits, Bishops

DAILY SAINTS WHOSE ANCESTRY IS KNOWN

Later St. Paul went back to his native Tarsus, where he began to evangelize his own province. He stayed there until he was called by Barnabus to Antioch. After one only about one year, on the occasion of a famine, both Barnabus and Paul were sent with alms to the poor Christian community at Jerusalem. After having stayed a time they fulfilled their mission they returned to Antioch.

Paul and Barnabus made the first missionary journey, consisting of many stops, including visiting the island of Cypress, then Pamphylia, Pisidia, and Lycaonia. All sees missionary stops were in in Asia Minor, and he established churches at Pisidian Antioch, Iconium, Lystra, and Derbe.

Paul, accompanied by Silas and later also by Timothy and Luke, after the Apostolic Council of Jerusalem, made his second missionary journey. St. Paul first revisited the churches previously established by him in Asia Minor, and then passed through Galatia. It was at Troas that a vision of a Macedonian was seen by Paul. This vision impressed him as a call from God to evangelize in Macedonia. Therefore he accordingly sailed for Europe, and preached the Gospel in Philippi. Beroea, Corinth, Athens, and Thessalonica. Then he returned to Antioch by way of Ephesus and Jerusalem.

On his third missionary journey, Paul revisited nearly the same regions as on the second trip, but made Ephesus the center of his missionary activity where he remained nearly three years. He made plans also for another missionary journey, intending to leave Jerusalem for Rome and Spain. It was persecutions by the Jews that hindered him from accomplishing his purpose. St. Paul was imprisoned for two years at Caesarea after that he finally reached Rome, where he was kept for an additional two years in chains.

The Acts of the Apostles gives us no further information on the life of the Apostle.

From the Pastoral Epistles and from tradition that at the end of the two years St. Paul was released from his Roman imprisonment, and St. Paul then traveled to Spain. He then

SAINTS DAILY
Kings, Queens, Popes, Princes, Princesses, Emperors, Hermits, Bishops

DAILY SAINTS WHOSE ANCESTRY IS KNOWN

traveled later to the East again, and then back to Rome. It was in Rome where he was imprisoned a second time and in the year 67, was beheaded.

Fourteen canonical Epistles have been given by St. Paul who showed untiring interest in and paternal affection for the churches that he established. St. Paul undoubtedly however, wrote other letters which are no longer extant. In his letters or Epistles, St. Paul shows himself to be a profound religious thinker and he has had an enduring formative influence in the development of Christianity. The centuries only make more apparent his greatness of mind and spirit. His feast day is June 29th.

June 30   Saint Eurgen Of Llan Ilid

Country: England   **Date:**

Family: Father: Caradoc Ap Bran King Of Britain
                Mother: Eurgain
Spouse: Unknown   Siblings: Gladys (Claudia) Britain; Linus Bishop of Rome Saint; Cyllin (Coellyn or Cyllinus) ap Caradog Saint

Ancestors: Ancestors that were the Kings of Siluria. Generations previous to this they were the Kings of Britain. The line then goes back to Zerah, whose father is Judah. This line also marries Anna Arimathea who is the daughter of Joseph of Arimathea. A little know fact of the biblical character of Joseph of Arimathea is that he is the son of Mathat, who is in the line of Nathan that is listed in the New Testament book of Luke. So Saint Cyllin is descended from the Davidic line of Nathan and so from Judah thru Perez, and also as previously mentioned thru Judah's son Zerah. Saint Cyllin is the Ancestor of Saint Helen of the Cross. Israelites Judah, Levi, Zebulon and Joseph are all ancestors of King David.

Branches of the Tree: This is the branch of the tree right on top of Saint Paul, Rufus Pudens (husband of Gladys).

SAINTS DAILY
 Kings, Queens, Popes, Princes, Princesses, Emperors, Hermits, Bishops

DAILY SAINTS WHOSE ANCESTRY IS KNOWN

Biography: This Saint lived very near biblical times, and his grandfather was the husband of Anna of Arimathea, whose Father Joseph was mentioned in the bible. Siblings include Gladys(Claudia) and Linus who was a Pope. Also Cyllin ap Caradog is a Sibling Saint. Virgin foundress of Wales. The daughter of chieftain Caradog of Glamorgan, Wales, she founded Cor-Eurgain, later called Llanwit.

June 30   *Saint Clotsind*
Country: Franconia, Prussia   **Date:** 714

Family: Father: Adalbald I De Artois Saint   Mother: Saint Rictrudis
Spouse: Unknown   Siblings: Adalbald II De Artois, Eusebia Saint, Adalsind Saint, and Mauront Saint

Ancestors: None known

Branches of the Tree: This branch is the branch near Saint Gertrude of Hamage.

Biography: Clotsind and Glodesind are names Saint Clotsind is also called. She was a Benedictine abbess. She was born circa 635, the daughter of Sts. Adalbald and Rictrudis. Saint Clotsind was educated by her mother. Her mother was the abbess of Machiennes Abbey in Flanders, in Belgium and France. In 688 Saint Clotsind became the abbess of Machiennes Abbey.

SAINTS DAILY
Kings, Queens, Popes, Princes, Princesses, Emperors, Hermits, Bishops

DAILY SAINTS WHOSE ANCESTRY IS KNOWN

Saints of July

FEAST DAY	SAINT	COUNTRY	BORN	DIED
1-Jul	Saint Leonorius			c. 570
1-Jul	Saint Veep	Wales		6th
2-Jul	Blessed Peter of Luxemborg	Luxemborg	1371	1399
2-Jul	Saint Oudoceus		536	625
4-Jul	Saint Isabel of Aragon	Portugal	1271	1336
5-Jul	Saint Gwen	Brittany		5th
5-Jul	Saint Morwenna	Wales		6th
5-Jul	Saint Fracan	Brittany		5th
6-Jul	Saint Sexburga	Kent		c 699
7-Jul	Saint Aubierge (Ethelburga)	England		c 647
7-Jul	Saint Ethelburga	England		664
7-Jul	Saint Ercongotha	England		660
8-Jul	Saint Withburga	England		c 743
11-Jul	Saint Pius	Rome		155
11-Jul	Saint Olga of Kiev	Russia	879	969
13-Jul	Saint Henry II of Germany	Germany	972	1024
13-Jul	Saint Mildred Of Thanet	England		c 700
14-Jul	Blessed Boniface of Savoy	France		1270

SAINTS DAILY
Kings, Queens, Popes, Princes, Princesses, Emperors, Hermits, Bishops

193

DAILY SAINTS WHOSE ANCESTRY IS KNOWN

Date	Saint	Place		
15-Jul	Blessed Bernard of Baden	France	1429	1458
15-Jul	Saint Vladimir of Kiev	Russia	956	1015
15-Jul	Saint Edith of Polesworth	Viking		
16-Jul	Blessed Ermengard	Germany	c. 832	c. 866
16-Jul	Saint Reineldis	Belgium		680
17-Jul	Saint Cynwl	Wales		6th
17-Jul	Saint Kenelm	England		821
18-Jul	Saint Arnulf Bishop of Metz	Metz		635
18-Jul	Saint Edburga of Bicester	England		7th
20-Jul	Saint Etheldwitha	England	852	905
20-Jul	Saint Joseph Barsabas Apostle	Israel		1st
21-Jul	Saint Praxedes	Rome		mid 2nd
22-Jul	Saint Mary Magdalene	Israel		1st
22-Jul	Saint Wandrille	France	635	665
23-Jul	Blessed Cunegund	Hungary	1224	1292
23-Jul	Saint Bridget of Sweden	Sweden	1303	1373
24-Jul	Blessed Louisa of Savoi	France	1461	1503
24-Jul	Saint Boris	Russia		1010
24-Jul	Saint Gleb	Russia		1010
24-Jul	Saint Menefrida	Wales		6th
25-Jul	Saint James the Greater	Israel		1st
28-Jul	Saint Sampson	Britain		565

SAINTS DAILY
Kings, Queens, Popes, Princes, Princesses, Emperors, Hermits, Bishops

DAILY SAINTS WHOSE ANCESTRY IS KNOWN

29-Jul	Blessed Urban II Pope		1042	1099
29-Jul	Saint Olaf of Norway	Norway		1030
30-Jul	Saint Olaf of Skottkonung	Sweden	c 950	c 1024
30-Jul	Blessed Mannes	Spain		c. 1230
31-Jul	Saint Germannus d'Auxerre	Britain		6th
31 –Jul	Saint Neot	Britain		9th

TABLE EIGHT SAINTS OF JULY

July 1   *Saint Leonorius*

Date: c. 570   **Feastday:** July 1

Family:
Parents: Father- Hoel I Mawr ('the Great') de Bretagne Mother- Alma Pompea de Domnonée Saint
Siblings: Hoel II Fychan ('the Small') de Bretagne
Children: None

Ancestry: Saint Leonorius is eight generations the descendent of Conan and Saint Dareca. He is also descended thru Conan and Saint Ursula. Therefore Saint James the son of Saint Joseph is an ancestor and the line of David thru Solomon. Therefore the Israelites Joseph, Benjamin, Levi, Zebulon and Judah are ancestors. Also King Coel of Britain is an ancestor.

Branches of the Tree:
Saint Leonorius is located near King Budig II.

SAINTS DAILY
Kings, Queens, Popes, Princes, Princesses, Emperors, Hermits, Bishops

DAILY SAINTS WHOSE ANCESTRY IS KNOWN

Biography:
Saint Leonorius is also known as Lunaire. He studied under Saint Illtyd, went to Brittany and founded Pontual Monastery.

July 1   Saint Wennap or Veep

Date: d. Sixth Century   Feastday: July 1

Family:
Parents: Father-Saint Brychan   Mother- Rigrawst b: 0450

Children: Unknown

Biography:
Also called Veep Patron Saint of Saint Veep in Cornwall England. Also called Veepu.

July 2   Blessed Peter of Luxemborg

Feastday: July 2   Date: b. 1371 d. 1399

Family: Father: Guy Of Luxemburg, Cte De St Pol, Roussy, Fienne   Mother: Mahaut de Chatillon, Comtesse de St Pol Spouse: Unknown   Siblings: Valerian.

Ancestors: Many generations back Baldwin V of Flanders is found.

Branch of the Tree: This is a branch of the tree near the Counts of Luxemborg and of Ghent.

Biography: Blessed Peter was the son of the Count of Ligny and was orphaned when four years old. He studied at Paris where he became a canon at Notre Dame. He was held hostage for his brother by the English at Calais. Antipope Clement VII named

SAINTS DAILY
Kings, Queens, Popes, Princes, Princesses, Emperors, Hermits, Bishops

DAILY SAINTS WHOSE ANCESTRY IS KNOWN

him bishop of Metz and cardinal although he was only fiftenn and a deacon. The followers of Pope Urban VI entered his see and he required the armed intervention of his brother Valerian. He was driven from Metz by political unrest in 1386 and joined Clement at Avignon. He was known for his holiness and charities. When he was eighteen he died at a Carthusian monastery at Villeneuve on July 2 and was beatified in 1527.

July 2   Saint Oudoceus
Feastday: July 2   **Date:** b 536   d. 625

Family:
Parents: Father: Budig Emyr Llydaw ap Erich II   Mother: Anowed verch Ensich
Spouse: None Children: None   Siblings: Ysfael Ap Budic, Theodoric Ap Budic, Tyfain Ap Budic

Ancestry: Saint Brychan is an ancestor as is his daughter Saint Mereri. Saint Brychan's wife is a descendent of Conan, therefore David is an ancestor, and the five Israelites Benjamin, Joseph, Levi, Judah, and Zebulon are ancestors.

Branches of the Tree: This is the branch near Saint Brychan.

Biography: Saint Oudoceus was the nephew of Saint Teilo. His mother then was the sister to Saint Teilo. He was the abbot that replaced Saint Teilo at Llandeilo Fawr, Carmarthenshire. Later he became a bishop and is one of the four saints that the Cathedral of Llandaff Wales is dedicated.

July 4   Saint Isabel of Aragorn
Country: Spain   Patron of the third order of Saint Francis.
            Date: 1271- 1336

SAINTS DAILY
Kings, Queens, Popes, Princes, Princesses, Emperors, Hermits, Bishops

DAILY SAINTS WHOSE ANCESTRY IS KNOWN

Family: Parents: Father- Pedro Of Aragon III Mother- Konstanze Of Sicilies
Husband: Dionysius Of Portugal   Children: Constanza Of Portugal, Affonso IV of Portugal

Ancestry: Saint Isabel (or Elizabeth of Portugal) ancestry is not known.

Descendents: Descendents Include King Edward IV Plantagenet of England, King Peter the Cruel of Castile and Leon, and King Alphonso IV of Portugal.

Biography: She was very beautiful and very lovable. Elizabeth was a Spanish princess who was given in marriage to King Denis of Portugal at the age of twelve She was also very devout, and went to Mass every day. Elizabeth was a holy wife, but although her husband was fond of her at first, he soon began to cause her great suffering. In fact, his sins of impurity gave great scandal to the people. Though a good ruler, he did not imitate his wife's love of prayer and other virtues.

Later, to make matters worse, the King believed a lie told about Elizabeth and one of her pages by another page. This page was jealous of his companion. In great anger the King ordered the one he believed guilty, to be sent to a lime-burner. The lime-burner was commanded to throw into his furnace the first page that came. The good page set out obediently. On his way he stopped for Mass, not knowing death was waiting for him, since he had the habit of going daily. The first Mass had begun, so he stayed for a second one. In the meantime, the King sent the wicked page to the lime-burner to find out if the other had been killed. And so it was this page that was thrown into the furnace! When the King learned what had happened, he realized that God had saved the good page, punished the liar, and proven Queen Elizabeth to be innocent.

SAINTS DAILY
Kings, Queens, Popes, Princes, Princesses, Emperors, Hermits, Bishops

DAILY SAINTS WHOSE ANCESTRY IS KNOWN

He apologized to his wife in front of everyone and began to have a great respect for her. This amazing event helped greatly to make the King live better. In his last sickness, she never left his side, except for Mass, until he died a holy death. St. Elizabeth lived for eleven more years, doing even greater charity and penance. She was a wonderful model of kindness toward the poor and a successful peacemaker between members of her own family and between nations.

Because St. Elizabeth was faithful to daily Mass, she found strength to carry her many great crosses. And because her page was faithful to daily Mass, he escaped death. We should try our best to make it a habit to go to Mass daily.

July 5   *Saint Morwenna*

Date: d. Fifth Feastday: November 8 or July 5

Family:
Parents: Father-Saint Brychan   Mother- Rigrawst b: 0450
Husband: Unknown
Children: Unknown

Biography:
Virgin. Of Cornish Origin. Titular patron of several sites in the Cornish region. Her emblem was a tall cross. She was also depicted teaching children how to read. There is a legend that when the people built a church, Morwenna carried a stone on her head up from beneath the cliff; when she put it down to rest, St. Morwenna's well sprang up; when she finally deposited it in the place she wanted, the church as built there; although the first choice for its site was elsewhere.

SAINTS DAILY
Kings, Queens, Popes, Princes, Princesses, Emperors, Hermits, Bishops

DAILY SAINTS WHOSE ANCESTRY IS KNOWN

July 5 *Saint Fracan*

Country: Brittany France   **Date:** 6th Century

Family: Father: Selfy   Mother: Wenna Gwen
Spouse: Gwen   Siblings: Unknown
Children: Saint Wethoc, Saint Iocab, Chreirbia

Ancestors: Saint Constantine, Saint Joseph of Arimathea.

Branches of the Tree: This is the branch that leads to Saint Judicael

Descendents: Saint Judicail, King Edward IV

Biography: *Given Name:* Welsh-Fragan, Latin-Bracanus, English-Bracan .Fragan and Gwen went to Brittany from Wales to escape the pagan barbarians of England. They are the parents of Sts. Jacut, Guithem and Winwaloe. Churches in Brittany and France are dedicated to them. The name is equivalent to the Welsh Brychan. Certainly a cousin of King Cado of Dumnonia, it seems most likely that Fr acan was a younger son of King Salom of Cerniw. He fled Britain, with his wife, Gwen Teirbron (the Triple-Breasted) and their children, when a pestilence spread through the land . They landed on the Gouet Estuary in Brittany and Fracan established a large estate now named after him, at Ploufragan. He went on to found a church there and at Saint-Frégan (near Lesneven). Hence his saintly reputation. Fracan once had a stormy argument with King Riwal of Domnonée concerning the speed of their two horses. Fracan organised a race, but there was an accident and his jockey was injured. Luckily however, his son, St.Winwaloe, was on hand to heal the poor lad.

July 5   *Saint Gwen*
Country: Brittany France   **Date:** 6th Century

SAINTS DAILY
Kings, Queens, Popes, Princes, Princesses, Emperors, Hermits, Bishops

DAILY SAINTS WHOSE ANCESTRY IS KNOWN

Family: Father: Budig II   Mother: Elaine
Spouse: Fragan   Siblings: Unknown
Children: Saint Wethoc, Saint Iocab, Chreirbia

Ancestors: James the bishop of Jerusalem son on Saint Joseph. Saint Constantine the Great, Saint Darerca, Saint Ursula.

Branches of the Tree: This is the branch that leads to Saint Judicael

Descendents: Saint Judicail, King Edward IV

Biography: Princess Gwen the Triple-Breasted was one of the daughte s of King Budic II of Brittany. She was known to the French as St. Blanche, and sometimes, in written Latin, as Alb a Trimammis. She married twice, first to Fracan, a cousin f King Cado of Dumnonia , by whom she was mother of Saints Wethnoc, Iacob and Winwaloe. Hence the reason for her being born with three breasts was revealed. Together they cro sed the Channel to escape a pestilence that was ravaging the Dumnonian countryside, and settled at PlouFracan in Domnonée. Gwen later bore Fracan a daughter, Chreirbia, also. After Fracan's death, Gwen married Eneas Ledewig (the Breto n) and became the mother of St. Cadfan. Gwen was twice kidnapped by Anglo-Saxon pirates and carried off to England. Each time, however, she escaped by walking back across the Channel to Brittany. In the twilight of her life, she retired to Whitchurch Canonicorum (Dorset) in Eastern Dumnonia. Here she lived for many years in her small hermitage, before the Saxons had their revenge at last, ransacked her home and murdered her. St. Wite's shrine remains there still in the church built over her grave. It was one of only two in the whole of Britain to survive the Reformation. St. Gwen Teirbron (Triple-Breasted) should not be confused with other St. Gwens: the Queen of Elmet, St. Gwen ferch Brychan B rycheiniog and the Queen of Cerniw, St. Gwen ferch Cynyr Ceinfarfog (Fair-Beard).

SAINTS DAILY
Kings, Queens, Popes, Princes, Princesses, Emperors, Hermits, Bishops

DAILY SAINTS WHOSE ANCESTRY IS KNOWN

July 6   Saint Sexburga

Country: England   *Date:* d 699

Family: Parents: Father- Anna King of East Anglia Mother- Saint Hereswitha
Husband: Earconbert Kent King Kent   Children: Egbert Kent King Kent

Ancestry: Saint Sexburga mother is Saint Hereswitha. Further back ancestry is not known. Saint Sexburga married King Erconbert of Kent. Also included is Joseph of Arimathea. Also King David of Judah and Israel is an ancestor thru Nathan his son. Woden and Frigg are Ancestors.

Descendents: Sainted descendants include Saint Adele of Blois, Saint Louis IX of France, Saint Fernando III of Spain, Saint Cunigunda of Luxemborg, Saint Leopold III of Austria, Saint Henry II of Germany, and Saint David and Saint Margaret of Scotland. Royal descendents include King Edward III Plantagenet of England, King of Naples Charles II, King of France Philip IV, and King of Scotland William the Lion. Also Casimir King of Poland, Alphonso Enriquez I King of Portugal and Henry IV Holy Roman Emperor of Germany.

Biography: Benedictine Abbess. Sister to Sts. Etheldreda, Ethelburga, Erconwald and Withburga and half sister of St. Saethryth. She married King Erconbert of Kent in 640 bearing two saints Ermengilda and Ercongota. She was widowed in 664 and entered the convent at Sheppey before going to Ely Abbey in 670 as abbess after her sister Etheldreda. She assisted the founding of the convent of Minster on Sheppey Island. Her shrine at Ely Abbey survived until the Reformation.

SAINTS DAILY
Kings, Queens, Popes, Princes, Princesses, Emperors, Hermits, Bishops

DAILY SAINTS WHOSE ANCESTRY IS KNOWN

July 7 *Saint Ethelburga*
Country: England   **Date:** 664

Family: Father: Anna King of East Anglia   Mother: Hereswitha Saint
Spouse: Unknown   Siblings: Sexburga Princess Of East Anglia Saint; Etheldreda Saint; Erconwald Saint; Withburga Saint; Jurmin Saint

Ancestors: Saint Ethelburga mother is Saint Hereswitha. Further back ancestry is not known. Woden and Frigg are Ancestors. Saint Cyllin is an Ancestor. Ancestors include the Kings of Siluria. Generations previous to this they were the Kings of Britain. The line then goes back to Zerah, whose father is Judah. This line also marries Anna Arimathea who is the daughter of Joseph of Arimathea. A little know fact of the biblical character of Joseph of Arimathea is that he is the son of Mathat, who is in the line of Nathan that is listed in the New Testament book of Luke. So Saint Cyllin is descended from the Davidic line of Nathan and so from Judah thru Perez, and also as previously mentioned thru Judah's son Zerah.

Branches of the Tree: Kings of East Anglia.

Biography: Saint Ethelburga was the daughter of Anna, King of the East Angles. She was the abbess of Farmountiersen-Brie, France, although she was English. Saint Burgundofara, directed her to France to become a nun with her half sister Saint Sethrida. She is from a large family of Saints, seven in all counting herself.

July 7 *Saint Ercongotha*
Country: England   **Date:** 660

Family: Father: Unknown   Mother: Sexburga Princess Of East Anglia Saint
Spouse: Unknown   Siblings: Unknown

SAINTS DAILY
Kings, Queens, Popes, Princes, Princesses, Emperors, Hermits, Bishops

DAILY SAINTS WHOSE ANCESTRY IS KNOWN

Ancestors: Saint Sexberga is the daughter of Saint Hereswitha. Further back ancestry is not known. Woden and Frigg are Ancestors. Saint Cyllin is an Ancestor. Ancestors include the Kings of Siluria. Generations previous to this they were the Kings of Britain. The line then goes back to Zerah, whose father is Judah. This line also marries Anna Arimathea who is the daughter of Joseph of Arimathea. A little know fact of the biblical character of Joseph of Arimathea is that he is the son of Mathat, who is in the line of Nathan that is listed in the New Testament book of Luke. So Saint Cyllin is descended from the Davidic line of Nathan and so from Judah thru Perez, and also as previously mentioned thru Judah's son Zerah.

Branches of the Tree: Kings of East Anglia.

Biography: Saint Sexburga was the mother and a King of Kent the father of Saint Ercongotha. She was a Benedictine nun. She is sometimes called Ercongota. Saint Ercongotha was a nun in France at Faremoutiers-en-Brie. It is likely she died there at a young age.

July 8   *Saint Withburga*
Country: England   **Date:** 743

Family: Father: Anna King of East Anglia
         Mother: Hereswitha Saint
Spouse: Unknown   Siblings: Sexburga Princess Of East Anglia Saint; Etheldreda Saint Erconwald Saint Withburga Saint

Ancestors: Saint Ethelburga mother is Saint Hereswitha. Further back ancestry is not known. Woden and Frigg are Ancestors. Saint Cyllin is an Ancestor. Ancestors include the Kings of Siluria. Generations previous to this they were the Kings of Britain. The line then goes back to Zerah, whose father is Judah. This line also marries Anna Arimathea who is the daughter of

SAINTS DAILY
Kings, Queens, Popes, Princes, Princesses, Emperors, Hermits, Bishops

DAILY SAINTS WHOSE ANCESTRY IS KNOWN

Joseph of Arimathea. A little know fact of the biblical character of Joseph of Arimathea is that he is the son of Mathat, who is in the line of Nathan that is listed in the New Testament book of Luke. So Saint Cyllin is descended from the Davidic line of Nathan and so from Judah thru Perez, and also as previously mentioned thru Judah's son Zerah.

Branches of the Tree: Kings of East Anglia.

Biography: Saint Withburga was a Benedictine nun. She was the youngest daughter of King Anna of East Anglia and Saint Hereswitha. She was from a family of Saints, with mother and siblings Saint Sexburga, Saint Erconwald, Saint Withburga, and Saint Etheldreda. King Anna died in battle so she moved to Dereham where she started a church and established a nunnery. On March 17 she died with the Church unfinished. Monks later stole her remains and enshrined them in Ely. At her grave in Dereham a fresh spring called Withburga's Well sprang up.

July 11   Saint Pius the First the 10th Bishop of Rome (Pope)

Date: ruled the papacy 140-155

Family: Father: Jude 15th Bishop of Jerusalem
Mother: Unknown
Unknown Spouse: Unknown   Siblings: unknown
Children: Unknown

Country: Israel

Ancestors: See Saint Joseph's ancestry.

Branches of the Tree: This is the branch of the tree right on the descent of Saint Joseph.

Biography: Saint Pius the 10th Pope was the son of Jude the 15th Bishop of Jerusalem, who was the son of Benjamin the 6th Bishop of Jerusalem, who was the son of John, who was the son of James

SAINTS DAILY
Kings, Queens, Popes, Princes, Princesses, Emperors, Hermits, Bishops

205

DAILY SAINTS WHOSE ANCESTRY IS KNOWN

the Just, who was the son of Saint Joseph Foster Father of the Lord. Pope Pius made several decrees, one being that a Priest must make 40 days of penance if any of the precious blood to reach the ground during Mass. The blood must be taken up by the Priests lips, the dust gathered and burned, and the ashes thrown into consecrated ground. He ordered that Easter must be celebrated on a Sunday. Churches were made by Pope Pius from the houses of Pudens and Praxedes. Pope Pius is known to have welcomed Saint Justin Martyr, and was himself martyred. Feastday July 11.

July 11   *Saint Olga of Kiev*

Country: Russia   **Date:** 879-969

Family: Parents: Oleg Veshchi, Great Prince & Tsar of Novgorod   Husband: Igor, Grand Duke of Kiev   Children: Svatislav I, Grand Duke of Kiev

Ancestry: Saint Olga's ancestry is not known.

Descendents: Her Grandson is Saint Vladimir of Russia and Saint Louis IX is her descendant.

Biography: Prince Igor I wife, married in 903 has been described as a cruel and barbarous woman. Saint Olga scalded the murderers of her husband to death in 945 and killed hundreds of the murderers followers. Until her baptism in Constantinople in 957 she is said to have remained cruel. She requested missionaries from Emperor Otto I to be sent to Kiev. Out of Magdeburg Saint Adalbert was sent and attempts to convert Saint Olga's son Svyatoslav were made. Saint Adalbert was unsuccessful, as was the misson to convert Kiev. Saint Olga's grandson, Saint Vladimir was converted however many years later and is credited as introducing Christianity in Russia. So the

SAINTS DAILY
Kings, Queens, Popes, Princes, Princesses, Emperors, Hermits, Bishops

DAILY SAINTS WHOSE ANCESTRY IS KNOWN

mission was successful, although a generation later. Saint Olga's feastday is July 11.

July 13   Saint Henry II of Germany
Country: Germany   **Date:** 972- c 1024

Family: Parents: Father-Henry II The Wrangler Duke of Bavaria Mother- Gisele of Burgundy
Wife: Cunigunda Luxemburg Saint Children: Agatha von Braunschweig

Ancestry: Saint Henry II ancestors include Saint Mathilda. Also Charlemange is an ancestor thru his mother Gisele. Also Henry the Fowler holy Roman Emperor is his ancestor (married Saint Mathilda.). Also included is Joseph of Arimathea. Also King David of Judah and Israel is an ancestor thru Nathan his son. King Solomon of Israel and Judah is also an ancestor. Sainted Ancestors include Saint Ethelbert, Saint Itta, Saint Arnulf, Saint Sigebert, Saint Dagobert, Saint Beggue, Saint Liuthwin, Saint Beggue, Saint Sexburga, Blessed Pepin, Saint Clodulf, , and Saint Sexburga.

Descendents: Descendents include Saint David and Margaret of Scotland, Saint Louis IX of France, and Saint Fernando III of Spain. Royal Descendents include King Edward Plantagenet III of England, King Philip IV of France, King of Naples Charles II, and William I of Scotland.

Biography: Pope St. Pius X declared Saint Henry the patron saint of the Benedictine Oblates. Saint Henry II was an Emperor, called the Good. On May 3, 973 he was probably born in Hildesheim, Bavaria, Germany. He became the Duke of Bavaria in 995 when his father died, and Emperor in 1002 when his cousin Otto III died. Saint Herisbert was his chancellor and his wife was Saint Cunegundis from Luxemborg. Pope Benedict VIII crowned him Holy Roman Emperor. He was a Patron of the Benedictines. Henry wanted to be a Benedictine, and lived as an

SAINTS DAILY
Kings, Queens, Popes, Princes, Princesses, Emperors, Hermits, Bishops

DAILY SAINTS WHOSE ANCESTRY IS KNOWN

Oblate so Tradition states. Pope Eugene III canonized him in 1146.

July 13　　　*Saint Mildred Of Thanet*

Country: Great Britain　　**Date:** d. c. 725

Family:　Father: Merewald of Mercia　　Mother: Saint Ermenburga
Spouse: Unknown　　Siblings: Milburga Saint; Mildgytha Saint;

Ancestors: The line of the King of Mercia Penda who is the grandfather goes to Woden and Frigg.

Biography: Saint Mildred was the daughter of Merewald, an Anglian ruler Mercia. She was from a family of Saints, her mother was Saint Ermenburga, a Kentish princess and her sisters were Saint Milburga and Saint Mildgytha. Near Paris at Chelles Saint Mildred was educated. A young man sought her for marriage, however she entered a monastery called Minster. This monastery had been founded by her mother Saint Ermenburga. Saint Theodore of Canterbury received her into the community that was located on the Isle of Thanet. Saint Mildred eventually became abbess. She developed a great reputation for holiness and for generosity. She was very compassionate to the poor and rejected. Saint Mildred died about the year 700.

July 13　　　*Saint Dogfan*

Family:
Parents: Father-Saint Brychan　　Mother-Unknown
Wife: Unknown
Children: Unknown

Biography:
Welsh martyr, He was slain by pagan invaders at Dyfed, Wales. His memory is honored in a church there.

SAINTS DAILY
Kings, Queens, Popes, Princes, Princesses, Emperors, Hermits, Bishops

DAILY SAINTS WHOSE ANCESTRY IS KNOWN

July 14 Blessed Boniface of Savoy

Country: France **Date:** d. 1270

Family: Father: Thomas I Count of Savoy   Mother: Margaret De Geneva and Faucigny
Spouse: Unknown   Siblings: Beatrice De Savoy

Ancestors: The Counts of Savoy and Blessed Humbert are ancestors

Branches of the Tree : This branch of the tree is connected to the Kings of Portugal and Savoy, and Saint Fernando is very near in this branch of the tree. Blessed Humbert is very near Blessed Boniface as an Ancestor

Biography: The Count of Savoy Thomas had Blessed Boniface Of Savoy as his son. He became the Chartreuse in his youth and was made prior of Mantua. He served seven years as ambassadors of the diocese of Belley in 1241 and then of Valence. He was elected Archbishop of Canterbury in 1241 thru the influence of his niece Eleanor wife of King Henry the third of England but did not go to the holy see until 1244. He attempted to reform the see and effect economies in the heavily indebted see, and this was met with strenuous opposition. He excommunicated the bishop of London and the clergy of St. Bartholomew's and while an appeal to Rome upheld his visitation rights he was forced to rescind his excommunications, and his visitations had restrictions placed on them. He acted as regent for Henry while the King was out of the country. He also accompanied the king on a diplomatic mission to France. He peacefully negotiated a succession in his native Savoy. On the way to a crusade with Edward I he died at the castle of Sainte-Helene des Millieres in Savoy. Boniface's cult was confirmed in 1838.

SAINTS DAILY
Kings, Queens, Popes, Princes, Princesses, Emperors, Hermits, Bishops

DAILY SAINTS WHOSE ANCESTRY IS KNOWN

July 15   *Blessed Bernard of Baden*

Feastday: July 15   Date: 1429-1458

Family: Father: James I Margrave Of Baden   Mother: Catherine of Lorraine
Spouse: Unknown   Siblings: Karl\Charles I Zähringen Margrave of Baden, Margaret (of Baden) Zähringen

Country: France

Ancestors: On his mothers side counts of Blois and Chatillon lead to King Phillip III son of Saint Louis IX King of France. Blessed Bernard of Baden is seven generations the descendent of Saint Louis IX.

Branches of the Tree: This is the branch of the tree of the French Kings.

Biography: Military interest and literature as a young man led Blessed Bernard to turn over his right to succession to participate in a crusade against the Turks. In Moncalieri Italy he died on the way to see Pope Callistus about his plan. Miracles were reported at his tomb and he was beatified in 1479.

July 15   *Saint Vladimir of Kiev*

Country: Russia   *Date:* 956- c 1015

Family: Parents: Father-Svyatoslav Grand Duke of Kiev Mother-Debrima
Wife: Rogneida of Polotsk   Children: Jaroslav   I Wladymirovitch Grand Duke

Ancestry: Saint Vladimir grandmother was Saint Olga. Much more is not known.

Descendents: Titled descendents include Edward Stafford 3rd Duke of Buckingham, Hugh Magnus Duke of France and

SAINTS DAILY
Kings, Queens, Popes, Princes, Princesses, Emperors, Hermits, Bishops

210

DAILY SAINTS WHOSE ANCESTRY IS KNOWN

Burgundy, Thomas De Berkeley Lord Berkeley, and Humphrey De Bohun Earl of Hereford.

Biography: Saint Vladimir was the grandson of Saint Olga who is credited with bringing Christianity to Russia. He was the illegitimate son of Sviastoslav, Grand Duke of Kiev, and his mistress, Malushka. His father gave Novgorod to Saint Vladimir to rule. Vladimir's half-brothers got into a civil war, and Yaropolk defeated and killed Oleg, making himself ruler. When he captured Novgorod, Saint Vladimir was forced to flee to Scandinavia in 977. Vladimir defeated and slew Yaropolk at Rodno in 980, after he returned with an army and captured Novgorod. Russia was now under one monarch, Saint Vladimir, and he was notorious for his barbarism and immorality. He became impressed by the progress of Christianity after his conquest of Kherson in the Crimea in 988, and asked Eastern Emperor Basil II for the hand of his daughter Ann. He married Anne, was converted and reformed his life. He built schools and churches when he returned to Kiev and invited Greek missionaries to Russia. He led his people to Christianity, and canonical features were borrowed from the West. He had two sons who became martyrs with Ann, both saints, Romanus and David. Later years were troubled by sons of his first marriages rebellions. He marched against his rebellious son Yaroslav in Novgorod in 1014, fell ill, and on the way died at Beresyx, Russia. Russian Catholics hold him as their Patron. Feastday July 15.

July 15   Saint Edith of Polesworth

Country: Viking   *Date:* unknown

Family: Parents: Unknown   Husband: Sitric Caoch (Sigtryggr Gale) Dublin and York
Children: Olafsson, Sihtric Silkbeard King of Dublin; Harald Sihtricsson King of Limerick

SAINTS DAILY
Kings, Queens, Popes, Princes, Princesses, Emperors, Hermits, Bishops

DAILY SAINTS WHOSE ANCESTRY IS KNOWN

Ancestry: Saint Edith's ancestry is not known.

Descendents: Descendents include Olafson King of Dublin, Rhys Ap Gruffydd Lord of South Wales, Olaf II Godredson King of Man and Isle.

Biography: St. Edith of Polesworth was the sister of King Athelstan of England. She married Viking king Sihtric at York in 925. When he died the next year, she became a Benedictine nun at Polesworth, Warwickshire. She was noted for her holiness and may have become Abbess. She may also have been the sister of King Edgar and aunt of St. Edith of Wilton, or possibly these were two different woman of Polesworth. Her feast day is July 15th.

July 16   Saint Reineldis
Country: Belgium   **Date:** d. 680

Family: Father: Theuderic (Thierry) III (King of Neustria)
     Mother: Amalaberga de Neustria Saint
       Spouse: Unknown   Siblings: Chrotlind des Francs; Saint Gudula

Ancestors: Saint Bathildis is the grandmother, and Saint Amalberga is the mother. Notable ancestors include Clovis I and Saint Clotidle who started the merovigian dynasty.

Branches of the Tree: This is the branch of Clovis the Frankish King and Saint Bathildis.

Biography: Saint Reineldis was also called Raineldis and Reinildis. She had a Saint for her mother, Saint Amalberga, and her sister Gudula also became a Saint. Her parents both decided to enter the religious life. Her father was at Lobes Abbey in France, and she was unsuccessful at joining. She made a pilgrimage to the Holy Land. She then returned home and

SAINTS DAILY
Kings, Queens, Popes, Princes, Princesses, Emperors, Hermits, Bishops

DAILY SAINTS WHOSE ANCESTRY IS KNOWN

devoted herself to a life of charitable work at Saintes. She became a martyr with Frimoald, a deacon and her servant Gundulf, when barbarians invaded.

July 16   Blessed Ermengard

Feastday: July 16   Date: c. 832-c. 866

Family: Father: Louis The German   Mother: Emma of Bavaria
Spouse: Unknown   Siblings Hedwige of Germany

Country: Germany

Ancestors:. Louis I the son of Charlemagne, so Joseph the Vizier of Egypt and Israel, Issac, and Abraham.

Branches of the Tree This is branch of the tree that contains Saint Arnulf and Charlemagne.

Biography: Blessed Ermengard was German and had Louis as a father. Emma of Bavaria was her mother. Little else is known except the lineage relationships found in Saints in the Tree. She was appointed abbess of Buchau and of the royal abbey of Chiensee in Bavaria.

July 17   Saint Kenelm

Country: Great Britain   **Date:** 821

Family: Father: Kenulf of Mercia   Mother: Elfleda
Spouse: Unknown   Siblings: Unknown

Ancestors: His direct ancestors are not known.

Branches of the Tree: Saint Kenelm is one generation up the tree and four generations down a branch to King Alfred the Great Saint.

SAINTS DAILY
Kings, Queens, Popes, Princes, Princesses, Emperors, Hermits, Bishops

DAILY SAINTS WHOSE ANCESTRY IS KNOWN

Biography: Saint Kenelm was a martyr. He was also a King, so he was a martyred King. He was the son of King Kenulf. Henchman of Cynefrith a relation killed Saint Kenelm. He had succeeded to the throne at age seven. Possibly his other relation Quendreda bribed his tutor to slay him. In Gloucestershire in Winchcombe Abbey he is buried. Reportedly miracles took place there. It is also possible he died before his father died. Saint Kenelm is mentioned in Canterbury Tales.

July 17   *Saint Cynwl*

d. sixth   Feastday: July 17

Family: Father: Dynod Bwr König Von South Pennines
        Mother: Dwywai ferch Llaennog
Spouse: Unknown   Siblings: Saint Deinol

Ancestors: Saint Gwenillian ferch Brychan is an ancestor of this Saint.

Biography:
Saint Cynwl was a hermit. He was the brother of Saint Deinol. He lead an austere life if southern Wales. Several Churches in the region were dedicated to Cynwl.

July 18   Saint Arnulf Bishop of Metz

Country: France   *Date:* 635

Family: Parents: Father- Arnoul Metz Bishop Metz Mother- Oda Savoy
Wife: Doda Saxony   Children: Anchises Metz

Ancestry: Saint Arnulf had a Son Saint Cloudulph Bishop of Metz and his line also goes back to Zerah. Also King David of

SAINTS DAILY
Kings, Queens, Popes, Princes, Princesses, Emperors, Hermits, Bishops

DAILY SAINTS WHOSE ANCESTRY IS KNOWN

Judah and Israel is an ancestor thru Joseph of Arimathea and to the line of Nathan King David's son. .

Descendants: Sainted descendants include Saint Adele of Blois, Saint Adelaide of Italy, Saint Louis IX of France, Saint Fernando III of Spain, Saint Cunigunda of Luxemborg, Saint Leopold III of Austria, Saint Henry II of Germany, Saint Lazlo King of Hungary, Saint Raymond Berenger IV. and Saint David and Saint Margaret of Scotland. Royal descendents include King Edward III Plantagenet of England, King of Naples Charles II, King of France Philip IV, and King of Scotland William the Lion. Also Casimir King of Poland , Alphonso Enriquez I King of Portugal and Henry IV Holy Roman Emperor of Germany.

Biography: Member of the court of Theodebert II of Austasia, the Frankish King Arnulf of Metz was a Bishop. Arnulf married Doda, being a noble and had a son named Ansegisel. Ansegisel marred the daughter of Pepin of Landen, Beggia, which started the Carolingian dynasty of France. Arnulf made plans to enter a monastery but was named the bishop of Metz around 616 and Doda became a nun. Clotaire of Neustria became the King of Austrasia as Arnulf continued his court services. King Clotaire's son was Dagobert whom Arnulf served as counselor. Arnulf took part in the councils of hy and Rheims. His friend Romaricus and Arnulf retired to a hermitage at Remiremont, France in 626.

July 18   Saint Edburga of Bicester

Country: Great Britain   **Date:** 7th Century

Family: Father: King Penda of Mercia   Mother: Princess Cynewise of Northumbria
Spouse: Unknown   Siblings: Princess Wilburga of Mercia; Kyneburga Saint; Kyneswide Saint; King Wulfhere Of Mercia; Merewald of Mercia

Ancestors: The line of the King of Mercia Penda goes to Woden and Frigg.

SAINTS DAILY
Kings, Queens, Popes, Princes, Princesses, Emperors, Hermits, Bishops

DAILY SAINTS WHOSE ANCESTRY IS KNOWN

Biography: Saint Edburga was the daughter of Penda, the pagan King of Mercia. She was a nun at Salisbury, Buckinghamshire, England. Her relics were taken to Flanders Belgium. Her shrine is at Stanton Harcourt, Oxfordshire.

July 20   Saint Joseph Barsabas the Apostle
Country: Israel

Family: Father: unknown   Mother: Mary Alphaews   Spouse: Unknown   Siblings: Saint Judas the apostle, Saint Simon the apostle, Saint James the Lesser apostle

Ancestors: Saint Joseph of Arimathea is an ancestor. A little know fact of the biblical character of Joseph of Arimathea is that he is the son of Mathat, who is in the line of Nathan that is listed in the New Testament book of Luke. His ancestors then must be King David of Israel and Judah, and so the Israelites Joseph, Levi, Zebulon, and Judah. Anna married Saint Joseph of Arimathea, and her ancestry is an unbroken male line to Levi the Israelite. Saint Joseph of Arimathea's mother may have been the daughter of Eleazor, who was of the Davidic line of Solomon. Eleazor was the Grandfather of Joseph who married the Virgin Mary and this line is listed in the Gospel of Mathew. The Israelite Benjamin was an ancestor of King Davids wife Maacah (Sauls daughter) whose line married in the line from Solomon joined by the marriage of Reheboam to Maacah. Therefore Saint Joseph of Arimathea has five Israelites as ancestors.

Branches of the Tree: This is a branch of the tree that has Saint Joseph of Arimathea in it. He is the Father of Cleopas who is the Father of Mary Alphaws. He is three generations the ancestor of Saint Joseph Barsabas. This line also marries Anna Arimathea who is the daughter of Joseph of Arimathea.

Biography: Saint Joseph Barsabas was the relative of the lord. He is a disciple, although not one of the twelve. He was listed in

SAINTS DAILY
Kings, Queens, Popes, Princes, Princesses, Emperors, Hermits, Bishops

DAILY SAINTS WHOSE ANCESTRY IS KNOWN

Acts as the person not chosen to replace the apostle that betrayed the Lord.

July 20   Saint Etheldwitha
Country: Great Britain   **Date:** 852-905

Family: Parents: Father- Ethelred Mucel   Mother-Eadburh   Husband: Alfred the Great King of England Children: Ethelfleda and Edward I King of England

Ancestry: Only goes back a few generations.

Descendents: King Edgar the Peaceful is a descendent, as well as Edward I and Edmund I "The Elder" both kings of England. Also King Edward IV Plangagenet is a descendent.

Biography: Saint Etheldwitha was married to King Alfred the Great. She became widowed and founded a convent at Winchester. She was also called Ealsitha, and she was an Anglo-Saxon princess. She became the abbess at the convent she founded in the Benedictine rule.

July 21   Saint Praxedes
Country: Italy (Rome)   **Date:** 1st Century

Family: Father: Rufus Pudens Saint   Mother: Gladys (Claudia) Britain
Spouse: Unknown   Siblings: Timotheus; Prudentiana Saint; Novatus Saint

Ancestors: Bran the Blessed is an Ancestor, as is his wife Anna of Arimathea. Saint Joseph of Arimathea and so the Line of Nathan Son of David King of Israel and Judah. King David's ancestors include the Israelites, Zebulon, Levi, Joseph, and Judah. Also Anna of Arimathea, daughter to Joseph of Aramathea married Bran the Blessed whose line goes to Tros and

SAINTS DAILY
Kings, Queens, Popes, Princes, Princesses, Emperors, Hermits, Bishops

217

DAILY SAINTS WHOSE ANCESTRY IS KNOWN

so to Epraim son of Joseph the Israelite. Also the line from Anna of Arimathea's mother goes thru Simon the Just thru many High Priests to Judah the Israelite.

Branches of the Tree: Go up three generations to Bran the Blessed and Anna of Arimathea. The Apostle Paul is very near in this branch of the tree.

Biography: She was the sister of St. Pudentiana, who sought Christians out to relieve them with care, money, and every charitable aid. When the Emperor Marcus Antoninus was hunting down Christians. Praxedes was a Roman maiden. She buried the dead and hid some Christians in her house. She helped the christians in prison and who were slaves. Finally she died after no longer being able to bear the cruelties inflicted on Christians. She died on July 21. In the cemetery of Priscilla on the Salarian Way her body was laid by the priest Pastor in the tomb of her father, Pudens, and her sister Pudentiana. This saint was probably buried in the catacomb of Priscilla, near to St. Pudentiana. A separate church was built in her honour. She has been venerated as a martyr in connection with the ECCLESIA PUDENTIANA.

July 22   Saint Mary Magdalene

Country: Israel   **Date:** 1st Century

Family: Father: Mathew Syro (Syrus the Jarius)
Mother: Eucharia
Spouse: Unknown   Siblings: Unknown

Ancestors: Levi the Israelite is an Ancestor as is also Zebulon the Israelite. Simon the Just is an ancestor.

Biography: Mary Magdalene is 70 generations from Adam the son of God. Her lineage is very interesting, and there are many heresies and books written about her relationship to Jesus,

SAINTS DAILY
Kings, Queens, Popes, Princes, Princesses, Emperors, Hermits, Bishops

DAILY SAINTS WHOSE ANCESTRY IS KNOWN

although there seems to be little evidence to support any real claims.

July 22   Saint Wandrille

Country: France   **Date:** b. c. 635 d. c. 665

Family: Father: Walchigise of METZ   Mother: Unknown
Spouse: Unknown   Siblings: Valtrude of Verdun

Ancestors: Saint Arnulf is a Grandfather, so also Saint Mary Magdalene, the Israelite Levi, The Israelite Joseph, and Judas of Gamla. Because of Judas of Gamla the line of Solomon from Mathan the son of Eleazor to Solomon are ancestors, as is King David, the Israelites Benjamin, Judah, and Zebulon.

Biography: Wandrille was the uncle of Saint Godo. WANDREGISEL (-21 Apr 665). The *Vita S. Wandregisili* names "*Walchisus…consobrinus…Pippini…Principis Francorum*" as father of "*Wandregisilus cognomento Wando*"[81]. The *Gesta Abbatum Fontanellensium* names "*Wandregisilus*" as the first abbot of Fontanelle and in a later passage specifies that he was son of "*Walchisus…patruus Pippini ducis Francorum filii Anchisi*"[82]. The *Vita Ansberti* names "*princeps Pipinus Ansegisili filius*" as "*consobrinus…beati patris Wandragisili*"[83]. The *Annales Xantenses* record the death in 665 of "*Sanctus Wandregisilus*"[84]. The *Vita S. Wandregisili* records the death "*menso quarto, die primo et vicesimo…annus…665*" aged 96 of "*Beatus Wandregisilus*"[85], although her age must be considerably exaggerated if her parentage is correctly shown here.

July 23   Blessed Cunegund

Country: Hungary   **Date:** 1224-1292

SAINTS DAILY
Kings, Queens, Popes, Princes, Princesses, Emperors, Hermits, Bishops

219

DAILY SAINTS WHOSE ANCESTRY IS KNOWN

Family: Father: Bela IV (King of Hungary)   Mother: Marie Lascarina
Spouse: Boleslaus V Of Poland   Siblings: Stephen V (King of Hungary); Margaret of Hungary Saint; Jolenta Blessed

Ancestors: The Kings of Hungary

Branches of the Tree   This branch of the tree contains Kings of Hungary, branches to Royalty of Russia, and then the Byzantine empire.

Biography: Blessed Cunegund was raised at her father's court. When she was sixteen she was married to King Boleslaus V of Poland. She took a vow of perpetual chastity with Boleslaus. She ransomed many Christians from the Turks and built churches and hospitals. She also helped the poor and sick. When Boleslaus died in 1279 she became a poor clare nun at a convent she founded at Sandek. In 1287 when Tartars invaded Poland she was not there however did spend the remainder of her life in the convent. Her prayers were credited with their abandoning the siege of the castle of Pyenin when the Tartars invaded Poland. In 1690 her cult was approved.

July 23   *Saint Bridget of Sweden*
Country: Sweden   **Date:** 1303-1373
   Patron: Sweden

Family: Father: Ulf Godmarsson   Mother: Birgitta
Spouse: Unknown   Siblings: Saint Catherine; Cecilia Ulfsdotter; Charles Ulfsdotter, Martha Ulfsdotter

Ancestors: Svend II Ulfsson (Estridssen) King Of Denmark;

Branches of the Tree: This branch goes up many generations before it joins with the Kings of Denmark who are the royal link.

SAINTS DAILY
Kings, Queens, Popes, Princes, Princesses, Emperors, Hermits, Bishops

DAILY SAINTS WHOSE ANCESTRY IS KNOWN

Biography: Saint Bridget was the daughter of Birger, the royal Prince of Sweden and of Ingeburdis, whose ancestors where the Gothic Kings. Her father conscrated all Fridays to special acts of penance, and from childhood mediatation upon the Passion of Christ was loved by Saint Bridget. Her daughter Saint Catherine became a Saint when she married at the age of fourteen the Prince of Nericia in Sweden. She had eight children the last one was Saint Catherine. Finally the holy couple took a vow of chastity and made a pilgrimage to Compostela in Galicia. When they returned to Sweden Ulfo with his wife's consent entered a Cistercian monastery. He died in the odor of sanctity very soon after he joined the monastery. After Ulfo died Saint Bridget renounced her royalty and changed her habit. The great monastery of Wastein was built by Saint Bridget in 1344 and became the motherhouse of the new Order called the Brigittines. She next undertook a pilgrimage to Rome and to Palestine. She returned to Rome after her devotional pilgrimages were satisfied and she lived one year longer. During this time she was sorely afflicted by sickness, but she endured it. In her last moments her son Birger and her daughter Saint Catherine were with her. She gave them her final instructions and she received the Last Sacraments and died in 1373. Her feast day is July 23 and she is patroness of Sweden.

July 24   Blessed Louisa of Savoi
Date: b. 1461 - 1503   **Feastday**: July 24

Family:
Parents: Father: Amadeus IX De Savoi Duke Of Savoy Blessed
Mother: Yolande de Valois
Spouse: Hugh de Chalons Lord of Nozeroy   Siblings: None

Country: France

SAINTS DAILY
Kings, Queens, Popes, Princes, Princesses, Emperors, Hermits, Bishops

DAILY SAINTS WHOSE ANCESTRY IS KNOWN

Ancestors: Charles VII King of France was his grandfather on his mothers side.

Branch of the Tree: This branch is the Kings of France.

Biography: Blessed Louisa of Savoi was the niece of King Louis XI of France. Her father died when she was nine so her mother raised her. When she was eighteen she married Hugh de Chalons lord of Nozeroy. She became a Franciscan tertiary when her husband died after nine years of married life. She became a poor clare at Orbe, Switzerland after she distributed her fortune. In 1839 her cult was approved.

July 24   Saint Boris

Country: Russia   **Date:** 1010
       Patron: Moscow

Family: Father: Vladimir I "the Great" Grand Duke of Kiev Saint   Mother: Rogneda Princess of Polotsk
       Spouse: None   Siblings: Gleb Saint, Jaroslav "the Wise" Grand Duke of Kiev

Biography: Saint Boris and Saint Gleb, both brothers were the sons of Vladimir the Great Grand duke of Kiev. Both were martyrs and their brother was the one who did the deed. Their lineage is found in Saints in the Tree.

July 24   Saint Gleb

Country: Russia   **Date:** 1010

Family: Father: Vladimir I "the Great" Grand Duke of Kiev Saint   Mother: Rogneda Princess of Polotsk
       Spouse: None   Siblings: Boris Saint, Jaroslav "the Wise" Grand Duke of Kiev

SAINTS DAILY
Kings, Queens, Popes, Princes, Princesses, Emperors, Hermits, Bishops

DAILY SAINTS WHOSE ANCESTRY IS KNOWN

Biography: Saint Boris and Saint Gleb, both brothers were the sons of Vladimir the Great Grand duke of Kiev. Both were martyrs and their brother was the one who did the deed. Their lineage is found in Saints in the Tree.

July 24   *Saint Menefrida*

Family:
Parents: Father-Saint Brychan   Mother-Unknown
Husband: Unknown
Children: Unknown

Biography:
Patron saint of Tredresick, in Cornwall, England.

July 25   *Saint James the Greater*

Country: Israel   **Date:** 1st Century   **Patron:** Laborers, Hatmakers, Rheumatoid sufferers, Chile, Guatemala, Nicaragua. Spain, Spanish Conquistadors

Family: Father: Zebedee   Mother: Mary
Spouse: Unknown   Siblings: Saint John Zebedee

Ancestors: Saint Joseph of Arimathea is an ancestor. A little know fact of the biblical character of Joseph of Arimathea is that he is the son of Mathat, who is in the line of Nathan that is listed in the New Testament book of Luke. His ancestors then must be King David of Israel and Judah, and so the Israelites Joseph, Levi, Zebulon, and Judah. Anna married Saint Joseph of Arimathea, and her ancestry is an unbroken male line to Levi the Israelite. Saint Joseph of Arimathea's mother may have been the daughter of Eleazor, who was of the Davidic line of Solomon. Eleazor was the Grandfather of Joseph who married the Virgin Mary and this line is listed in the Gospel of Mathew. The Israelite Benjamin was an ancestor of King David's wife Maacah

SAINTS DAILY
Kings, Queens, Popes, Princes, Princesses, Emperors, Hermits, Bishops

DAILY SAINTS WHOSE ANCESTRY IS KNOWN

(Sauls daughter) whose line married in the line from Solomon joined by the marriage of Reheboam to Maacah. Therefore Saint Joseph of Arimathea has five Israelites as ancestors.

Branches of the Tree: This is a branch of the tree that has Saint Joseph of Arimathea in it. He is three generations the ancestor of Saint James. This line also marries Anna Arimathea who is the daughter of Joseph of Arimathea.

Biography: Saint James is the apostle that is mentioned in various places in the bible. He was one of the twelve disciples. His grandfather was Saint Joseph of Arimathea, and so was related to the house of David. He is called James the Greater, and was one of the two "Sons of Thunder". Saint James was one of the first martyrs of the church, as told in the biblical book of Acts, died by the sword becoming a Martyr.

July 28 *Saint Sampson*
Date: 565 **Feastday:** July 28

Family:
Parents: Father: Amwn Ddu ap Budic , Abbot of Southill, Prince Mother: Anna verch Gwerthefyr gan Oxenhall, Princess Wife: None Children: None Siblings: None

Ancestry: Saint Sampson is six generations the grandson of Conan and Dareca. Thus King David thru Nathan and Saint Joseph of Arimathea is an Ancestor, and thru Saint Dareca the line from Solomon because Eurgain was the sibling to Saint Cyllin. Also thru Bran the Blessed the Cornwall Kings of Britain are Ancestors.

Branches of the Tree: Saint Umbrafael was his uncle, and Budig ap AldrienI, King of Vannetais was his Grandfather. This is the Branch of the Tree in the vicinity on King Arthur, son of Uther Pendragon.

SAINTS DAILY
Kings, Queens, Popes, Princes, Princesses, Emperors, Hermits, Bishops

DAILY SAINTS WHOSE ANCESTRY IS KNOWN

Biography: Saint Sampson was the Bishop of Dol. He also founded a Monastery at Penda. He became a disciple of Saint Illtyd at Lianwit monastery in the south of Glamorgan. He lived as a monk on Caldey Island in a community. Saint Sampson cured his father Amon of a mortal illness. He is known for his evangelization of Brittany after he left England.

July 29 *Blessed Urban II Pope*

Feastday: July 29 **Date:** b c. 1042 d. 29 Jul 1099

Family:
Parents: Father: Gui I de Chatillon Mother: Unknown
Spouse: None Children: None Siblings: None

Ancestry: Blessed Urban II was ten generations the grandson of Charlemange. He was from Louis I and Charles II who were Frankish Descendents of Charlemange. Thus he was on the Line of David, Descended from five Israelites, Benjamin, Joseph, Judah, Levi, and Zebulon, was of the Epraim princes and descended from Joshua son of Nun, and also from Saint Joseph of Arimathea and so related to many of the apostles.

Branch of the Tree: Close to Arnaud Count & Bishop of Cambray and after ten generations to Charlemange.

Biography: Otto (Pope Urban II) de CHATILLON Blessed was born at Chatillons-sur-Marne, Champagne France. He was a monk at Cluny after he studied with Saint Bruno at Rheims and became an archdeacon at Rheims. In 1078 was named Cardinal Bishop of Ostia after assisting Pope Gregory VII reform. Emperor Henry IV briefly imprisoned him when he was legate to Germany. He elected Pope on March 12 1088. Antipope Clement III held Rome at the time and was supported by Henry IV. Finally in 1094 after a synod that denounced lay investiture, simony and clerical marriages Pope Urban II sat on the papal throne in Rome. He was in conflict with King Philip I of France

SAINTS DAILY
Kings, Queens, Popes, Princes, Princesses, Emperors, Hermits, Bishops

DAILY SAINTS WHOSE ANCESTRY IS KNOWN

about his wife Bertha who was put aside when King Philip I of France took Bertrada to wife at the request of Eastern Emperor Alexis I. Pope Urban II preached the first crusade that led to the capture of Jerusalem in 1099 and then Emperor Henry IV and his party of antipope Clement III left from Pope Urban had won. In his pontificate Pope Urban II had excommunicated Henry, and King Philip I of France. He was beatified by Pope Leo XIII in 1881.

July 29   Saint Olaf of Norway

Country: Norway   *Date:* c 1030
       Patron: Norway

Family: Parents: Father- Harold Gudrodsson Underling of Vestfold   Mother- Asta Gudbranddottir   Wife: Astrid Olafsdottir   Children: Magnus I Olavsson the Good King of Norway

Ancestry: Saint Olaf ancestors include Joseph of Arimathea and Saint Helena of the Cross of Rome. Also King David of Judah and Israel is an ancestor thru Nathan his son.

Descendents: Descendents with Titles include Harold II Maddadarson Earl of Caithness Orkney, Charles Howard Earl of Nottingham, and Magnus I the Good King of Norway.

Biography: King of Norway and a martyr, also called Olaf Haraldsson. The son of a Norwegian lord King Harold Grenske of Norway, he spent most of his youth as a Norse raider engaging in war and piracy in the Baltic until 1010 when he was baptized at Rouen. In 1013, he journeyed to England and offered his services to King Ethelred against the invading Danes and did battle. Returning home in 1015 after succeeding to the throne due to the absence of his rivals and his military prowess, he embarked upon a war to free Norway from the domination of the Danes and the Swedes, defeating Earl Sweyn at Nesje in 1016. He gave his subjects peace and harmony. He also immediately requested that

SAINTS DAILY
 Kings, Queens, Popes, Princes, Princesses, Emperors, Hermits, Bishops

DAILY SAINTS WHOSE ANCESTRY IS KNOWN

missionaries be sent from England to advance the Christianization of Norway which under his rule he used force and persuasion. Owing to the harsh nature of his rule, he faced a rebellion of nobles in 1029. Through the aid of the formidable King Canute of Denmark, the rebels overthrew him and drove him into exile in Russia in 1029. Olaf returned in 1030 but was slain in battle at Stiklestad, Norway, on July 29. Olaf was soon revered after death owing to reports of miracles occurring at his tomb. One of his missionaries built a church on the site of his grave and declared him a Saint. After King Cnut died in 1035 Olaf's son Magnus became king and his cause for sainthood greatly increased. He was greatly respected as a champion of Norwegian independence, and his shrine became the foundation of the cathedral of Trondheim, which was a popular place of pilgrimage during the Middle Ages. He is the patron of Norway, and was canonized in 1164. He is shown to carry emblems of a battle axe and loaves of stone.

July 30   Saint Olaf of Skottkonung

Country: Sweden   **Date:** 950- c 1024

Family: Parents: Father- Erik VIII Seiersal Bjornsson King of Sweden   Mother- Swietoslava Or Sygryda Sweden Norway Denmark   Wife: Astrid Inegrid Obotrites Queen of Sweden
Children: Ingrid Olafdotter Princess of Sweden

Ancestry: King of Sweden ancestry is traced for a few generations.

Descendents: Descendents include Duke Henry De Stafford of Buckingham and for the most part do not include any Saints or other nobles or Royalty.

Biography: Olaf Skottkonung is the name otherwise used for Saint Olaf. He is a martyred Swedish King ruling Sweden from 993-1024 as heir and son of Eric the Conqueror. With the aid of

SAINTS DAILY
Kings, Queens, Popes, Princes, Princesses, Emperors, Hermits, Bishops

DAILY SAINTS WHOSE ANCESTRY IS KNOWN

King Sweyn of Denmark and Eric, Jarl of Lade, he defeated King Olaf I Tryggvason of Norway at Svolder in 1000. This was the main event of his reign. St. Sigfrid converted Saint Olaf to Christianity and attempted to introduce the faith to all of Sweden. Pagans put up a strong resistance, and Saint Olaf was martyred at Stockholm by rebels. He had refused sacrifice to pagan idols.

July 30 *Blessed Mannes*
Country: Spain   **Date:** d.c. 1230

Family: Father: Felix Guzman   Mother: Joan Of Aza Blessed
Spouse: Unknown   Siblings: Dominic Saint

Ancestors:. Many Nobles of Spain, Including the Nunez, the Rodriques, the Kings of Len

Branches of the Tree This branch of the tree will eventually lead to the Kings of Leon and the Castillo.

Biography: Blessed Mannes was the brother to Saint Dominic and was the son of Blessed Joan of Aza and Felix Guzman. Little else is known of Blessed Mannes except the lineage relationships found in Saints in the Tree.

July 31 *Saint Neot*
Country: England   **Date:** Ninth

Family: Father: Aelwolf   Mother: Unknown Mistress
Spouse: Unknown   Siblings: Half brother to King Alfred the Great

Ancestors: Same as King Alfred.

SAINTS DAILY
Kings, Queens, Popes, Princes, Princesses, Emperors, Hermits, Bishops

DAILY SAINTS WHOSE ANCESTRY IS KNOWN

Branches of the Tree: This is the branch of the tree in the vicinity of King Alfred, the father of King Edward I of England.

Biography: Half brother to King Alfred. He was a hermit and monk. He departed to become a hermit in Cornwall (he was a hermit in Glastonbury first) and was ordained before he left. King Alfred may have visited him for his counsel as tradition states.

July 31 Saint Germannus d'Auxerre

Country: Gaul (Spain) **Date:** 378-448

Family: Father: Decimus Junius Rusticus (Prefect of Gaul)
 Mother: Unknown
Spouse: Unknown Siblings: Daughter of Decimus Junius Rusticus (Prefect of Gaul)

Ancestors: Not much ancestry is known, as the tree connects thru the siblings descent.

Branches of the Tree: This is the branch of the tree in the vicinity of King Arthur of the Round Table. Saint Kentigern is in this branch of the Tree.

Biography: Also known as Germain, and born at Auxerre, Gaul of Christian parents he studied at Gallic schools and then law at Rome. He then became a lawyer. He married Eustochia, and was named governor of the Amorican border provinces of Gaul and in 418 was named bishop of Auxerre. He embraced poverty as a life style and built a monastery, and endowed various poor churches in the diocese. Saint Germanus and St. Lupus, bishop of Troyes in 429 combatted the Pelagian heresy in Britain, after being sent there. They were successful in restoring orthodoxy. On this trip it was reported that the Saint saved a force of Britons from destruction by Picts and Saxons who were marauding. He had the Britons shout Alleluia from a high mountain pass in a ravine and the echoes were so great that the Saxons thought they

SAINTS DAILY
Kings, Queens, Popes, Princes, Princesses, Emperors, Hermits, Bishops

DAILY SAINTS WHOSE ANCESTRY IS KNOWN

were outnumbered and so fled the scene. So Germanus is said to have baptized many of the Britons in the army. When he returned to Gaul he convinced Auxilliaris prefect of Gaul, to reduce taxes. It is said this was done by healing Auxiliaris's sick wife. In 440 he again returned to Britain to combat Pelagainism. He again eliminated the heresy and founded numerous schools to teach true doctrine. Aetius, a Roman general had dispatched a barbarian army under Goar, he found as he returned to Gaul to put down a revolt in Amorica. Fearful of the savagery of the barbarian forces, Germanus tried to persuaded Goar to desist and even went to see the Emperor Valentinian III to call off the attack. None of this stopped the attack however and news of another uprising reached the ears of the Emperor. On July 31 Saint Germanus died while he was still in Ravenna.

SAINTS DAILY
Kings, Queens, Popes, Princes, Princesses, Emperors, Hermits, Bishops

DAILY SAINTS WHOSE ANCESTRY IS KNOWN

Saints of August

FEAST DAY	SAINT	COUNTRY	BORN	DIED
1-Aug	Saint Rioch	Ireland		c 480
1-Aug	Saint Almedha	Wales		6th
2-Aug	Saint Ethelritha	England		835
3-Aug	Saint Waltheof	Scotland		1160
7-Aug	Saint Claudia	Rome		1st
8-Aug	Blessed Joan of Aza	Spain		c 1190
8-Aug	Saint Dominic	Spain	1170	1221
9-Aug	Saint Oswald	England	c. 605	642
12-Aug	Saint Merewenna	Wales		6th
13-Aug	Saint Radegund	Franks	499	
13-Aug	Blessed Gertrude of Altenburg	Hungary	1227	1297
16-Aug	Saint Stephen of Hungary	Hungary	977	1038
18-Aug	Saint Helena of Rome	Rome	250	330
19-Aug	Saint Louis of Toulouse	France		1297
20-Aug	Saint Oswin	England		651
20-Aug	Saint Bernard of Clairvaux	France	1090	1153
21-Aug	Saint Apollinaris Sidonius	Rome		480
22-Aug	Saint John Wall	England		1679
22-Aug	Saint Tydfil	Wales		6th

SAINTS DAILY
Kings, Queens, Popes, Princes, Princesses, Emperors, Hermits, Bishops

231

DAILY SAINTS WHOSE ANCESTRY IS KNOWN

23-Aug	Saint Zaccaeus	Israel		116
24-Aug	Saint Batholomew	Israel		1st
25-Aug	Saint Louis IX of France	France	1214	1270
25-Aug	Saint Ebbe	England		683
28-Aug	Saint Rumwald	England		c 650
29-Aug	Saint Sebbi	England		695
30-Aug	Saint Pammachius	Italy		410
31-Aug	Saint Waltheof of Huntington	Northumbria	1045	1076

TABLE NINE SAINTS OF AUGUST

SAINTS DAILY
Kings, Queens, Popes, Princes, Princesses, Emperors, Hermits, Bishops

DAILY SAINTS WHOSE ANCESTRY IS KNOWN

August 1   *Saint Rioch*
Country: Ireland   **Date:** 480

Family: Father: Conan (Cynan) Meriadoc (King of Dumnonia)   Mother: Saint Darerca
Spouse: Unknown   Siblings: Gradlon Maw ('the Great') (King of Bretagne); Ystrafael; Melchu, Munis, Mel Saint

Ancestors: Saint Joseph of Arimathea is an Ancestor, as is Bran the Blessed King of Britain around 10 AD. Bran the Blessed ancestors include Camber and Tros, sons of Dardanus, who is the son of Zerah son of the Isralite Judah. Dardanus mother is also listed as Electra wife of Tarah, son of Ephriam who is the son of Joseph the Israelite. Saint Patrick is then descended from both Joseph and Judah, thru Dardanus and from David the King of Israel and Judah thru his son Nathan and the line leading to Matthat, father of Saint Joseph of Arimathea.

Branches of the Tree: The line of ancestry of Saint Patrick is sixteen generations from his ancestor Joseph of Arimathea, and fifteen generations from Bran the Blessed, whose ancestors are from the Israelites.

Biography: Saint Patrick had a nephew and it was Saint Rioch. His brothers were Melchu and Muinis and Saint Mel. He became the Bishop Abbot of Inisboffin Ireland. Saint Rioch and his brothers were the sons of Conis and Saint Darerca. He was a missionary bishop.

August 1   *Saint Almedha*
Feastday: August 1

Family:
Parents: Father-Saint Brychan   Mother- Unknown
Husband: Unknown

SAINTS DAILY
Kings, Queens, Popes, Princes, Princesses, Emperors, Hermits, Bishops

233

DAILY SAINTS WHOSE ANCESTRY IS KNOWN

Children: Unknown

Biography:
Virgin and Martyr. She took a vow of virginity and dedicated her life to Christ. She fled to a neighboring kingdom when the King found a suitor for her. She went to Llandrew, Llanfillo, and Llechfaen. The people all turned her away and she promised that dreadful thing calamites would befall anyone who denied her sanctuary. She took up residence in a small hut when she reaches Brecon, but the king arrived and demanded her return. She refused him so he beheaded her. All three of the villages had disasters, and a spring was sprung at the site of her murder.

August 2   *Saint Ethelritha*

Feastday: August 2   Date: d.835

Family: Father: Offa   Mother: Quendrida (Petronilla)
Spouse: Unknown   Siblings: Elfleda, Eadburga

Country: Britain

Ancestors: Not Known

Branches of the Tree: This branch of the tree is near the King Saint Alfred of England who is a Great Great Descendent.

Biography: Also known as Alfritha, Aelfnryth, Afreda, and Etheldreda. She was a Virgin and Hermit. Saint Ethelbert came to marry her but was killed by Ethelritha queen Cynethritha. She was the daughter of King Offa of Mercia. Alfreda Left the court and went to the marshes of Crowland. She became a hermitess. Her sister Aelfreda also lost a husband in the court of Offa and his queen due to political intrigue.

SAINTS DAILY
Kings, Queens, Popes, Princes, Princesses, Emperors, Hermits, Bishops

DAILY SAINTS WHOSE ANCESTRY IS KNOWN

August 3   Saint Waltheof
Feastday: August 3   Date: d.1160

Family: Father: Simon I de Saint Liz Earl of Huntington
        Mother: Matilda (Maud) Huntington
Spouse: Unknown   Siblings: Simon De Saint Liz

Country: Scotland

Ancestors: The kings of Denmark, and some nobility of France.

Branches of the Tree: This branch of the tree is near the King Saint David of Scotland. Saint Waltheof's mother Matilda Huntinton had married King David of Scotland.

Biography: After his fathers death his mother married King David of Scotland. In King David's court Saint Waltheof was influenced by Saint Aelred. Saint Waltheof left the court and joined the Nostelle Monastery in Yorkshire becoming an Augustine Canon. He became abbot of Kirkham and then joined the Cistercians at Wardon, Bedfordshire. King David of Scotland founded a monastery at Melrose and Saint Waltheof was named abbot. In 1154 he was named archbishop of Saint Andrews but refused the honor. Saint Waltheof was known for hid kindness to the poor, and was credited with performing miracles.

August 7   Saint Claudia
Country: Britain   **Date:** 1st Century

Family: Father: Unknown   Mother: Unknown
Spouse: Caradoc Ap Bran King Of Britain   Siblings: Unknown
        Children: Eurgaine Of BRITAIN; Gladys (Claudia) Britain; Cyllin (Coellyn or Cyllinus) ap Caradog; Saint Eurgen Of Llan Ilid Saint Linus; Bishop Of Rome Saint

Ancestors:. Unknown

SAINTS DAILY
Kings, Queens, Popes, Princes, Princesses, Emperors, Hermits, Bishops

DAILY SAINTS WHOSE ANCESTRY IS KNOWN

Branches of the Tree This branch of the tree has Saint Linus Bishop of Rome as a descendent of Saint Claudia.

Biography Tradition has Saint Claudia the daughter of British King Caractacus. He was sent to Rome with his family in chains and enslaved when he was defeated by Aulus Plautius. Claudia was the mother of Linus, who became the second Pope. When King Caractuacus was released by Emperor Claudius, one of his daughters took the name Claudia, remained in Rome. She was baptized, and is the Claudia mentioned in St. Paul's second letter to Timothy. This is one tradition. Another tradition has her the daughter of a British ally of Claudius, a man named Cogidubnus, who took the Emperor's name. Still another tradition states that Martial mentions a British lady, Claudia Rufina, and says she was married to his friend Aulus Pudens, a Roman senator. Another tradition has this senator the Pudens also mentioned in St. Paul's second letter to Timothy. Her feast day is August 7.

August 8   *Blessed Joan Of Aza*
Country: **Portugal**   *Date:* d. c. 1190

Family: Father: Unknown   Mother: Unknown
         Spouse: Felix Guzman   Siblings: Unknown
         Offspring: Saint Dominic; Blessed Mannes

Ancestors: Unknown

Branches of the Tree: This branch of the tree will eventually lead to the Kings of Leon and the Castillo.

Biography: Mother to Saint Dominic and Blessed Mannes she is the wife of Felix Guzman. Born in the castle of Aza, near Arnada, Old Castile, she was married to Felix Guzman. He was warden of Calaruega in Burgos. Four children where born to her, one of which is Saint Dominic. She was known for her spiritual and physical beauty, and on her death a cult developed, which

SAINTS DAILY
Kings, Queens, Popes, Princes, Princesses, Emperors, Hermits, Bishops

DAILY SAINTS WHOSE ANCESTRY IS KNOWN

was confirmed in 1828. There is a legend that says she prayed for a son when her two eldest boys were grown and dreamed she bore a dog in her womb, while she was bearing Dominic, which would set the world afire with the torch in its mouth. The symbol of the Dominicans became a dog, and gave rise to the expression Domini Canes to describe the Dominicans. This expression is translated Watchdogs of the Lord.

August 8   *Saint Dominic*

Country: Spain   Patron of Astronomers   **Date:** b. 1170 d. 1221

Family: Father: Felix Guzman   Mother: Joan Of Aza Blessed
Spouse: Unknown   Siblings: Blessed Mannes

Ancestors:. Many Nobles of Spain, Including the Nunez, the Rodriques, the Kings of Len

Branches of the Tree This branch of the tree will eventually lead to the Kings of Leon and the Castillo.

Biography: Saint Dominic was born at Calaruega Spain. He studied at the Univ at Palencia, and was probably ordained there while pursuing his studies. He was the son of Felix Guzman and Blessed Joan of Aza. He was appointed canon at Osma in 1199. It was there were he became prior superior of the chapter. This chapter was noted for the rule of Saint Benedict. He preached against the Albigensians and in 1203 he accompanied Bishop Diego de Avezedo of Osma to Languedoc where his preaching helped reform the Cistercians. An institute for women at Prouille in Albigensian territory in 1206 and attached several preaching friars to it. The Albigensians got a crusade launched against them in 1208 when papal legate Peter of Castelnan was murdered by them. The crusade was ordered by Pope Innocent III and headed by Count Simon IV of Montfort and continued for seven hears. Dominic followed the army and preached to the heretics

SAINTS DAILY
Kings, Queens, Popes, Princes, Princesses, Emperors, Hermits, Bishops

DAILY SAINTS WHOSE ANCESTRY IS KNOWN

but with no great success. In 1214 Dominic and six followers founded an order at Casseneuil that Simon had given him. He failed to gain approval for his order of preachers at the fourth General Council of the Lateran in 1215 but was approved by Pope Honorius III in 1216. This was the year the Order of Preachers was founded. Dominic spent the last years of his life founding new houses and traveling all over Italy, Spain and France. The order was successful with conversions. Saint Dominic convoked the first general council of the order at Bologna in 1220 and died there in 1221 after returning from Hungary. He was canonized in 1234 and is the patron saint of astronomers. Feast day is August 8.

August 9   *Saint Oswald*

Country: England   **Date:** 605-42

Family: Father: Aethelfrith Of Northumbria   Mother: Acha Of Deira
Spouse: Unknown   Siblings: Eanfrith; Oswiu; Saint Ebbe, Saint Elfleda

Ancestors: Aethelfrith line is unknown, but Acha of Deira goes back many generations to Woden (Norse God of ancient legend.) Ancestors go back to the Anglo-Saxons around the year 100 AD. Also the line of the Kings of Deira lead to the Lords of the Anglo Saxons.

Branches of the Tree: This branch of the tree connects to the Mercia Kings, and the Kings of Penda. Also Acha of Deira the Saints mother is the sister to Saint Edwin of Northumbria. His line is known

Biography: Saint Oswald was the nephew of Odo of Fleury who was an Archbishop in France. It was in his household that Saint Oswald studied, although he was a dane by birth. It was in France that he was ordained. In 959 he returned to England and

SAINTS DAILY
Kings, Queens, Popes, Princes, Princesses, Emperors, Hermits, Bishops

DAILY SAINTS WHOSE ANCESTRY IS KNOWN

in 962 was made Bishop of Worcester by Saint Dunstan. Many monasteries were built, including the famous abbey of Ramsey in Huntingdonshire. Archbishop of York by 972 Saint Oswald also retained the see of Worcester. King of Mercia Elfhere attacked his reforms in his monasteries in Worcester. Perhaps this is why he retained the see. Saint Oswald wrote two treatises and several synodal decrees and always tried to increase his clergy's theological knowledge, and keep his clergy moral. In 992 Saint Oswald died and was associated with Saint Dunstan and Saint Ethelwold since popular veneration joined his name to theirs. He is considered one of the three Saints who revived English monasticism.

August 12   Saint Merewenna

Date: b. 479   Feastday: August 12

Family:
Parents: Father-Saint Brychan Mother- Unknown
Husband: Unknown
Children: Unknown

Biography:
Patroness of Marharm Church, in Cornwall, England. Sometimes known as Merwenna and Merwinna, she was a daughter of Brychan of Brecknock. According to the Cornish lists, Morwenna was one of the many holy daughters of King Brychan Brycheiniog. She was trained in Ireland before becoming one of the Welsh saints who crossed over to Cornwall. Morwenna made her home in a little hermitage at Hennacliff (the Raven's Crag), afterwards called Morwenstow. It stands near the top of a high cliff looking over the Atlantic, where the sea is almost constantly stormy, and from where, in certain atmospheric conditions, the coast of Wales can be seen. She built a church there, for the local people, with her own hands. She carried the stone, on her head, from beneath the cliff and where she once stopped for a rest, a spring gushed forth. It can

SAINTS DAILY
Kings, Queens, Popes, Princes, Princesses, Emperors, Hermits, Bishops

DAILY SAINTS WHOSE ANCESTRY IS KNOWN

still be seen to the west of the church. When she was dying, her brother, St. Nectan, came to see her from Hartland and she bade him raise her up that she might look once more on her native shore. This occurred sometime in the early 6th century, possibly on 24th July. An interesting, but much defaced, polychrome wall-painting was found on the north wall of the chancel of Morwenstow church, thought to represent this lady. It shows a gaunt female clasping to her breast, with her left hand, a scroll or volume; the right arm is raised in blessing over a kneeling monk. She is sometimes identified with St. Merryn, whose feast day is 7th July, but Doble believes that this was originally a male saint. She should also not be confused with her sister, St. Marwenna.

August 13 Blessed Gertrude of Altenburg

Feastday: August 13   Date: b. 1227 d. 1297

Family: Father: Louis IV Landgrave of Thuringia Saint
Mother: Elizabeth Of Hungary Saint   Spouse: Unknown   Siblings: Sophia of Thuringia

Country: Hungary

Ancestors: Not much is known past the Kings of Thuringia

Branches of the Tree: Kings of Hungary and Thuringia are in this branch of the tree.

Biography: Blessed Gertrude was born two weeks after her father Saint Louis was killed in a crusade. When two years old she as placed in the Praemonstratensian abbey at Altenburg. She was raised as a nun and when twenty two years old she was elected Abbess. She built a church and an almshouse and she is credited as beginning the feast of Corpus Cristi in Germany in her monastery. Pope Clement VI approved her cult.

August 13   Saint Radegund

Country: France   *Date:* b. 499

SAINTS DAILY
Kings, Queens, Popes, Princes, Princesses, Emperors, Hermits, Bishops

240

DAILY SAINTS WHOSE ANCESTRY IS KNOWN

Family: Parents: Father- Berthar Half King of Thuringia Mother- Unknown   Husband: King Clotaire   Children: Charlbert I King of Paris

Ancestors: Only her father is known.

Descendents: Descendents include Saint Adelaide of Italy Empress, Saint Adele Countess of Blois, Saint Arnolf Bishop of Metz, Blessed Charlemange, Saint Cunigunda of Luxemborg, Saint David and Saint Margaret of Scotland, Saint Edgar of England, Saint Ferdinand III of Spain, Saint Louis IX of France, Saint Raymond Berenger Count, Saint Henry II King of Germany, Saint Lazlo King of Hungary, and Saint Leopold III of Austria.

Biography: Berthaire, pagan king of a portion of Thuringia, was Radegunde's father. Erfurt, Thuringia, Germany is likely her birthplace. Her uncle Hermenefrid, murdered her father. He was defeated in 531 by King Theodoric or Austarasia and King Clotaire of Neustria, and Clotaire took Radegunde captive although she was only twelve years old. When she was eighteen Clotaire married her. She founded a leper hospital, devoted herself to the poor, the sick, and captives, and when Clotaire murdered her brother, Unstrut, she stopped bearing Clotaire's cruelties without complaint. She left the court, received the deaconess habit from Bishop Medard at Noyon, and at Saix became a nun. The double monastery of the Holy Cross was built at Poitiers about 557 where she retired and where she developed in into a great center of learning. She secured a relic of the True Cross for the Church of her monastery, and was active in peacemaking roles, and lived in great austerity. She died at the monastery on August 13 living the last years of her life in seclusion. Venantius Fortunatus wrote her biography. He was a priest at Poitiers.

SAINTS DAILY
Kings, Queens, Popes, Princes, Princesses, Emperors, Hermits, Bishops

DAILY SAINTS WHOSE ANCESTRY IS KNOWN

August 16   *Saint Stephen of Hungary*

Country: Hungary   **Date:** 977-1038

Family: Parents: Father-Geza King of Hungary   Mother-Adelajda of Poland   Wife: Giselle of Bavaria   Children: Eminilde Arpad, Hedwig of Hungary

Ancestry: Saint Stephen's ancestry goes back a few generations and then is not known.

Descendents: Descendents include Saint Cunigunda of Luxemborg, Saint Louis IX of France, Saint David and Margaret of Scotland, and Saint Fernando III of Spain. Royal Descendents include King Edward Plantagenet III of England, King Philip IV of France, King of Naples Charles II, William I of Scotland, and King Casimir I of Poland.

Biography: Son of the Magyar chieftain Geza, Stephen succeeded him as leader in 997. He is the Patron Saint of Hungary and the first King in Hungary. He wed the daughter of Duke Henry II of Bavaria Gissell of Bavaria. He was raised a Christian, and devoted much of his time as King to the promotion of the faith of Christianity. The Black Hungarians created a pagan counter reaction to Christianity, so Saint Stephen crushed their failed rebellion. He was a proponent of the rights of the Holy See, helped build churches, and gave his patronage to Church leaders. He received the cross and crown from Pope Sylvester II in recognition of his efforts, thus the anointed King of Hungary in 1000. The remainder of his time as King was occupied by consolidation of the Christian hold on the region. Beloved symbols of the Hungarian nation, his crown and regalia are held still venerated today. The ideal Christian King is said to be fulfilled by Saint Stephen. He became the patron saint of Hungary as he was canonized in 1083 by Pope St. Gregory VII.

SAINTS DAILY
Kings, Queens, Popes, Princes, Princesses, Emperors, Hermits, Bishops

DAILY SAINTS WHOSE ANCESTRY IS KNOWN

August 18   *Saint Helenus*

Country: Rome   *Date:* 250-330

Family: Parents: Father-Coel II King of Colchester Mother- Strada ferch Cadfan
Husband: Constantius I Roman Emperor   Children- St.Constantine I The Great Flavius Valerius Rome

Ancestry: King of Britain and Romans including Mark Antony and Julia of Rome. Also Joseph of Arimathea so David thru Nathan. Also Saint Cyllin so Zerah thru the Kings of Siluria and Tros King of Troy. Tros is a few generations away from Zerah the son of Judah.

Descendents: Descendents include Saint Margaret of Scotland, Saint Adele of Blois, Saint Olav of Norway, Saint Leopold III of Austria and Saint Louis IX of France.

Biography: Empress mother of Constantine the Great married the then Roman general Constantius I Chlorus about 270. She was a native of Bithynia, who mothered Constantine who was born soon after, and in 293, Constantius was made Caesar, or junior emperor. He divorced Helena to marry co Emperor Maximian's stepdaughter. After the fateful victory at Milvian Bridge, Constantine became emperor in 312 and Helena was named Augusta, or empress. She converted to Christianity and performed many acts of charity, including building churches in Rome and in the Holy Land. Helena discovered the True Cross on a pilgrimage to the Holy Land. She is believed to have died in Nicomedia. Geoffrey of Monmouth, England, started the legend that Helena was the daughter of the king of Colchester, a tradition no longer upheld. In liturgical art Helena is depicted as an empress, holding a cross. Her porphyry sarcophagus is in the Vatican Museum. Helenus is the Mother of Constantine the Great who made Christianity the official religion of the Roman Empire.

SAINTS DAILY
Kings, Queens, Popes, Princes, Princesses, Emperors, Hermits, Bishops

DAILY SAINTS WHOSE ANCESTRY IS KNOWN

August 19   *Saint Louis of Toulouse*

Country: Italy   **Date:** 1297

Family: Father: Charles II King of Naples   Mother: Maria Princess of Hungary
Spouse: Unknown   Siblings: Marguerite Princess of Sicily and Naples

Ancestors: Saint Louis of Toulouse ancestors include Saint Fernando and so Muhamed, Ishmael and Abraham. Also Charlemagne and so Zerah. Also Joseph of Arimathea and Saint Helena of Rome. Also King David of Judah and Israel is an ancestor thru Nathan his son. King Solomon of Israel and Judah is also an ancestor. These are Saint Ethelbert, Saint Arnulf, Saint Itta, Saint Sigebert, Saint Dagobert, Saint Beggue, Saint Liuthwin, Saint Bathildis, Saint Sexburga, Blessed Pepin, Saint Clodulf, Saint Olga, Saint Matilda, Saint Elgiva, Saint Edgar, Saint Henry II, Saint Cunigunda, Saint Stephen, Saint Margaret, and Saint David. Also thru his mothers side ancestors include

Branches of the Tree: Saint King Louis the Ninth is in this branch of the tree, as well as King Alfred the Great

Biography :   Saint Louis of Toulouse was the son of Charles II of Anjou who was the King of Naples. He was a Franciscan bishop. He was related to Saint Elizabeth of Hungary and Saint Louis IX of France. For seven years Saint Louis was held as a hostage for his father. Ordained at twenty-three he became a Franciscan and later served as bishop of Toulouse France. He served only six months. At a young age he died. Saint Louis was canonized in 1317.

SAINTS DAILY
Kings, Queens, Popes, Princes, Princesses, Emperors, Hermits, Bishops

DAILY SAINTS WHOSE ANCESTRY IS KNOWN

August 20 *Saint Oswin*
Country: Northumbria   **Date:** d. 951

Family: Father: Prince Osric Of Diera
         Mother: Rhiainfelt verch Rhoedd
Spouse: Unknown   Siblings: Oswy of Northumbria, King of Northumbria

Biography: Welsh King Cadwallon in 633 killed Saint Oswin's father King Osric of Deira. So Saint Oswin was taken to Wessex, baptized and was educated there. When Saint Oswald was killed in battle against King Penda of Mercia in 642, the King of Deira became Osein. When Oswy, Oswald's brother had become King in Bernicia, Oswald had united Deira with Bernicia. However Oswy declared war on Oswin, so Oswin went into hiding at the estate of Earl Hunwald at Gilling near Richmond, York, rather than make a bloody battle. Ethelwin murdered him there after he was betrayed by Hunwald on orders from Oswy. He died August 20.

August 20 *Saint Bernard of Clairvaux*
Country: **Date:** b. 1090 d. 1153
Patron: Gibraltar, Queens College Cambridge

Family: Father: Tescelin Of Sorus Mother: Aleth Blessed
Spouse: None   Siblings: Humbeline De Troyes Saint

Biography: St. Bernard was born of noble parentage in Burgundy, France, in the castle of Fontaines near Dijon. St. Bernard was an Abbot and Doctor of the Church. He was sent at an early age to a college at Chatillon under the care of his pious parents. He was conspicuous for his remarkable piety and spirit of recollection. At the same place he entered upon the studies of theology and Holy Scripture. He also persuaded his brothers and several of his friends to follow his example. His Mother died so he fearing the snares and temptations of the world embraced the newly established and very austere institute of the Cistercian

SAINTS DAILY
Kings, Queens, Popes, Princes, Princesses, Emperors, Hermits, Bishops

DAILY SAINTS WHOSE ANCESTRY IS KNOWN

Order. He was destined to become the greatest ornament of this order.

In 1113, St. Bernard, presented himself to the holy Abbot, St. Stephen, with thirty young noblemen, at Citeaux. He made his profession in the following year after a novitiate spent in great fervor. Seeing the great progress he had made in the spiritual life, his superior sent him with twelve monks to found a new monastery, which afterward became known as the celebrated Abbey of Clairvaux.

St. Bernard was at once appointed Abbot and began that active life which has rendered him the most conspicuous figure in the history of the 12th century. He composed a number of works and undertook many journeys, founded numerous other monasteries, for the honor of God. He refused Several Bishoprics that were offered him. The reputation of St. Bernard spread far and wide; even the Popes were governed by his advice. He was commissioned by Pope Eugene III to preach the second Crusade. He aroused the greatest enthusiasm for the holy war among the masses of the population. In obedience to the Sovereign Pontiff he traveled through France and Germany. The failure of the expedition raised a great storm against the saint, but he attributed it to the sins of the Crusaders. St. Bernard was eminently endowed with the gift of miracles. His feast day is August 20. He died on August 20, 1153.

August 21 Saint Appollinaris Sidonius

Country: Italy

Date: 480

Family: Father: Unknown   Mother: Unknown
Spouse: Papianilla   Siblings: Unknown

Ancestors: Unknown

Branches of the Tree: Son in law of Avitus of Rome who was son of Julius Agricola

SAINTS DAILY
Kings, Queens, Popes, Princes, Princesses, Emperors, Hermits, Bishops

DAILY SAINTS WHOSE ANCESTRY IS KNOWN

Biography: Born in Lugdunum about 423 Daius Sollius Apollinaris Sidonius was a Bishop and classical scholar. He received an education in the classical style and was from a noble family. The daughter of Avitus, Papianilla became his wife as he entered the military. Avitus became emperor of the West in 455. When Avitus was deposed in 456 Apollinaris survived and served as the chief senator and prefect of Rome from 468 to 469. He carried on a vast correspondence from Gaul where he retired that gives considerable insight into the political period. He was both unwilling and not ordained but was appointed Bishop of Avernum. He was the only one able to defend the people from the invading Goths under Alaric, and this is why he was appointed Bishop. He learned much about being a Bishop and was soon recognized as an authority. He was exiled briefly when he opposed King Euric of the Goths in 474. He was a poet and orator and introduced the days of public prayer called "Rogation Days". A valuable resource on the period is the twenty-four of his letters and poems that survived. The great classical culture of Rome was being overrun by the Germanic invasions, and Saint Apollinaris is considered to be the last representative of the time.

August 22   Saint John Wall

Country: England   **Date:** 1679

Family: Father: William Wall   Mother: Joane Eaves
Spouse: Unknown   Siblings: Unknown

Ancestors: The line goes back to the Singletons around 1100.

Branches of the Tree: This line goes back many gereations to the Singletons around 1000 show descendents join with the tree.

Biography: Ordained in 1645, Saint John Wall was one of the forty Martyrs of England and Wales. He was educated at Douai and Rome. He became a Franciscan in 1651 with the name Father Joachim of Saint Anne. In 1656 he returned to Worcester England. In December 1678 he was arrested and imprisoned for

SAINTS DAILY
Kings, Queens, Popes, Princes, Princesses, Emperors, Hermits, Bishops

five months. He was hanged drawn and quartered at Redhill. Pope Paul VI canonized him in 1970.

August 23   *Saint Tydfil ferch Brychan*

Country: England   **Date:** 6th

Family:
Parents: Father-Saint Brychan Mother- Unknown
Husband: Unknown
Children: Unknown

Biography:
Welsh martyr. She was slain by a group of pagan Picts or Saxons. She is venerated at Merthyr-Tydfil, Glamorgan. Wales.

August 23   *Saint Zaccaeus*

Country: Israel   **Date:** 116

Family: Father: Simon   Mother: Unknown
Spouse: Unknown   Siblings: Unknown   Children: Mathias 5th Bishop of Jerusalem, Tobias 8th Bishop of Jerusalem, Ephres 13th Bishop of Jerusalem

Ancestors: The line leads to Simon son of Saint Joseph

Branches of the Tree: this branch is around Saint Joseph.

Biography: Also known as Zacharias he was described by Saint Epiphanius and others as the fourth Episcopal head of Jerusalem. He died about 116.

SAINTS DAILY
Kings, Queens, Popes, Princes, Princesses, Emperors, Hermits, Bishops

DAILY SAINTS WHOSE ANCESTRY IS KNOWN

August 24 — *Saint Bartholomew Apostle*

Country: Israel			**Date:** 1st Century

Family:		Father: Tolmai		Mother: Unknown
Spouse: Unknown				Siblings: Unknown

Country:		Israel

Ancestors: Tolmai's father was Judas of Gamla, who was the brother to Jacob who was the father of Saint Joseph. Therefore he has the same ancestry as Saint Joseph.

Branches of the Tree: Area of the Tree about Jacob who married Cleopatra of Jerusalem.

Biography: Saint Bartholomew may have been Nathaniel who was called under the fig tree in the scripture. He is counted as one of the twelve disciples. His relationship to his fellow apostles James the Lesser and the Zebeddee's would be second cousins.

August 25 — *Saint Louis IX King of France*

Country: France		*Date:* 1214-1270		*Patron:* French Monarchs

Family:
Parents: Father- Louis VIII of France   Mother- Blanca Alphonsa Princess Castile
Wife: Margaret De Provence		Children: Philip III "the Bold" King of France

Ancestry:

SAINTS DAILY
Kings, Queens, Popes, Princes, Princesses, Emperors, Hermits, Bishops

DAILY SAINTS WHOSE ANCESTRY IS KNOWN

Saint Louis IX ancestors include Saint Fernando and so Muhamed, Ishmael and Abraham. Also Charlemange and so Zerah. Also Joseph of Arimathea and Saint Helena of Rome. Also King David of Judah and Israel is an ancestor thru Nathan his son. King Solomon of Israel and Judah is also an ancestor. Sainted Ancestry includes more saints than any other saint. These are Saint Ethelbert, Saint Arnulf, Saint Itta, Saint Sigebert, Saint Dagobert, Saint Beggue, Saint Liuthwin, Saint Bathildis, Saint Sexburga, Blessed Pepin, Saint Clodulf, Saint Olga, Saint Matilda, Saint Elgiva, Saint Edgar, Saint Henry II, Saint Cunigunda, Saint Stephen, Saint Margaret, and Saint David.

Descendents:
Descendents include King Edward III Plantagenet of England, and the Kings of France.

Biography:
He succeeded to the throne at the age of twelve under the regency of his mother. Louis IX was born in Poissy, France in 1214 to Louis VIII and Blanche of Castille. On his twenty-first birthday he assumed full kingship. Louis generally remained neutral in international disputes. He was well known for protecting the French clergy from secular leaders and for strictly enforcing laws against blasphemy. However, because of a dispute between the Count of Le Marche and the Count of Poitiers, in which Henry III supported the Count of Le Marche, he was forced to go to war with England. In 1242 Louis defeated Henry III at Tailebourg. After the war, he made restitution to the innocent people whose property had been destroyed. Louis led two crusades, the Sixth and the Seventh Crusades. He established the Sorbonne (1252) and the monasteries of Rayaumont, Vavert, and Maubuisson. He was captured and imprisoned during the Sixth (1244-1249). At the onset of the Seventh Crusade in 1270, Louis died of dysentery. Boniface VIII canonized him in 1297.

SAINTS DAILY
Kings, Queens, Popes, Princes, Princesses, Emperors, Hermits, Bishops

DAILY SAINTS WHOSE ANCESTRY IS KNOWN

August 25   Saint Ebba The Elder
Country: England   **Date:** d. 683

Family: Father: Aethelfrith Of Northumbria   Mother: Acha Of Deira
Spouse: Unknown   Siblings: Eanfrith; Oswiu; Saint Oswald

Ancestors: Aethelfrith line is unknown, but Acha of Deira goes back many generations to Woden (Norse God of ancient legend.) Ancestors go back to the Anglo-Saxons around the year 100 AD. Also the line of the Kings of Deira lead to the Lords of the Anglo Saxons.

Branches of the Tree : This branch of the tree connects to the Mercia Kings, and the Kings of Penda. Also Acha of Deira the Saints mother is the sister to Saint Edwin of Northumbria. His line is known

Biography: Saint Ebbe was from Northumbria. Aethelfrith was the father and Acha of Deria the mother. Saint Oswald was the sibling who was a Saint and other siblings include Eanfrith and Oswiu. Not much else is known of Saint Ebbe other than the lineage relationships found in Saints in the Tree. She refused to marry the King of the Scots and was habited by St. Finan at Lindisfarne. Her brother donated some land and she built the monastery of Ebbchester. She then built a double monastery on the coast of Berwick at Coldingham. Here she was first abbess, although her enforcement of discipline was notoriously lax.

August 26   Blessed Thomas Percy
Country: England   **Date:** 1672

Family: Father: Thomas Percy   Mother: Eleanor Harbottle
Spouse: Unknown   Siblings: Unknown

SAINTS DAILY
Kings, Queens, Popes, Princes, Princesses, Emperors, Hermits, Bishops

251

DAILY SAINTS WHOSE ANCESTRY IS KNOWN

Ancestors: King Edward III of England, thus Charlemagne and the French Kings.

Branches of the Tree : This branch of the tree is the Percy Line that has an ancestor five generations back King Edward III of England.

Biography: Blessed Thomas Percy was in good graces with Queen Elizabeth and he also served Queen Mary. However he went to the north and got involved with the Scottish Uprising and was sold to Queen Elizabeth for 2000 pounds. He was in prison three years and would not abjure his faith and then was beheaded. He was beautified in 1896.

August 28   Blessed Robert Morton

Country: England   **Date:** 1672

Family: Father: Thomas Percy   Mother: Eleanor Harbottle
Spouse: Unknown   Siblings: Unknown

Ancestors: King Henry I of England, thus Charlemagne and the French Kings.

Branches of the Tree : This branch of the tree is the Conyers whose ancestors were the Constable's. Notable Houses include the Spencers and the Wentworths.

Biography: Blessed Robert Morton studied for the priesthood at Reirns and Rome. In 1587 he was ordained. He had been born in Bawtry Yorkshire in England however his studies took him out of England. He returned to England and was arrested soon after. In 1588 he was executed at Lincoln's Inn fields, London. He was beatified in 1929.

SAINTS DAILY
Kings, Queens, Popes, Princes, Princesses, Emperors, Hermits, Bishops

DAILY SAINTS WHOSE ANCESTRY IS KNOWN

August 28   *Saint Rumwald*
Country: Great Britain   **Date:** 650

Family: Father: Alchfrith Of, UnderKing Of Deira
Mother: Saint Kyneburga
Spouse: Unknown   Siblings: Unknown

Ancestors: The line of the King of Mercia Penda goes to Woden and Frigg.

Biography: Saint Rumwald was a prince. He was the son of King Aldfrith and Queen Cuneburga. He was prince of Northumbria, England. He was baptized at only three days old, and it is said he declared the profession of faith and then died. For centuries in parts of England he is said to be venerated, but this tradition is highly in doubt.

August 29   *Saint Sebbi*
Country: Great Britain   **Date:** 694

Family: Father: Saeward (Joint-King of Essex - 617-623)
Mother: Unknown
Spouse: Unknown   Siblings: Unknown

Ancestors: Saint King Ethelbert is an ancestor, as is Woden or Odin of Asgard.

Branches of the Tree: This branch is the branch of the kings of Kent and of Essex.

Biography: Saint Sebbi became the king of the East Saxons or the King of Essex. Actually Saint Cedd converted the Kingdom in 664 and Saint Sebbi became King after that. The kingdom was under the domination of Mercia, and there was a period of peace

SAINTS DAILY
Kings, Queens, Popes, Princes, Princesses, Emperors, Hermits, Bishops

DAILY SAINTS WHOSE ANCESTRY IS KNOWN

during his rule. After thirty years rule he abdicated and in London became a monk. He was buried in old St. Paul's.

August 30   *Saint Pammachius*

Country: Italy (Rome)   **Date:** d. 404

Family: Father: Unknown   Mother: Unknown
Spouse: Paulina   Siblings: Unknown

Ancestors: Very few generations known.

Branches of the Tree: Go up the tree three generations and down ten to find Saint Arnulf Bishop of Metz.

Biography: Friend of Saint Jerome and Roman Senator, Pammachius was of the Furii family. In 385 he married Saint Paula's daughter Paulina. Saint Jerome wrote a treatise against Jovianian's teachings which Pammachius critized. Pope Saint Siricius heard Pammachius denunciation of Jovinism. Pammachius devoted his life after his wife Paulina died in 397 to study and charitable works. At Porto he built a hospice with Fabiola for pilgrims who came to Rome and also for the poor and sick. He had a church in his house. The site of his house is now occupied by the Passionists SS. Peter and Paul Church. Jerome was urged by Pammachius to translate Origen's De Principiis. Saint Pammichius wrote a letter to tenants on his estaste in Numidia. This letter was about abandoning Donatism and he got a letter from Saint Augustine thanking him. He was called from this life while in Rome.

August 30   *Saint Rumon*

Country: England   **Date:** b. 515

Family: Father: Hoel I   Mother: Alma Pompeia

SAINTS DAILY
Kings, Queens, Popes, Princes, Princesses, Emperors, Hermits, Bishops

DAILY SAINTS WHOSE ANCESTRY IS KNOWN

Spouse: Unknown   Siblings: Bishop Tudwal Saint, and many others found on internet, see gedcom.

Ancestors: Saint Joseph is an ancestor thru his son Bishop James of Jerusalem. Therefore his ancestry includes King David of Israel and Judah.

Branches of the Tree: This is the branch near Saint Judicael.

Biography: Other names he is known as include Ruan, Ronan, Ruadan. Not much is known, he may have been an Irish missionary with many churches in Devon and Cornwall in England named after him. Some believe that he and Saint Kea were British Monks who founded a monastery at Street Somerset.

August 30   *Saint Agilus*
Country: France   **Date:** 650

Family: Father: Chagnoald   Mother: Unknown
Spouse: Unknown   Siblings: Unknown

Ancestors: Pharamond and Frotmund are ancestors.

Branches of the Tree: This is the branch near the Franks.

Biography: Became Abbot of Rebais. Educated at Saint Columvanus at Luxeuil France, he was from a noble family. He was also called Ayeul, and served as a missionary in Bavaria Germany.

SAINTS DAILY
Kings, Queens, Popes, Princes, Princesses, Emperors, Hermits, Bishops

DAILY SAINTS WHOSE ANCESTRY IS KNOWN

August 31 Saint Waltheof of Northumbria

Country: England *Date:* 1045- 1076

Family: Parents: Father- Siward Earl of Huntingdon Mother- Aelflaed II of Northumbeland
Wife: Judith de Lens Children: Maud de Huntingdon; Alice Adeliza Huntingdon

Ancestry: His known ancestry goes back only a few generations.

Descendents: King Edward the Fourth Plantagenet of England is a descendent, and two of his children are Maud de Huntingdon and Alice de Huntingdon. Rosamond Clifford a descendent married King Henry II of France and their child was William Longspee.

Biography: Siward had a son named Waldef or Watheof. He was the Earl of Northumbria or the count of Northhampton and Huntingdon. In 1066 he fought with distinction against the Normons and also fought well at the siege of York years later. William the Conqueror pardoned him, gave his niece as his wife, and restored his lands. Judith was happily married to Waldef in 1070. Waldef went to Normandy to ask pardon of the king and obtain mercy after the rebellion of the Earls in 1075. William did not grant pardon and Waltheof was imprisoned for a year and then beheaded for treason at Winchester. His feastday is August 31. Incorruptibility of his body was claimed, miraculous cures were reported on patients, and a Norman monk was struck dead when deriding him. A cult was formed calling him a traitor to the Normans and a martyr to the Anglo Saxons. It is said he completed the Lord's Prayer at his beheading, the last sentence while his head was severed and flying thru the air.

SAINTS DAILY
Kings, Queens, Popes, Princes, Princesses, Emperors, Hermits, Bishops

DAILY SAINTS WHOSE ANCESTRY IS KNOWN

Saints of September

FEAST DAY	SAINT	COUNTRY	BORN	DIED
1-Sep	Saint Nivard	France		c 670
3-Sep	Saint Hereswitha	Wessex		690
3-Sep	Saint Cuthburga	England		c. 725
4-Sep	Saint Ida d'Autun of Herzfeld	England	770	840
7-Sep	Saint Alchmund	Britain		781
7-Sep	Saint Madelberta	England		7th
7-Sep	Saint Clodoald	France	c 520	560
8-Sep	Saint Adela	Flanders	1009	1077
9-Sept	Blessed Seraphina Sforza	Italy	1432	1478
9-Sep	Saint Isaac Pahlav the Great	Armenia	351	438
10-Sep	Saint Edward Ambrose Barlow	England	1585	1681
11-Sep	Saint Deniol	Wales	c 535	584
12-Sep	Saint Eanswida	England		c. 640
12-Sep	Saint Eanswythe	England		640
16-Sep	Saint Ludmilla of Bohemia	Bohemia		
16-Sep	Saint Edith of Wilton	England		984

SAINTS DAILY
Kings, Queens, Popes, Princes, Princesses, Emperors, Hermits, Bishops

257

DAILY SAINTS WHOSE ANCESTRY IS KNOWN

16-Sep	Saint Victor III	Italy	c 1027	1087
18-Sep	Saint Richardis	Franks		c 895
20-Sep	Saint Vincent Madelgaire de Hainault	Hainault	635	677
21-Sep	Saint Michael of Cheringov	Russia		1246
21-Sep	Saint Mathew Apostle	Israel		1st
23-Sep	Saint Linus Bishop of Rome	Rome		c 76
28-Sep	Saint Wenceslaus I Vaclav	England	907	10th
28-Sep	Saint Blesilla	Rome	363	383
28-Sep	Saint Eustochium Julia	Rome	c 368	491
30-Sep	Saint Gregory the Enlightened	Armenia	c 240	c 326

TABLE TEN SAINTS OF SEPTEMBER

September 1   *Saint Nivard*

Country: France   **Date:** c. 670

Family: Father: Sigebert III   Mother: Immachilde
Spouse: Unknown   Siblings: Bilichild

Biography: Saint Nivard was Archbishop of Reims. His father was Sigebert III and he was brother in law of Childeric II of Austrasia the Frankish King. He was enshrined in Hautvilliers Abbey, the abbey that he restored.

SAINTS DAILY
Kings, Queens, Popes, Princes, Princesses, Emperors, Hermits, Bishops

DAILY SAINTS WHOSE ANCESTRY IS KNOWN

September 3   Saint Hereswitha

Country: England   **Date:** d 690

Family: Parents: Father- Hereric   Mother- Breguswith   Husband: Anna King of East Anglia
Children: Saint Sexburga, Saint Ethelreda   Siblings: Saint Hilda

Ancestry: Unknown.

Descendents: Sainted descendants include Saint Adele of Blois, Saint Louis IX of France, Saint Fernando III of Spain, Saint Cunigunda of Luxemborg, Saint Leopold III of Austria, Saint Henry II of Germany, and Saint David and Saint Margaret of Scotland. Royal descendents include King Edward III Plantagenet of England, King of Naples Charles II, King of France Philip IV, and King of Scotland William the Lion. Also Casimir King of Poland, Alphonso Enriquez I King of Portugal and Henry IV Holy Roman Emperor of Germany.

Biography: Saint Hereswitha was a benedictine princess of Northumbria, England, sister of St. Hilda and mother of Sts. Sexburga, Withburga, and Ethelburga. Hereswitha spent the last years of her life as a Benedictine in Chelles, France, she was a widow.

September 3   Saint Cuthburga

Country: Wessex England   **Date:** d. c. 725

Family: Father: Prince of Wessex Cenred   Mother: Unknown
Spouse: Unknown   Siblings: Prince of Wessex Ingild; Ina of Saxe-Wessex; Quenburga Saint

Ancestors: King Of Wessex Caedwalla, and Wig and Woden.

SAINTS DAILY
Kings, Queens, Popes, Princes, Princesses, Emperors, Hermits, Bishops

DAILY SAINTS WHOSE ANCESTRY IS KNOWN

Branches of the Tree: This branch of the tree is the rulers of Wessex

Biography: Saint Cuthburga as the daughter of the Prince of Wessex Cenred and sister to Saint Quenburga. She was the first abbess of Wimborne. She wanted to become a nun so she left her husband. She joined under St. Hildelitha at Barking. About 705 or a short time after a double monastery was founded by Saint Cuthburga and her sister, St. Quenburga. This monastery had a band of missionary nuns set out for Germany where they worked with Saint Boniface. Saint Cuthburga died c 725, and she is known for being hard on herself but kind to others.

September 4   Saint   Ida (Redburga) d'Autun of Herzfeld

Date: 770 - 840

Family:
Parents: Father- Makhir (Theuderic) (Thierry d'Autun) Mother- Auda Aldane Martel
Husband: Egbert I (King of England - 802-839)
Children: Æthelwulf (King of England - 839-858)

Ancestry:
Saint Arnulf Bishop of Metz is an ancestor, also many Kings of Persia are ancestors. Pepin is an ancestor, as is the family of Martel.
This line also goes back to Zerah. Also King David of Judah and Israel is an ancestor thru Joseph of Arimathea and to the line of Nathan King David's son.

Descendents:
Saint Leopold III, Saint Louis IX, Saint Margaret of Scotland, Saint Irene of Hungary, and Saint Isabella of Aragon are all

SAINTS DAILY
Kings, Queens, Popes, Princes, Princesses, Emperors, Hermits, Bishops

DAILY SAINTS WHOSE ANCESTRY IS KNOWN

descendents. King of Naples Charles II and King of England Edward III and King of France Louis VIII are all descendents.

Biography:
Noblewoman of Charlemagne's court, widow, d. 813 Founder of a Monastery and Great-granddaughter of Charles Martel. King Egbert of England was her husband but she was widowed at a young age. She moved from her estate at Hofstadt, and founded in Westphalia the convent of Herzfeld. Warin, her son, also became a monk at Corvey. Feast day: September 4

September 7 Saint Madelberta

Country: England **Date:** 7th Century

Family: Father: Vincent Madelgaire de Hainault Saint   Mother: Waldetrudis de Loomis Saint   Spouse: Unknown   Siblings: Adeltrude de Hainault Saint; Adeltrudis Saint; Dentlin Saint

Ancestors: Only one generation is known and is listed above.

Branches of the Tree: Saint Adeltrude Descendents are known.

Biography: Saint Madelberta was the daughter of two Saints, Vincent and Waldetrudis, and had three siblings all Saints. Saint Madelberta was a Benedictine abbess. Saint Aldegund was her aunt and she founded Maubeuge. This was where Saint Madelberta took the veil, and her aunt who founded the abbey was her superior. In 697 she became abbess.

September 7 Saint Clodald

Country: Orleans France **Date:** b. 520 d. 560

Family: Father: Clodomir Of Orleans King   Mother: Guntheuque Queen

SAINTS DAILY
Kings, Queens, Popes, Princes, Princesses, Emperors, Hermits, Bishops

DAILY SAINTS WHOSE ANCESTRY IS KNOWN

Spouse: None Siblings: Theobald Of Orleans Prince, Gonthaire Of Orleans Prince

Ancestors: Grandmother is Saint Clothilde Burgundy and Grandfather is Clovis King of the Franks. Saint Arnulf of Metz is an Ancestor. Clovis has the Israelite Joseph as an ancestor. This ancestry also goes back to Zerah. Also King David of Judah and Israel is an ancestor thru Joseph of Arimathea and to the line of Nathan King David's son.

Branches of the Tree: Early Franks, with Saint Clothilde, and Bishop of Metz Arnulf very close in the tree.

Biography: St. Cloud the youngest son of King Clodomir of Orleans of Orleans was a grandson of King Clovis of the Franks. He was born in 524. Queen of the Franks St. Clotilda raise all Saint, Cloud, and his brothers. She was their grandmother. At the ages of nine and 10. The brothers Theodoald and Gunther were slain by their uncle, Clotaire King of the Franks. St. Cloud survived by being sent to France to Providence. Saint Severinus accepted him as a disciple and he became a hermit. Near Paris, he remained at Nogent. St. Cloud became a place name of Nogent.

September 7   *Saint Alchmund*
Country: England   **Date:** 781

Family: Father: Alchred Of Northumbria King Of Northumbria   Mother: Osgyfu
Spouse: Unknown   Siblings: Osred II Of Northumbria King Of Northumbria

Ancestors: Ancestors include Odin and Frigg and the Kings of Bernicia.

Branches of the Tree: This branch of the tree is where the kings of Northumbria are. Going up to the Kings of Bernicia you can go down to the Kings of Scotland.

SAINTS DAILY
Kings, Queens, Popes, Princes, Princesses, Emperors, Hermits, Bishops

DAILY SAINTS WHOSE ANCESTRY IS KNOWN

Biography: Saint Alcmund was a bishop and miracle worker. Saint Wilfrid established the see of Hexham in Northumberland, England, in 767 Saint Alcmund succeeded to this see. He was bishop until his death in 781. Near Saint Acca beside the Hexham church he was buried, but the Danes invaded and the grave was forgotten. A parishioner saw Saint Alcmund appear in the eleventh century, telling him to move the bones. He told Alfred the sacrist of Durham but Alfred kept one bone when the grave was opened. The remains of Saint Alcmund could not be moved until that one bone was replaced. In 1154 all the Hexham Saints were gathered into one shrine as Hexham was again invaded. Finally in 1296 when Scottish Highlanders attached the region the remains were destroyed.

September 8 *Saint Kingsmark*

Country: Wales **Date:** d. 612

Family: Father: Meirchaum Gul   Spouse: Nefyn daughter of Saint Brychan II (Also listed as Saint Nyfain the daughter of Saint Brychan) Siblings: unknown Children: Urien who married Morganna le Faye twin to Efdryll. (See Saint Nyfain's Children)

Ancestors: Saint Ceneu of Britain son of King Coel

Branches of the Tree: This is the branch very near King Arthur of the Round Table.

Biography: Saint Kingsmark lived in Wales where he is venerated. However his origin was Scottish as he is refered to as a Scottish Cheiftain.

SAINTS DAILY
Kings, Queens, Popes, Princes, Princesses, Emperors, Hermits, Bishops

DAILY SAINTS WHOSE ANCESTRY IS KNOWN

September 8 Saint Adela of Flanders

Country: Flanders   *Date:* c 1009- 1077

Family: Parents: Father- Robert II of France Mother- Constance De Toulouse   Husband: Count Baldwin IV of Flanders   Children: Maud of Flanders

Ancestors: Ancestry past parentage is unknown.

Descendents: Edward I Longshanks King of England. Edward III Plantagenet, and Edward IV Plantagenet of England.

Biography: Adela was the wife of Count Baldwin IV of Flanders. She was a Benedictine noblewoman. When the count died, she entered the Benedictines, receiving the habit from Pope Alexander II. Adela served as a nun until her death, retiring to the Benedictine convent near Ypres.

September 9 Blessed Seraphina Sforza

Feastday: Sept 9   Date: 1432-1478

Family: Father: Guidantonio Montefeltro Lord Of Urbino
     Mother: Rengarda Malatesta
Spouse: Alexander Sforza   Siblings: Duke Federico Of Montefeltro-Urbino

Country: Italy

Ancestors: Eight Generations the descendent of King Edward I of England. Thus King David, the five Israelites Joseph, Benjamin, Judah, Levi, and Zebulon are ancestors.

Branches of the Tree: This is the branch of the tree of the Dukes of Montefletro and Urbino Italy.

SAINTS DAILY
 Kings, Queens, Popes, Princes, Princesses, Emperors, Hermits, Bishops

264

DAILY SAINTS WHOSE ANCESTRY IS KNOWN

Biography: She was orphaned as a child and raised in the household of her Uncle Prince Colonna. She married Alexander Sforza at sixteen who was the duke of Pesaro. Her husband had an affair and so tried to poison blessed Seraphina he drove her from his home so she joined the poor clares in 1457 at Pesaro taking the name Seraphina. (she was christened Sueva). She lived a life of great holiness and became abbess in 1475. Pope Penedict XIV approved her cult in 1754.

September 9   Saint Isaac Pahlav

Country: Armenia   *Date:* b. 351- d. 438

Family: Parents: Father-Narses I Nerseh Pahlav Saint b. 335 Mother- Sandukht
Wife: Unknown   Children: Hamazasp

Ancestry: Saint Gregory the Enlightened is an ancestor. Further ancestry is not known.

Descendents: Saint Fernando III is a descendent. Also Edward I Longshanks King of England is a descendent. Edward III and Edward IV Plantagenet are also descendents, with Thomas Prince of England. Edward Stafford 3rd Duke of Buckingham is also a descendent. Also William X Duke of Aquitane. Konstantinos Emperor of Byzantium is a descendent.

Biography: Saint Isaac the Great was the son of St. Nerses I of Armenia. Isaac the Great whose feast day is September 9 became a monk. He studied at Constantinople, married, and on the early death of his wife became a monk. He was appointed Catholicos of Armenia in 390 and secured from Constantinople recognition of the metropolitan rights of the Armenian Church, thus terminating its long dependence on the Church of Caesarea in Cappodocia. He at once began to reform the Armenian Church.

SAINTS DAILY
Kings, Queens, Popes, Princes, Princesses, Emperors, Hermits, Bishops

DAILY SAINTS WHOSE ANCESTRY IS KNOWN

He enforced Byzantine canon law, encouraged monasticism, ended the practice of married bishops, fought Persian paganism, and built churches and schools. He supported St. Mesrop in his creation of an Armenian alphabet, and was responsible for establishing a national liturgy and the beginnings of Armenian literature. He also helped to promote the translation of the Bible and the works of the Greek and Syrian doctors into Armenian. He was the founder of the Armenian Church and is sometimes called Sahak in Armenia.

When the Persians conquered part of his territory he was driven into retirement in 428 but returned at an advanced age to rule again from his See at Ashtishat, where he died in the year 439.

The Armenian Saints Isaac, Nerses and Gregory have a unique line of descent that leads to the Emperors of the Byzantine Empire. This line is pretty isolated from the known royal lines of Europe, and joins the existing royalty lines with Edward I Longshanks of England around the year 1000. The line is from the Mamokonian house and contains William Count of Toulouse and his wife Konstantinos. William Count of Toulouse will be mentioned again at the chapter that concerns the years 700-800. Saint Louis IX and Saint Fernando are also Descendents.

September 10   *Saint Ambrose*
Barlow Venerable

Country: England   **Date:** b. 1585   d. 10 Sep 1641

Family: Father: Alexander Barlowe   Mother: Mary Brereton
Spouse: Unknown   Siblings: Unknown

Ancestors: Henry Earl Of Northumberland King Of Scotland son of King David the Saint of Scotland who was son of Saint Margaret of Scotland. Saint Margaret ancestors include Charlemagne, Joseph of Arimathea, and Saint Helena of Rome. Also King David of Judah and Israel is an ancestor thru Nathan

SAINTS DAILY
Kings, Queens, Popes, Princes, Princesses, Emperors, Hermits, Bishops

DAILY SAINTS WHOSE ANCESTRY IS KNOWN

his son. King Solomon of Israel and Judah is also an ancestor. Sainted Ancestry includes Saint Ethelbert, Saint Arnulf, Saint Itta, Saint Sigebert, Saint Dagobert, Saint Beggue, Saint Liuthwin, Saint Bathildis, Saint Sexburga, Saint Clodulf, Blessed Pepin, Saint Matilda, Saint Elgiva, Saint Edgar, Saint Henry II, Saint Cunigunda, and Saint Stephen.

Branches of the Tree: This branch will go back many generations until it finds the Kings and Queens of Scotland.

Biography: Fourth of fourteen children of Sir Alexander Barlow, and christened Edward, he was born in Barlow Hall, Manchester England and brought up as a protestant. He was converted to Catholicism, went to Douai in 1614 and studied at Valladolid, Spain as well, then joined the Benedictines at St. Grefory's in Douai, taking the name Ambrose in 1615. He became ordained in 1617 and engaged in pastoral work in Lancashire England. Arrested four times in the next two and a half decades each time he was released. In 1641 when priests were ordered from England or be labeled traitors and suffer the consequences, he stayed and was arrested on Easter of that year. When he refused to discontinue his priestly duties if released he was condemned to be executed. In Lancaster on September 10 he was hanged, disemboweled and quartered a week after he had been named prior of Canterbury. He was canonized by Pope Paul VI in 1970 as one of the Forty Martyrs of England and Wales.

September 11   *Saint Deinol*

Feastday: September 11   Date: 584

Family: Father: Dynod Bwr König Von South Pennines
        Mother: Dwywai ferch Llaennog
Spouse: Unknown   Siblings: Saint Cynwl

Country: Great Britain

SAINTS DAILY
Kings, Queens, Popes, Princes, Princesses, Emperors, Hermits, Bishops

DAILY SAINTS WHOSE ANCESTRY IS KNOWN

Ancestors: Saint Gwenillian ferch Brychan is an ancestor of this Saint. Pabo Post Prydyn King of the Pennines Saint is his Grandfather.

Branches of the Tree: Cadwaladr Fendigaid, King of Gwynedd, Saint is a descendent of Pabo Post Pryden. This is the area of the tree around King Arthur and the Knights of the Round Table.

Biography: Saint Deinol was the Bishop of Bangor, Wales. The cathedral and other regional parishes bear his name. He is also called Daniel. He came of a Strathclyde family. Saint Deinol founded the monastery of Bangor Fawr. This monstaery was located on the Menai Straits. He also founded a monastery called Bangor Iscoed on the Dee. He was consecrated to be a bishop by either St. Dyfig, St Teilo, or St David. Saint David sent Saint Deinol into Gaul to fetch a bishop to help combat a recrudescence of Pelagianism. There are a number of Miracles attributed to Saint Deinol. He died and was buried at Ynys Ynlli, now called Bardsey. His feast is kept in the diocese of Menevia.

September 12 *Saint Eanswida*

Country: England   **Date:** 680

Family: Father: Eadbald Kent King Kent   Mother: Emma Austrasia
Spouse: Unknown   Siblings: Earconbert Kent King Kent

Ancestors:. Nobles and Kings of Kent; Saint Ethelbert who converted Kent to Christianity thru his wife Saint Bertha, who is of the Franks.

Branches of the Tree This branch of the tree is the Kings of Kent and the Franks.

SAINTS DAILY
 Kings, Queens, Popes, Princes, Princesses, Emperors, Hermits, Bishops

DAILY SAINTS WHOSE ANCESTRY IS KNOWN

Biography: Saint Eanswida is sometimes called Eanswith. She is depicted as a crowned nun holding a church or a fish. King of Kent Eadbald was her father, and her Grandfather was Saint Ethelbert. She founded a convent at Foldestone in Kent, about 630. Saint Eanswida refused to marry a pagan Northumbrian prince and so founded her convent. She died on August 31, the remainder of her life spent in her convent. In 1885 her relics were discovered when the convent church was restored. This church had been destroyed by Danes.

September 12   Saint Eanswythe
Country: Kent England   **Date:** 640

Family: Father: Eadbald (King of Kent - 616-640) Mother: Emma de Neustria
Spouse: Unknown   Siblings: Earcombryth (Earconbert) (Erconbert)

Ancestors: Saint Eanswythe has Saint Ethelbert and Saint Bertha as Grandparents. Saint Ethelbert of Kent ancestry traces back to Zerah thru the Kings of Troy. His wife Saint Bertha also is traced back to the lines of the Frankish Kings to Zerah whose father is Judah. Saint Bertha's ancestor is Saint Clotilde who converted the Frankish King Clovis to Christianity. Also included is Joseph of Arimathea. Also King David of Judah and Israel is an ancestor thru Nathan his son. His wife Saint Bertha also is traced back to the lines of the Frankish Kings to Zerah whose father is Judah. Saint Bertha's ancestor is Saint Clotilde who converted the Frankish King Clovis to Christianity. Also included is Joseph of Arimathea. Also King David of Judah and Israel is an ancestor thru Nathan his son.

Branches of the Tree: This vicinity of the Branch is closest to the Saints Ethelbert and Bertha.

SAINTS DAILY
Kings, Queens, Popes, Princes, Princesses, Emperors, Hermits, Bishops

DAILY SAINTS WHOSE ANCESTRY IS KNOWN

Biography: Saint Eanswythe was the daughter of a King of Kent King Eadbald. Not much else is known of Saint Eanswythe.

September 16 Saint Ludmilla of Bohemia

Country: Bohemia *Date:* unknown
Patron: Czechoslovakia

Family: Parents: Father- Slavibor   Mother- Unknown
Husband: Borziwas Przemysl Duke of Bohemia b. c. 842
Children: Vratislav (Uratislas) Duke of Bohemia

Ancestry: Her father is known as Slavibor in Melnik, Czechoslovakia

Descendents: Descendents include King of England Edward I Longshanks. Also King Edward III Plantagenent of England.

Biography: Daughter of a Slavic prince, Saint Ludmila married Duke Borivoy of Bohemia. She followed him into the Church. Building a church near Prajue and trying to force Christianity on their subjects they did not succeed. When Borivoy died, his sons Spytihinev and Ratislav, succeeded him, and Ratislav had married Drahomira. Ludmila brought to the latter son Venceslaus. When Ratislav died, Drahovira became the regent, and kept Wenceslaus from Ludmila. Drahomira reportedly caused Saint Ludmila to be strangled at Tetin. Her Feastday is September 16th.

SAINTS DAILY
Kings, Queens, Popes, Princes, Princesses, Emperors, Hermits, Bishops

DAILY SAINTS WHOSE ANCESTRY IS KNOWN

September 16   *Saint Edith of Wilton*
Country: England   **Date:** 984

Family: Father: Edgar "the Peaceable" King of England Saint Mother: Elfrida Spouse: Unknown Siblings: Aethelred II "The Unready"; Edward The Martyr Saint

Ancestors: Saint Edgar's ancestors include his mother Saint Elgiva, four generations previous Saint Alfred. Also included is Joseph of Arimathea. Also King David of Judah and Israel is an ancestor thru Nathan his son. King Solomon of Israel and Judah is also an ancestor.

Branches of the Tree: This is the branch of the tree of the English Kings.

Biography: Saint Edith of Wilton was sister to Saint Edward the Martyr and the daughter of King Edgar of England and Wulfrida. She was brought as a very young child to Abbey of Wilton being born at Kensing, England. Her mother brought her and became a nun there and eventually Abbess. Saint Edith became a nun when fifteen, and was offered three abbacies by her father, but refused each one. When her half-brother King Saint Edward died she refused to become Queen. She built the Church of Saint Denis at Wilton.

September 16   *Saint Victor III Pope*
Country: Italy   *Date:* d. 1125

Family: Father: Landolfo V Principe di Benevento Mother: Maria
Spouse: Unknown   Siblings: Maria (Marie) di Benevento

Ancestors: Pandulf III. di Capua e di Benevento and his parents are not known.

SAINTS DAILY
Kings, Queens, Popes, Princes, Princesses, Emperors, Hermits, Bishops

DAILY SAINTS WHOSE ANCESTRY IS KNOWN

Branches of the Tree: The Grandfather of Saint Victor III Pope is the fifth generation ancestor of Ramon Berenger III. de Barcelona, who is five generations the ancestor of Isabella of Aragon Saint

Biography: Saint Victor III was the only son of Duke Dauferius Benevento. He was born with the name Daufar and resisted efforts to have him marry. In 1047 when his father was killed in battle he became a hermit. After being forced to return home by his family he escaped a year later by his family and entered La Cava Monastery. He transferred to St. Sophia Abbey at Benevento, where the name Desiderius was given to him. He wandered about for a few years, a hermit in the Abruzzi, study of medicine at Salernok and some time at an island monastery. He helped to negotiate a peace with the Normans for Pope Leo IX in 1053. In 1054 he joined the court of Victor II in Florence. Later the same year he joined the Benedictines at Monte Cassino, and was elected abbot designate in 1057, and was on his way to Constantinople as papal legate when Pope St. Stephen died. He was installed as abbot in 1058. He rebuilt Monte Cassino and developed it into one of the great centers of learning and culture in Europe, noted for the strict rule of its monks and the art there as well as the magnificence of his buildings. On May 24 1086 he was elected Pope to succeed Gregory and was forcibly vested on May 24, 1086 with the name Victor III. Four days later he was forced to flee to Monte Cassino from the imperial prefect and was not consecrated until May 9, 1087, at which time Buibert of Ravenna (antipope Clement III), who had been occupying the city, was temporarily driven out by Norman Troops. He repeatedly attempted to expel and excommunicate the Anti Pope and finally died on September 16 with a reign of only four months. His cult was approved by Pope Leo XIII in 1887.

SAINTS DAILY
Kings, Queens, Popes, Princes, Princesses, Emperors, Hermits, Bishops

DAILY SAINTS WHOSE ANCESTRY IS KNOWN

September 17   *Saint Hildegard*

Country: France   *Date:* d 1179

Family: Parents: Sibling of Blessed Jutta Husband: unknown Children: Unknown

Ancestry: Nothing past the grandfather is known

Biography: Saint Hildegard had fragile health as a child. Saint Hildegard was cared for by her aunt blessed Jutta. Blessed Jutta formed a community of Nuns, which Saint Hildegarde joined. She became the prioress of the house when Blessed Jutta died in 1136. Saint Hildegarde moved the group to Rupertsburg and established another convent at Eibengen around the year 1165. Saint Hildegarde was known for visions and prophecies, which she recorded at her spiritual directors requested. They were set down in a work called Scivias and approved by the arch bishop of Mainz and Pope Eugenius III after Saint Bernard of Clairvaux recommended it. Saint Hildegarde corresponded with four popes, two emperors, King Henry II of England and famous clergy. She put her talents to work in a quest for true justice and peace. Her pronouncements attracted the fancy of populace, and she wrote on many subjects. She wrote commentaries on the Athanasian Cree, the Rule of Saint Benedict, the Gospels, and the Lives of the Saints as well as a medical book on the well-being of the body. Saint Hildegard is one of the greatest figures in the 12th Century and the first of the great German mystics as well as a poet, a physician and a prophetess. She has been compared to Dante and to William Blake. This remarkable woman of God died on September 17, 1179. She has been never formally canonized, but her name was inserted in the Roman Martyrology in the fifteenth century and miracles were reported at her death.

SAINTS DAILY
Kings, Queens, Popes, Princes, Princesses, Emperors, Hermits, Bishops

DAILY SAINTS WHOSE ANCESTRY IS KNOWN

September 18   Saint Richardis
Country: France   **Date:** d 895

Family: Parents: Father- Budwine of Italy Mother- Richilde of Arles Husband: Charles the Fat
Children: Rothilde De Neustria

Ancestry: Saint Richardis married Charles The Fat and four generations previous to Saint Richardis is her ancestor Charlemange thru Charles the Fat. Her father is known and her mothers line is known for four generations.

Biography: Wife of Emperor Charles the Fat and so empress, Saint Richardis was the daughter of the count of Alsace. She served the future emperor for nineteen years until the Bishop Lietword of Vercelli reportedly was infidel with Saint Richardis. After being accused Saint Richardis successfully endured the painful ordeal of fire, but after the ordeal left Charles. She lived as a nun at Hohenburg, Germany and the Andlau Abbey. She remained at Andlau until her death.

September 19   Saint Goeric
Country: France   **Date:** d. 647

Family: Father: Gamardus Babo Mother: Unknown Spouse: Unknown Siblings: Godin Cahors; Doda; Desiderius Bishop of Albi; Radbertus Children: unknown

Ancestors: Roman Ancestor Avitus; Sidonious Apolonarius; Flavius Africanus Syagrius \\ Consul

Branches of the Tree: This is the branch of the tree near Saint Leiutwin, and Saint Leger Bishop of Autun.

SAINTS DAILY
Kings, Queens, Popes, Princes, Princesses, Emperors, Hermits, Bishops

DAILY SAINTS WHOSE ANCESTRY IS KNOWN

Biography: Bishop of Metz. Saint Goeric succeeded Saint Arnulf as Bishop. Other names he is refered to as include Abbo or Goericus. Saint Goeric may have been a courtier at the court of King Dagobert, who became blind and was cured miraculously of his blindness. He is credited as becoming a priest and bishop and founding a convent.

September 20   Saint Vincent Madelgaire de Hainault

Country: Hainault   *Date:* d 677

Family: Parents: Father- Madelgaire de Hainault   Mother- Onuguera
Wife: Wautrude de Loomis   Children: Adeltrude de Hainault

Ancestry: Only one generation is known and is listed above.

Descendents: Descendents include Saint Adelaide of Italy, Saint Anglibert, Saint Lazlo of Hungary, Saint Irene, Saint Leopold III, Saint Louis IX, Saint Hedwig, Saint Isabel of Aragon, and Saint Nithard the Cronicler.
Royal Descendents include King of Naples Charles II, King of France Louis VIII, Alphonso IV of Portugal, and King Edward III Plantagenet of England.

Biography: Born at Strepy les Binches, Hainault, Belgium. Benedictine abbot, sometimes called Madelgarius and Madelgaire. About 635 he wed St. Waldetrudis by whom he fathered four children, all of whom were later venerated as saints: Aldegundis, Landericus, Dentlin, and Madalberta. He went to Ireland and returned with several Irish monks to serve as missionaries to the pagan areas of the kingdom on behalf of the Frankish king Dagobert I (r. 629-639). In 643, his wife entered a convent, and Madelgarus joined the Benedictines at Haumont under the name Vincent. He also founded a monastery at Hautmont, France, in 642. After serving as abbot at Haumont, he

SAINTS DAILY
Kings, Queens, Popes, Princes, Princesses, Emperors, Hermits, Bishops

DAILY SAINTS WHOSE ANCESTRY IS KNOWN

established another monastery on his estate at Soignies, Belgium, where he died on July 14.

September 21   *Saint Mathew*

Country: Israel   **Patron:** Bankers Accountants Bookkeepers; Customs Officers; Security Guards; Tax Collectors

Family: Father: unknown   Mother: Mary Alphaews   Spouse: Unknown   Siblings: Saint Judas the apostle, Saint Simon the apostle, Saint Joseph Barabas the apostle

Ancestors: Saint Joseph of Arimathea is an ancestor. A little know fact of the biblical character of Joseph of Arimathea is that he is the son of Mathat, who is in the line of Nathan that is listed in the New Testament book of Luke. His ancestors then must be King David of Israel and Judah, and so the Israelites Joseph, Levi, Zebulon, and Judah. Anna married Saint Joseph of Arimathea, and her ancestry is an unbroken male line to Levi the Israelite. Saint Joseph of Arimathea's mother may have been the daughter of Eleazor, who was of the Davidic line of Solomon. Eleazor was the Grandfather of Joseph who married the Virgin Mary and this line is listed in the Gospel of Mathew. The Israelite Benjamin was an ancestor of King Davids wife Maacah (Sauls daughter) whose line married in the line from Solomon joined by the marriage of Reheboam to Maacah. Therefore Saint Joseph of Arimathea has five Israelites as ancestors.

Branches of the Tree : This is a branch of the tree that has Saint Joseph of Arimathea in it. He is the Father of Cleopas who is the Father of Mary Alphaws. He is three generations the ancestor of Saint James. This line also marries Anna Arimathea who is the daughter of Joseph of Arimathea.

Biography: Saint Mathew was an apostle of the lord. He was one of the twelve disciples. He wrote the Gospel of Mathew. His mother was Mary and his grandfather was Cleopas, who was the son of Saint Joseph of Arimathea. He was called Levi.

SAINTS DAILY
Kings, Queens, Popes, Princes, Princesses, Emperors, Hermits, Bishops

DAILY SAINTS WHOSE ANCESTRY IS KNOWN

September 21   Saint Michael of Chernigov

Feastday: Unknown   Date: c.1246

Family: Father: Vsevolod III Prince of Kiev
Mother: Daughter of Poland
Spouse: Unknown   Siblings: Unknown

Country: Russia

Ancestors: Ancestors include the Kings of Poland, Casimir II and his ancestry as well as Saint Vladimir and his ancestry.

Branches of the Tree : This the branch of the tree that has Saint Vladimir and Saint Olga. This is the branch of the tree of West Europe and East Asia, or Russia.

Biography: Very little is known of this Saint other than what is in the lineage relationships found in Saints in the Tree.

September 23 Saint Linus Bishop of Rome

Country: England   **Date:** c 67

Family: Father: Caradoc Ap Bran King Of Britain   Mother: Eurgain
Spouse: Unknown   Siblings: Gladys (Claudia) Britain; Eurgen Of Llan Ilid Saint; Cyllin (Coellyn or Cyllinus) ap Caradog Saint

Ancestors: Ancestors that were the Kings of Siluria. Generations previous to this they were the Kings of Britain. The line then goes back to Zerah, whose father is Judah. This line also marries Anna Arimathea who is the daughter of Joseph of Arimathea. A little know fact of the biblical character of Joseph of Arimathea is that he is the son of Mathat, who is in the line of Nathan that is listed in the New Testament book of Luke. So

SAINTS DAILY
Kings, Queens, Popes, Princes, Princesses, Emperors, Hermits, Bishops

DAILY SAINTS WHOSE ANCESTRY IS KNOWN

Saint Cyllin is descended from the Davidic line of Nathan and so from Judah thru Perez, and also as previously mentioned thru Judah's son Zerah. Saint Cyllin is the Ancestor of Saint Helen of the Cross. Israelites Judah, Levi, Zebulon and Joseph are all ancestors of King David.

Branches of the Tree: This is the branch of the tree right on top of Saint Paul, Rufus Pudens (husband of Gladys).

Biography: He is mentioned in the second letter to Timothy. The second pope was Saint Linus about the years 67. St. Peter gave the papal seat to Saint Linus according to Saint Ireanus. He is mentioned in the second letter to Timothy.

September 26   Saint Colman of Elo

Country: Ireland   **Date:** d. 612

Family: Parents: Sibling to Saint Columba
   Spouse: Unknown   Siblings: unknown

Ancestors: Fergus is an Ancestor, and the Monarchs of Ireland are ancestors.

Branches of the Tree: Saint Colman was nephew to Saint Columba.

Biography: Also called Colman Lann Elo. He was the nephew of Saint Columba born about 555 at Glenelly, Tyrone, Ireland. Saint Colman was an Abbot and Bishop of Connor. He built a monastery at Offaly and the Muckamore Abbey was founded by Saint Colman. He wrote the Alphabet of Devotion (book about devotion that Saint Colman was author of), and died at Lynally on December 26.

SAINTS DAILY
Kings, Queens, Popes, Princes, Princesses, Emperors, Hermits, Bishops

DAILY SAINTS WHOSE ANCESTRY IS KNOWN

September 28   *Saint Wenceslaus*

Country: Armenia   **Date:** 907- 10th Century
   Patron: Bohemia; Brewers; Czechoslovakia; Moravia

Family: Father: Vratislav (Uratislas) Bohemia Duke Of
   Mother: Drahomira Von Stoder
Spouse: Unknown   Siblings: Boleslav I The Cruel King Of Bohemia

Ancestors: Saint Ludmilla is an ancestor.

Branches of the Tree: Bohemia is in this branch of the Tree in the vicinity of Saint Ludmilla.

Biography: Saint Wenceslaus was born near Prague. He was also known by the name Vaclav. Saint Ludmilla was his grandmother and by her he was taught Christianity. Saint Ludmilla and the Duke of Bohemia Vratislav (Saint Weneslaus father) were murdered by the Magyars, and Drahomira, who were anti-christian. They took over the government. After a coup in 922 Saint Wenceslaus was declared the new ruler. Saint Wenceslaus encouraged Christianity. His brother, Boleslaus joined a group of noble Czech dissenters when Wenceslaus's son was born. Because Boleslaus was no longer successor to the throne, they invited Wenceslaus to a religious festival. On his was there they trapped and killed him on the way to Mass. He is the patron saint of Bohemia. His Feast day is September 28.

September 28   *Saint Blesilla*
Country: Italy (Rome)   *Date:* 419

Family: Father: Julius Toxotius, Roman senator
   Mother: Saint Paula

SAINTS DAILY
Kings, Queens, Popes, Princes, Princesses, Emperors, Hermits, Bishops

DAILY SAINTS WHOSE ANCESTRY IS KNOWN

Spouse: Unknown   Siblings: Saint Eustachium Julia; Paulina; Rufina; Toxotius

Ancestors: Very few generations known

Branches of the Tree: Go up the tree four generations and down ten to find Saint Arnulf Bishop of Metz.

Biography: Saint Blesilla was the daughter of Saint Paula and the Roman Senator Julius Toxotius. She had four siblings, one of which was a saint, Eustachium Julia.

September 28 Saint Eustochium Julia

Country: Italy (Rome)   **Date:** 419

Family: Father: Julius Toxotius, Roman senator
            Mother: Saint Paula
Spouse: Unknown   Siblings: Saint Blesilla; Paulina; Rufina; Toxotius

Ancestors: Very few generations known

Branches of the Tree: Go up the tree four generations and down ten to find Saint Arnulf Bishop of Metz.

Biography: She took her veil in 382 from St. Jerome, and was born c. 370. She stayed with her mother the third daughter of St. Paula. Concerning the Keeping of virginity was written for her by Saint Jerome in 384. She was involved with Saint Jerome while he translated the bible in Bethlehem Israel having traveled there with her mother. Three convents were founded by Saint Jerome in Bethlehem and Eustochium became abbess of all three in 404. Eustochium never recovered from the experience of having marauders destroy the convent. She died in Bethlehem.

SAINTS DAILY
Kings, Queens, Popes, Princes, Princesses, Emperors, Hermits, Bishops

DAILY SAINTS WHOSE ANCESTRY IS KNOWN

September 29 Saint Leutwinus

Date: b 655

Family:
Parents: Father- Warinus Mother- Kunza
Wife: Unknown
Children: Rotrude (Chrotude), Duchess Austrasia

Ancestry:
Saint Liuthwin can trace ancestry thru his mother to Saint Arnulf Bishop of Metz and thus to Zerah. Also King David of Judah and Israel is an ancestor thru Nathan his son.

Descendents:
Sainted descendents include Saint Adele of Blois, Saint Adelaide of Italy, Saint Louis IX of France, Saint Fernando III of Spain, Saint Cunigunda of Luxemborg, Saint Leopold III of Austria, Saint Henry II of Germany, Saint Lazlo King of Hungary, Saint Raymond Berenger IV. Saint Edgar King of England and Saint David and Saint Margaret of Scotland. Royal descendents include King Edward III Plantagenet of England, King of Naples Charles II, King of France Philip IV, and King of Scotland William the Lion. Also Casimir King of Poland , Alphonso Enriquez I King of Portugal and Henry IV Holy Roman Emperor of Germany.

Biography:
Benedictine bishop, founder of Mettlach Abbey, Germany. He was the bishop of Trier, Germany.

SAINTS DAILY
Kings, Queens, Popes, Princes, Princesses, Emperors, Hermits, Bishops

DAILY SAINTS WHOSE ANCESTRY IS KNOWN

September 30 Saint Gregory the Enlightened

Country: Armenia　　　　　　**Date:** b 240　d .326

Family:　　Parents: Unknown　Wife: Unknown
Children: Yusik Patriach of the Armenian Church

Ancestry:　　Even parentage is unknown.

Descendents: Saint Fernando III is a descendent. Also Edward I Longshanks King of England is a descendent. Edward III and Edward IV Plantagenet are also descendents, with Thomas Prince of England. Edward Stafford 3rd Duke of Buckingham is also a descendent. Also William X Duke of Aquitane. Konstantinos Emperor of Byzantium is a descendent.

Biography: Surnamed the Illuminator, Gregory the Enlightener is of unknown origins. Anok a Parthian who murdered King Khosrov I or Armenia may be his father, the murder happening when Gregory was a baby. Gregory, smuggled to Caesarea, was baptized, and had two sons after marriage. He was smuggled as the dying Khosrov's ordered to murder the entire family. Tiridates, King Khosrov's son, regained his father's throne, and Gregory was permitted to return. Support of the Armenian Christians and his conversion activities incurred the King's displeasure. Tiridates was converted to Christianity in time by Gregory and the Official religion of Armenia became Christianity. Consecrated bishop of Ashtishat, Gregory set about organizing the Church in Armenia. Evangelization and building a native clergy working untiringly was what kept Gregory busy as bishop. When his son Aristakes was consecrated to the episocopate he set into motion the process that made his See a hereditary position. Gregory then retired to a hermitage on Mount Manyea in Taron and remained there until his death. Miracles and Extravagent legends were attributed to him, many becoming celebrated feasts by the Armenians.

SAINTS DAILY
Kings, Queens, Popes, Princes, Princesses, Emperors, Hermits, Bishops

DAILY SAINTS WHOSE ANCESTRY IS KNOWN

Gregory the Enlightener is considered the apostle of Armenia. Feast day is September 30th.
He is the ancestor of Saint Narses Pahlav.

September 30 *Saint Enghendel*

Country: Wales   **Date:** b 697

Family: Father: Elise   Mother: Unknown
Spouse: Unknown   Siblings: Brochwel Ap Elise

Ancestors: King Coel is an ancestor, and so the lineage will lead to Jose son of Saint Joseph who was heir to the house of David.

Branches of the Tree: This is near the lineage of King Arthur and the Knights of the Round Table

Biography: In Anglesey Wales this Saint is venerated in a church.

SAINTS DAILY
Kings, Queens, Popes, Princes, Princesses, Emperors, Hermits, Bishops

DAILY SAINTS WHOSE ANCESTRY IS KNOWN

Saints of October

FEAST DAY	SAINT	COUNTRY	BORN	DIED
1-Oct	Saint Umbrafael	England		505
1-Oct	Saint Remi	France	730	770
1-Oct	Saint Bavo	France		7th
2-Oct	Saint Leodegar	France	616	679
2-Oct	Saint Thomas de Cantelou	Italy	1218	1282
3-Oct	Saint Hesychius of Vienne	Italy		c. 6th
5-Oct	Saint Apollinaris of Vienne	Rome		520
5-Oct	Saint Galla			c. 550
6-Oct	Saint Ephipanes	France		800
6-Oct	Saint Gregory of Utrecht	Austrasia		800
6-Oct	Blessed Adalbero		1045	1090
7-Oct	Saint Osyth of Penda	Penda	650	700
7-Oct	Saint Osyth	England	650	699
10-Oct	Saint Francis Borgia	Italy		16th
11-Oct	Saint Firminus of Uzes	France		553
12-Oct	Saint Edwin of Wessex	Northumbria	584	633
13-Oct	Saint Comgan	England		8th
13-Oct	Saint Gerald of Aurillac	France		909
13-Oct	Saint Edward the Confessor	England		1066

SAINTS DAILY
Kings, Queens, Popes, Princes, Princesses, Emperors, Hermits, Bishops

284

DAILY SAINTS WHOSE ANCESTRY IS KNOWN

Date	Saint	Place		
16-Oct	Saint Hedwig	Silesia		
16-Oct	Saint Balderic	France		7th
17-Oct	Saint Ethelred	Kent		670
17-Oct	Saint Ethelbricht	Kent		670
18-Oct	Saint Keyna	Wales		
18-Oct	Saint Gwen	Wales		5th
19-Oct	Saint Elfleda	England		1000
19-Oct	Saint Phillip Howard	England	1556	1595
21-Oct	Saint Ursula	Dumonia	305	
22-Oct	Saint Mary Salome	Israel		1st
23-Oct	Saint Anicius Manlius Severius	Italy	480	524
23-Oct	Saint Ignatius of Constaninople		799	877
23-Oct	Saint Ode	Aquitaine		688
23-Oct	Saint Clether	Wales		6th
24-Oct	Saint Maglor	England		6th
26-Oct	Saint Alfred the Great	England		899
26-Oct	Saint Eadfrid	Great Britain		675
26-Oct	Saint Evatistus	Rome		105
28-Oct	Saint Judas Apostle	Israel		1st

TABLE ELEVEN SAINTS OF OCTOBER

SAINTS DAILY
Kings, Queens, Popes, Princes, Princesses, Emperors, Hermits, Bishops

285

DAILY SAINTS WHOSE ANCESTRY IS KNOWN

October 1   *Saint Umbrafael*

Feastday: October 1   Date: b 505

Family: Father: Meliau (Maeliaw) Ap Budig Mother: Aurelia De Broerec
Spouse: Afrella ferch Gwerthefyr Saint Siblings: Amwn Ddu ap Budic , Abbot of Southill, Prince; Meliau (Maeliaw) AP BUDIG Children: Maglor ap Umbraphel Saint

Country: Britain

Ancestors: Saint Umbrafael is related to ancestry. Conan is six generations Saint Melar's ancestor and so Judah, Benjamin, Joseph, Levi, and Zebulon are ancestors, because Conan is a descendent of King David of Judah and Israel.

Branches of the Tree: This branch of the tree is the branch around King Arthur.

Biography: Saint Umbraphel is the Uncle of Saint Sampson Bishop of Dol. There are many Saints Umbraphel is related to, however there is a lack of knowledge about his life. It is known he was the husband of Saint Afrella.

October 1   *Saint Remi*

Feastday: October 1   Date: b. c. 730 d. 14 Jan 770/71

Family: Father: Charles ('the Hammer') Martel (Mayor of the Palace) Mother: Unknown
Spouse: Unknown Siblings: Auda Aldane Martel, Pepin III 'the Short', King of the Franks, Carloman I (Mayor of the Palace of Austrasia)

Country: France (Austrasia)

Ancestors: This Ancestry contains Walter, Sunno, Joshua son of Non, and Joseph the Israelite.

SAINTS DAILY
Kings, Queens, Popes, Princes, Princesses, Emperors, Hermits, Bishops

DAILY SAINTS WHOSE ANCESTRY IS KNOWN

Branches of the Tree: This is the branch that is the Frankish Kings, as Charles Martel is the Descendent of Pharamond, the early King of France. This line eventually leads to the Israelite Joseph and contains Joshua son of Non.

Biography: Very little is known of Saint Remi other than the lineage relationships found in Saints in the Tree. His father was Charles Martel whose sword was used many years latter by Saint Joan de Arc.

October 1 *Saint Bavo*
Feastday: October 1   Date: 7th Century

Family: Father: Pepin of Landen   Mother: Itte
Spouse: Unknown   Siblings: Saint Beggue

Country: France (Austrasia)

Ancestors: Pepin is an ancestor of Charlemagne, and his ancestry is unknown.

Branches of the Tree: This is the branch that is the Frankish Kings, as Charlemange is the Descendent of Pharamond, the early King of France. This line eventually leads to the Israelite Joseph and contains Joshua son of Non.

Biography: Saint Bavo was a nobleman and a famous hermit. He was also called Allowin. Saint Bavo was a native of the part of Brabant called Hesbaye. Saint Amand was heard by Saint Bavo at Ghent, and as Saint Bavo was left a widower he was moved to conversion to God. He gave all his money to the poor and went to the moastery at Ghent. At the monastery from the hand of Saint Amand he received the tonsure. Daily advancement in the fervor of his penance and practice of virtue he accompanied Saint Amand on his missionary journeys in France and Flanders. Saint Bavo had a great mortification of will, and humiliation of his heart and the regor os his austerities

SAINTS DAILY
Kings, Queens, Popes, Princes, Princesses, Emperors, Hermits, Bishops

DAILY SAINTS WHOSE ANCESTRY IS KNOWN

was an example on his missionary journeys. Saint Bavo was given leave by Saint Amand after some time to lead an eremitical life, living in a hollow trunk of a large tree first, and later he built a cell at Mendonck, using vegetables and water as his chief subsistence. Saint Bavo is known for doing penance for selling a man into serfdom by making the man lead him on a chain to the common lockup. Saint Amand had appointed Saint Floribert Abbot of the monastery at Ghent, Saint Bavo returned and got Saint Floribert's approval to build himself a new cell in a neighboring wood, where he lived until the end of his life as a recluse. Both Saint Amand and Saint Floribert attended him when Saint Bavo died with such a peaceful passage that all involved and present were impressed. Saint Bavo is titular of the Cathedral and patron of the diocese of Ghent in Haarlem in Holland.

October 2   *Saint Leodegar*

Feastday: Oct 2   Date: 616 - 679

Family: Father: Bodilon de Treves   Mother: Sigrada (Sigrade)
Spouse: Unknown (Warinus) de Treves   Siblings: Guerin

Country: France

Ancestors:. Unknown past parents.

Branches of the Tree Guerin (Warinus) is the sibling of Saint Leodegar is the ancestor of Saint Leutwinus.

Biography: Saint Leodegar was the offspring of Saigrad and Bodilon de Treves. Not mush else is known of Saint Leodegar.

SAINTS DAILY
Kings, Queens, Popes, Princes, Princesses, Emperors, Hermits, Bishops

DAILY SAINTS WHOSE ANCESTRY IS KNOWN

October 2 Saint Thomas de Cantelou

Country: England **Date:** 1282

Family: Father: William II de Cantelou Mother: Milicent (Melisende) de Gournay
Spouse: Unknown Siblings: Unknown

Ancestors: Baldwin V, and Kings and Queens of Flanders are Ancestors

Branches of the Tree: Baldwin V and the Flanders Line are in this branch of the tree.

Biography: Saint Thomas of Cantelou was the Bishop of Hereford. He was also called Cantilupe. In Buckinghamshire England about 1218 he studied at Oxford Paris, and Orleans. In 1261 he became chancellor of Oxford University and used his influence to help the barons in the struggle against King Henry III. In 1265 after the defeat of Henry's forces at the battle of Lewes, Saint Thomas became chancellor of England. After the Barons lost their grip on power he had to retire to Paris. He became chancellor of the university in 1273 at Oxford for the second time. After two years past he was appointed bishop of Hereford. He got a great reputation for sanctity and charity and was a most capable counselors of King Edward I. He also was a stern opponent of simony and was against all forms of secular encroachment upon his Episcopal rights. He had a relationship with Thomas John Peckham who was Archbishop of Canterbury but it deteriorated about jurisdiction and he was excommunicated by the Archbishop. Saint Thomas appealed to the papal court but died before any decision was reached by the pope. Despite the controversy, Saint Thomas of Cantelou was revered in England and miracles were reported at his tomb. He was canonized in 1320.

SAINTS DAILY
Kings, Queens, Popes, Princes, Princesses, Emperors, Hermits, Bishops

DAILY SAINTS WHOSE ANCESTRY IS KNOWN

October 3 *Saint Hesychius Of Vienne Bishop*

Date: 6th Century

Family: Father: Unknown   Mother: Unknown
Spouse: Audentia of Rome   Siblings: Unknown

Country: Italy

Ancestors: Unknown

Branches of the Tree: Julius of Agricola is related to Audentia of Rome, thus the family of Appollinaris Sidonius

Biography: Not very much is known about this Saint other than what is in the Saints in the Tree defining lineage relationships.

October 5   *Saint Galla*

Date: d. c. 550

Family: Father: Quintus Aurelius Memmius Symmachus
        Mother: Unknown
Spouse: Unknown   Siblings: Rusticana Symmacha, Proba
Children: None

Country: Italy

Ancestors: Many generations ending with Aurelius Julianus Tullienus Symmachus

Branches of the Tree: The branch of the roman Quintus Aurelius Memmius Symmachus

Biography: Saint Galla was widowed within a year of her marriage. She lived with some pious women on Vatican hill. While living there she cared for the sick and poor. She was

SAINTS DAILY
Kings, Queens, Popes, Princes, Princesses, Emperors, Hermits, Bishops

DAILY SAINTS WHOSE ANCESTRY IS KNOWN

praised by Pope Gregory I the Great and he wrote about her. Saint Fulgentius wrote a treastise on her. She died of cancer.

October 5 Saint Apollinaris Of Vienne

Country: Italy　　　　　　**Date:** 520

Family:　　Father: Hesychius of Vienne Saint　Mother: Audentia of Rome
Spouse: Unknown　　　　Siblings: Avitus Of Vienne Bishop Saint, Fuscina Of Vienne

Ancestors: Unknown

Branches of the Tree: Family of Saints including Hesychius of Vienne, and Avitus of Bienne both Bishops.

Biography: Saint Hesychius. the Bishop of Vienne, France was the father of Saint Apollinaris. About 492 he was consecrated Bishop by his brother Saint Avitus of Vienne, consecrated Bishop of Valence. Appollinaris was forced into exile when a synod of bishops condemned an official for an incestuous marriage. Other prelates were banned with Saint Apollinaris when King Sigismund of Burgundy defended his official. When Saint Apollinaris's cloak cured the King of a mysterious ailment he was recalled from exile.

October 6　　Saint Epiphania

Country: Franks　　　　　　　　　　**Date:** 800

Family:　　Father: Ratchis King Of The Lombards
　　　Mother: Unknown
Spouse: Unknown　　　　Siblings: Fastrada wife of Charlemagne

Branches of the Tree: This is the Franks branch of the tree

SAINTS DAILY
Kings, Queens, Popes, Princes, Princesses, Emperors, Hermits, Bishops

DAILY SAINTS WHOSE ANCESTRY IS KNOWN

Biography: Saint Epiphania was of Pavia Italy. She was a Benedictine nun. King Ratchis of the Lombards was her father. Her sister later married the Blessed Charlemagne. King Ratchis of the Lombards, her father later became a monk.

October 6 — Saint Gregory of Utrecht

Country: Austrasia   **Date:** 800

Family: Father: Son Of Saint Adele   Mother: Unknown
Spouse: Unknown   Siblings: Unknown

Ancestors: Saint Dagobert has King David of Judah and Israel is an ancestor thru Joseph of Arimathea and King David's son Nathan.

Biography: Saint Dagobert is his Great Grandfather and Saint Adele of Austrasia is Saint Gregory of Utrect's Grandmother.

October 6 Blessed Adalbero

Date: b 1045 d. 1090 **Feastday:** October 6

Family:
Parents: Father: Arnold II Von Wels   Mother: Reginlinde von Verdun
Spouse: None Children: None Siblings: Matilda Von Wels, Gottfried Von Wels

Ancestry: Parents of Blessed Adalbero ancestry not known.

Branch of the Tree: Matilda Von Wels is about four generations the ancestor of the Queen of France who married Louis VII. Thus she is the ancestor of King Phillip Augustus II of France.

SAINTS DAILY
Kings, Queens, Popes, Princes, Princesses, Emperors, Hermits, Bishops

DAILY SAINTS WHOSE ANCESTRY IS KNOWN

Biography: Bless Adalbero studied in Paris and supported the Pope Gregory VII in a dispute with Emperor Henry IV. He was driven from his see in 1085 from the Bishop of Wurzbury. He retired to the abbey of Lambach that was Benedictine. He died in 1090. In 1883 his cult was approved.

October 6   *Saint Nicetas*

Date: b 759   **Feastday:** October 6

Family:
Parents: Father: Constantine V Emperor   Mother: Eudocia
Spouse: None   Children: None   Siblings: Prince Kristophos, Nicephorus Saint, Eudoxius, Anthusa, Anthimus

Ancestry: Two Emperors for ancestors, know much else is known.

Branch of the Tree: Byzantine Emperors, and Saint Niketas is very near in this branch

Biography: Saint Nicetas was an opponent of Iconoclasticism. His fathers other wife, (not his mother) was empress Irene so he served in the royal court of Constantinople. He was the representative at the Council of Nicaea and was named prefect of Sicly. In 811 he became a monk, leaving politics behind. When Emperor Leo V the Armenian made some Iconoclast policies Nicetas fled with an icon of Christ but was caught and arrested. He was later (years later) exiled with other monks ending up at a farm in Katisia Paphlogonia. He died at the farm.

October 7   *Saint Osyth*

Country: England   Date: 700

Family: Father: King Frithwold of Surrey   Mother: Princess Wilburga of Mercia

SAINTS DAILY
Kings, Queens, Popes, Princes, Princesses, Emperors, Hermits, Bishops

DAILY SAINTS WHOSE ANCESTRY IS KNOWN

Spouse: King Sighere   Siblings: Unknown

Biography:
Saint Osyth was also known as Osith and Sytha. She was a martyred nun. Known mainly through legends, her mother was Wilburga, daughter of the King of Penda who was a pagan. She was also the daughter of a chieftain of the Mercian's in England. She was married against her will to King Sighere of Essex, she wanted to become a nun. She had a son by King Sighere. Permission was finally granted to enter a convent, and she established a monastery on land at Chich, Essex, where she was the abbess. The land was donated by King Sighere. Danish raiders came and it is reported she was slain. In art she carries her own head. Because Bede in his history does not make any mention of her there is historical difficulties associated with her existence.

October 10   Saint Francis Borgia

Country: Italy   **Date:** Sixteenth Century   Patron Earthquakes, Portugal

Family: Father: Giovanni (Juan) Duke of Gandia Borgia
              Mother: Juana de Aragon
Spouse: Unknown   Siblings: None

Ancestors: Ancestors include Pope Callistus III and Pope Alexander VI on the Borgia side of the family. Also found is Saint Fernando III and the Kings of Aragon and Spain.

Branches of the Tree: This is the branch of the tree that contains the Royalty of Spain.

Biography: Saint Francis Borgia was a young nobleman. He became a Duke at age thirty three. He was in the court of the King of Spain. He lived with his wife Eleanor and their eight children. He took holy communion often. Eventually his wife died so he gave up his Dukedom to his son Charles and became a Jesuit Priest. His first mass was so full they had to set up an altar

SAINTS DAILY
Kings, Queens, Popes, Princes, Princesses, Emperors, Hermits, Bishops

DAILY SAINTS WHOSE ANCESTRY IS KNOWN

outdoors. He helped with humble tasks like cooking, carrying wood, and sweeping the kitchen. He treated his fellow priests with humility and was only angry when anyone treated him with respect as if he were still a Duke. He spread the society of Jesus all over Spain and in Portugal. Saint Francis Borgia was made Superior General of the Jesuits and he sent missionaries all over the world. Saint Francis remained humble all his life. His feast day is October 10.

October 11   *Saint Firminus of Uzes*
Country: France   **Date:** 553

Family: Father: Ferroulus Senator of Rodez
       Mother: Dode abbess of St. Pierre of Rheims
Spouse: Unknown   Siblings: Ausbertus. Agibubfis Bishop of Metz, Gamardus Babo

Ancestors: Ancestors include the Franks and the line to Joseph the Israelite

Branches of the Tree: This is the branch of the tree where the House of David Joins the line from Jospeh the Israelite. Ausbertus descendents include Arnulph bishop of Metz and Charlemagne.

Biography: Saint Fiminus of Uzes was born in Narbonne France, and educated by an uncle. He succeeded this uncle as Bishop of Uzes. At twenty two he became bishop and died at thirty seven fifteen years later.

October 12   *Saint Edwin*
Country: England   *Date:* 584-633

Family: Parents: Father- King Aelli of Deira   Mother- Unknown   Wife: Princess Cwenburga of Mercia b. 585
       Children: Princess Cynewise of Northumbria

SAINTS DAILY
Kings, Queens, Popes, Princes, Princesses, Emperors, Hermits, Bishops

DAILY SAINTS WHOSE ANCESTRY IS KNOWN

Ancestors: Ancestors go back to the Anglo-Saxons around the year 100 AD. Also the line of the Kings of Deira lead to the Lords of the Anglo Saxons.

Descendents: Sainted Descendents include Saint Adele Countess of Blois, Saint Alfred the Great, Saint Cunigunda of Luxembory, Saint David and Saint Margaret of Scotland, Saint Louis IX, Saint Edgar the Peaceful, Saint Ferdinand III of Spain, Saint Leopold III of Austria, and Saint Henry II King of Germany. Royal descendents include King Edward III Plantagenet of England, King of Naples Charles II, King of France Philip IV, and King of Scotland William the Lion. Also Casimir King of Poland , Alphonso Enriquez I King of Portugal and Phillip II King of Germany.

Biography: He married Ethelburga, daughter of St. Ethelbert, King of Kent after promising to allow her to practice her Christian religion. St. Paulinus was sent as chaplain to the Queen and bishop for his converts. In the year 616, King Ethelfrith was slain in battle by Redwald, King of the East Angles. Edwin of Deira became king of the whole kingdom of Northumbria. After the death of Redwald, he had a certain lordship over the other English kings. When Queen Ethelburga gave birth to a daughter, she was baptized with twelve others on Whitsunday, and called Eanfleda; they were the first fruits of the Northumbrians. Paulinus continued to instruct him and to pray for his conversion. Edwin was a man of unusual wisdom and deliberated in his heart to which religion he should follow. King Edwin was baptized at York at Easter in the year 627, in the wooden church of St. Peter, on the site of the present York Minster, which he had caused to be built. This good king had reigned seventeen years when the Welsh Cadwalon a pagan marched in arms against him with Penda of Mercia. In the ensuing battle he was slain. King Edwin met them at Hatfield Chase on October 12, 633. St. Edwin was certainly venerated in England as a martyr, but though his claims to sanctity are else doubtful than those of some other royal saints, English and other, he has had no liturgical cults so far as is

SAINTS DAILY
Kings, Queens, Popes, Princes, Princesses, Emperors, Hermits, Bishops

DAILY SAINTS WHOSE ANCESTRY IS KNOWN

known. Churches were dedicated in his honor in London and at Brean in Somerset; his relics were held in veneration, and Pope Gregory XIII permitted him to be represented among the English martyrs on the walls of the chapel of the Venerable at Rome. His feast day is October 12th.

October 13   *Saint Comgan*

Country: Altdorf, Mittelfranken, Bavaria, Germany
      Date: Eighth Century

Family: Father: Garthrwys   Mother: Denyw
Spouse: None   Siblings: Saint Kentigern

Ancestors: King Pharamond of France about 370 AD is an ancestors also Sunno and the line to Joseph the Israelite and so a descendent of Abraham.

Branches of the Tree: The Frankish kings about 350 years before Charlemagne is where the branch ties into the tree.

Biography: Brother of Saint Kentigern and son of a prince of Leinster, Ireland he was an Abbot and founder in a battle, and was wounded by neighboring chieftains and fled with his sister and her children to Scotland he settled in Lochaise near Skye. There he built the monastery. Iona is his burial place.

SAINTS DAILY
Kings, Queens, Popes, Princes, Princesses, Emperors, Hermits, Bishops

DAILY SAINTS WHOSE ANCESTRY IS KNOWN

October 13   Saint Gerald of Aurillac
Feastday: October 13   Date: d. 909

Family: Father: Gerard II van Limousin   Mother: Unknown
Spouse: Unknown   Siblings: Unknown

Country: France

Ancestors: Saint Gerald grandfather married princess Hildegard the daughter of King Louis I of France.

Branches of the Tree: This is the branch near Charlemagne.

Biography: After the death of his parents Saint Gerald of Aurillac became Count, and he was known to give a large part of the revenue of his estate to the poor. He lived an austere life, going to Mass daily, and set a frugal table. He made a pilgrimage to Rome and founded a church to Saint Peter in place of the Church to Saint Clement which his father had built there. He also founded an abbey he populated with Monks from Vabres. He thought of becoming a monk, but was persuaded by Saint Gausbert, Bishop of Cahors to remain more useful to his dependents of the world as he was. The last seven years of his life he was blind, and he died iat Cezenac in Quercy in 909 and was buried at the abbey of Aurillac.

October 13 Saint Edward the Confessor
Country: Kent England   **Date:** 1066

Family: Father: Edgar "the Peaceful" King of England
        Mother: Elfrida (Elfthryth) Queen of England
        Spouse: Unknown   Siblings: Ethelred II (The Unready) King of England

SAINTS DAILY
Kings, Queens, Popes, Princes, Princesses, Emperors, Hermits, Bishops

DAILY SAINTS WHOSE ANCESTRY IS KNOWN

Ancestors: Saint Edgar's ancestors include his mother Saint Elgiva, four generations previous Saint Alfred. Also included is Joseph of Arimathea. Also King David of Judah and Israel is an ancestor thru Nathan his son. King Solomon of Israel and Judah is also an ancestor. Arnulf Sainted Bishop of Metz is an Ancestor and so the line from Him to Joseph the Israelite proves true. Also the line leading to Zerah, son of Judah. Thus Three Israelites are ancestors, Joseph, Zebulon, and Judah. (Zebulon is an Ancestor of King David of Judah and Israel, as is Judah).

Branches of the Tree: This vicinity of the Branch is closest to the English Kings.

Biography: Saint Edward the Confessor was the son of a Norman wife, Emma and King Ethelred III. Queen Emma was the daughter of Duke Richard I of Normandy. In 1013 when the Danes under Sweyn and his son Canute invaded England he was born. Canute remained in England and married Emma the year after Ethelred died, and so became King of England. Saint Edward remained in Normandy and finally in 1042 after his half-brother Hardicanute died, he was acclaimed King of England. This was done with the support of the powerful Earl Godwin. He married in 1044 Edith, the daughter of Earl Godwin. He used good rule and his reign was very peaceful, probably due to his favor of the Norman Barrons. Earl of Godwin was Saxon and Robert of Jumieges was Norman whom King Saint Edward named Archbishop of Canterbury in 1051. A rebellion was mustered when Earl of Godwin (who had been banished in 1051) returned with a fleet from Flanders. Peace was declared when the two men met in the presence of the Archbishop of Canterbury who was replaced by Stigand, and Robert returned to Normandy. Godwin's sons proved difficult after Godwin died in 1053. Harold and Tostig both wanted the throne since Saint Edward was childless. A revolt in 1065 drove Tostig away and he was banished to Europe by King Edward. So Harold became his successor. Saint Peter's Abbey at Westminster was built by King Edward at this time. Saint King Edward by now got interested in

SAINTS DAILY
Kings, Queens, Popes, Princes, Princesses, Emperors, Hermits, Bishops

DAILY SAINTS WHOSE ANCESTRY IS KNOWN

religious affairs. Due to his piety he was given the surname "The Confessor." On January 5 he died in London and was canonized in 1161 by Pope Alexander III. His feast day is October 13.

October 16   *Saint Hedwig*

Country: Silesia   **Date:** unknown

Family: Parents: Unknown   Husband: Henryk I "The Bearded" Prince Of Silesia
Children: Henryk II "The Pious" Prince Of Silesia

Ancestry: Saint Hedwig's ancestry is not known.

Descendents: Descendents include Stefan II Duke of Bavaria Landshut, and Henryk the Pious Prince of Silesia. Also Isabella of Bavaria wife of King Charles V of France is a descendent.

Biography: Hedwig was born in Andechs, Bavaria, Germany, the daughter of the Duke of Croatia and Dalmatia. Also called Jadwiga in some lists, she died in a Cistercain convent, having taken vows. Duchess and widow, the patroness of Silesia, a region of eastern Europe. She was the aunt of St. Elizabeth of Hungary. Hedwig was married to Duke Henry of Silesia, at the age of twelve, the head of the Polish Royal family. They had a happy marriage. She bore him seven children. Henry founded a Cistercian convent at Trebnitz, as well as hospitals and monasteries. Hedwig became a Cistercain at Trebnitz. Henry died in 1238. She had to leave her prayers to make peace among her offspring, and she buried a child who was killed fighting against the Mongols. She died in the convent on October 15. She was canonized in 1266. Many miracles were reported after her death.

October 16   *Saint Balderic*

Country: Frankish Kingdom (France)
     Date: 7th Century.

SAINTS DAILY
Kings, Queens, Popes, Princes, Princesses, Emperors, Hermits, Bishops

DAILY SAINTS WHOSE ANCESTRY IS KNOWN

Family: Father: Sigebert II King Of Franks Saint   Mother: Emnechilde
Spouse: None   Siblings: Dagobert II King Of Franks, Berswinde \France\ of

Biography:
Saint Balderic was a abbot and prince. He became the abbot-founder of a convent at Reims and Montfaucon Abbey in France. Brother of St. Bova. Balderie, or Baundry, and his sister were the children of Sigebert II, King of Austrasia.

October 17   Saint Ethelred and Saint Ethelbright

Feastday: October 17   Date: d. 760

Family: Father: Eormenred   Mother: Oslafa of Northumbria
Spouses: Unknown   Siblings: Eafa Eeormenburh Eangyth Athelthryth

Country: England Kent

Ancestors: Saint Ethelbert is the grandfather who was King of Kent. Thus the line to Odin and thru Thor to Priam to Zerah son of Judah.

Branches of the Tree: This is the branch of the tree near Kent

Biography: These saints where great grandsons of King Ethelbert of Kent. Other names for the Saints are Ethelbert and Etheired. They are not mentioned by Bede. Their uncle Erconbert ruled and was succeeded by their cousin in 664. Thunor Egbert's consellor murdered them at Eastry. Because Egbert was found responsible he founded the monastery of Minster. The princes sister Eormenburh as abbess of the monastery. In later years their bodies were taken outside Kent for political reasons to Wakering and later to Ramsey Abbey by

SAINTS DAILY
Kings, Queens, Popes, Princes, Princesses, Emperors, Hermits, Bishops

DAILY SAINTS WHOSE ANCESTRY IS KNOWN

Oswald of Worchester on the feast day of October 17. The feast was kept on this day at St. Augustine's Canterbury as well.

October 18   Saint Keyna or Keyne ferch Brychan

Feastday. October 18

Family:
Parents: Father-Saint Brychan Mother- Prawst verch Tudwal
Husband: Unknown
Children: Unknown

Biography:
Virgin. Once called Keyne or Ceinwen. On the banks of the Severn River in Somerset, England Saint Keyna became a hermitess. She was convinced to return to Wales by her nephew Saint Cadoc. In Corwall England and in southern Wales she founded Churches. Also possibly in Somerset.

- Saint Keyne verch Brychan
- *Sex:* F
- *Birth:* 0461
- *Death:* 0505
- *Note:*

> Note: Properly called Cain, though commonly known as St. Keyne, this saintly lady had a number of popular epithets: St. Cain Wyry(the Virgin), Cain Breit (the Bright) or Ceinwen (the Fair).She was the daughter of Brychan Brycheiniog, King of Brycheiniog in South Wales, a man of many saintly children: by some accounts, twenty-four daughters besides sons. Keyne was his most distinguished child. Many noble lords sought her hand in marriage but, wishing to remain a virgin, she crossed the Severn to find a wooded solitary abode. She travelled via

SAINTS DAILY
Kings, Queens, Popes, Princes, Princesses, Emperors, Hermits, Bishops

DAILY SAINTS WHOSE ANCESTRY IS KNOWN

Kentchurch, in Herefordshire, and settled in a place where now stands the town of Keynsham on the Avon in Somerset. It is said, however, that she was warned by the local King that the area was swarming with serpents and neither man nor beast could inhabit it. St. Keyne, addressing herself to her heavenly spouse, obtained of him by the fervor of her prayer, that all this poisonous brood should be changed into stones perfectly resembling the winding of serpents. Today, these are considered to be the fossilized remains of ammonites. A similar miracle is sometimes recorded of St. Hilda.

After living an austere and saintly life in Keynsham for some years, St. Keyne made a pilgrimage to Dinsol which is traditionally said to be St. Michael's Mount, but was probably St. Keyne, near St. Neots. She gave to the Cornish people here, a well which has the wonderful property of conferring the chief domestic authority on husband or wife, whichever first, after marriage, drinks of its waters. The parish of Kenwyn near Truro is probably named after her. Keyne's nephew, St. Cadog, son of her sister, Gwladys, was surprised to find her at Dinsoland tried to persuade her to return home with him. The locals were opposed to this, but she did eventually follow him some years later. Keyne made herself a small habitation at the foot of a mountain in her native country, almost certainly at Llangeinor in Glamorgan though possibly at Llangenny in Powys.She obtained, by her prayers, a spring of water which was helpful in divers infirmities and it remains at the former still. Here she stayed for many years and finally died on 8th October AD 505, a gracious smile and a beautiful rosy color

DAILY SAINTS WHOSE ANCESTRY IS KNOWN

appearing on her face. She was buried there by St. Cadog.

October 18   Saint Gwen

Country: Wales   **Date:** 5th Century

Family: Father: Cynyr Ceinfarfog The Fair   Mother: Sefin Verch Brychan Brycheiniog
Spouse: Unknown   Siblings: Saint Non

Ancestors: Saint Brychan is an Ancestor, of which only a few generations are known on father's side. Saint Helen of the Host is known as Mothers Ancestor of Saint Brychan.

Branches of the Tree: This branch is the Saint Brychan Branch. Saint Non is the mother of Saint Dewi (David) and Saint Brychan is the ancestor of King Edward IV Plantagenet.

Biography: Widowed martyr sometimes called Blanche, Wenn, or Candida. She was the descendent of a Chieftain, Brychan or Brecknock. Saxon pagans martyred Gwen at Talgrarth. Her sister was Saint Non, so Saint Dewi is her nephew. Also related to Saint Cybi.

October 19   Saint Phillip Howard

Country: England   **Date:** 28 Jun 1556
d. 19 Oct 1595

Family: Father: Thomas Howard   Mother: Mary (Arundel) Italian
Spouse: Unknown   Siblings: Unknown

Ancestors: The line goes back many generations of Howard's.

SAINTS DAILY
Kings, Queens, Popes, Princes, Princesses, Emperors, Hermits, Bishops

DAILY SAINTS WHOSE ANCESTRY IS KNOWN

Branches of the Tree: This branch of the line will intermarry with many English nobles and so join with the royalty of England.

Biography: Saint Phillip Howard was one of the Fory Martyrs of England and Wales. He is known for leading a religiously apathetic life until he was converted. After conversion he was a zealous Catholic in Elizabethan England. Saint Phillip was the Earl of Arundel. Arrested by authorities, he spent his final years in the Tower of London beginning in 1585 until he was condemned to death in 1589. He languished in the Tower until his death at the age of thirty eight. Beatified in 1929 he was included among the English martyrs canonized in 1970 by Pope Paul VI.

October 19   Saint Elfleda

Country: England   **Date:** 1000

Family: Father: Earl Ethelwold   Mother: Elfrida (Elfthryth) Queen of England
Spouse: Unknown   Siblings: Edward the Confessor Saint, Ethelred II (The Unready) King of England

Ancestors: Not much ancestry is known, as the tree connects thru the siblings descent.
Ordgar Ealdorman was Queen Elfrida (Elfthryth) father.

Branches of the Tree: Connects to the branch of the tree with King Edgar the Peaceful King of England as Queen Elfrida was the wife of King Edgar. (also Earl Ethelwold).

Biography: Saint Elfleda became the head of her Abbey. Her abbey was a Benedictine abbey in Ramses England. Saint Elfeleda was the half brother of King Edward the confessor and the daughter of Earl Ethelwold.

SAINTS DAILY
Kings, Queens, Popes, Princes, Princesses, Emperors, Hermits, Bishops

DAILY SAINTS WHOSE ANCESTRY IS KNOWN

October 20   *Saint Adelina*
Country: England   **Date:** 1125

Family: Parent: Unknown Child of William the Conqueror   Spouse: Unknown   Siblings: Vitalis Saint

Ancestors: William the Conqueror was from Normandy, and had Charlemange as an ancestor. Thus Judas of Gamla is an ancestor of the line of King Solomon and Joseph the Israelite is an ancestor.

Branches of the Tree: This is the branch of the tree near William the Norman Conqueror of England.

Biography: An abbess, the sister of St. Vitalis. Saint Adelina's grandfather was William the Conqueror. The Benedictine convent of La Blanche was the convent in which she was abbess. This religious community was founded by her sister Saint Vitalis.

October 21   *Saint Ursula verch Donaut of Dumnonia*
Country: England   *Date:* b. c. 305

Family: Parents: Father- Donaut (Dynod) (King of Dumnonia)   Mother- Unknown
Husband: Conan (Cynan) Meriadoc King of Dumnonia   Children: Cadfan (King of Gadeon) ap Conan (Cynan)

Ancestry: Only a few generations are known.

Descendents: Saint Cenue Ap Coel, Saint Custennin, Saint Erbin ap Custennin, Saint Gwelfyl verch Brychan, Saint Judicael, Saint Pabo Post Pryden are all Sainted Descendents. Edward IV of England is also a Descendent.

SAINTS DAILY
Kings, Queens, Popes, Princes, Princesses, Emperors, Hermits, Bishops

DAILY SAINTS WHOSE ANCESTRY IS KNOWN

Biography: Ursula was the daughter of a Christian king in Britain and was granted a three year postponement of a marriage she did not wish, to a pagan prince, according to a legend that appeared in the tenth century. With ten ladies in waiting, each attended by a thousand maidens, she embarked on a voyage across the North sea, sailed up the Rhine to Basle, Switzerland, and then went to Rome. When Ursula refused to marry their chieftain on their way back, they were all massacred by pagan Huns at Cologne in about 451. According to another legend, Amorica was settled by British colonizers and soldiers after Emporer Magnus Clemens Maximus conquered Britain and Gaul in 383. The ruler of the settlers, Cynan Meiriadog, called on King Dionotus of Cornwall for wives for the settlers, whereupon Dionotus sent his daughter Ursula, who was to marry Cynan, with eleven thousand maidens and sixty thousand common women. There fleet was shipwrecked and all the women were enslaved or murdered. The legends are pious fictions, but what is true is that one Clematius, probably at the beginning of the fourth century, a senator, rebuilt a basilica in Cologne that had originally been built, to honor a group of virgins who had been martyred at Cologne. Who they were and how many of them there were, are unknown. They were evidently venerated enough to have had a church built in their honor. From these meager facts, the legend of Ursula grew and developed. Feast day October 21.

October 22   Saint Mary Salome

Date: 1st

Family: Father: Joachim   Mother: Saint Joanne   Spouse: Zebedee   Siblings: Saint Mary Cleopas(Alphaeus) ; Escha Children: Saint James the Greater; Saint John Zebedee the Evangelist Mary

Country: Israel

SAINTS DAILY
Kings, Queens, Popes, Princes, Princesses, Emperors, Hermits, Bishops

DAILY SAINTS WHOSE ANCESTRY IS KNOWN

Ancestors: Thru father Joachim Zerubbabel is an ancestor and thus the line of Solomon. Hebrew names of Sirach and Haggai appear in the line between Joachim and Zerubbabel; On the Mothers side Saint Joanne is the daughter of Bianca the daughter of Matthat and Rachel. Matthat ancestor was Nathan son of David and Rachel is daughter of Eleazor of the line of Solomon.

Branches of the Tree: This is the branch of the tree in the vicinity Saint Joseph and the Blessed Virgin Mary.

Biography: Saint Mary Salome was present at the Cruxifix with Saint Mary the Mother of God and Saint Mary Magdalene. She was also at the burial place on the day of the Resurrection.

October 23   Saint   Anicius   Manlius Severinus Boethius

Feastday: October 23   Date: c. 480 c. 524

Family: Father: Anicius Manlius Torquatus Severinus Boethius   Mother: Rusticana Symmacha
Spouse: Rusticana   Siblings: Quintus Aurelius Memmius Symmachus Children: None

Country: Italy

Ancestors: About seven generations up we find Aurelius Julianus Tullienus Symmachus.

Branches of the Tree: Up about four generations and then down a few generations Rusticius de Lyon (Bishop of Lyon) Saint is found. Also Saint Veranus and Saint Salonius and Eucherius Bishop Of Lyon Saint are near in this branch of the tree.

Biography: Of the famous Anicia family Saint Severinus Boethius was the son of the proconsul Flavius Manlius Boethius. He was orphaned as a child and raised by Q. Aurelius Syummachus who had a daughter Rusticana that he married. He became a translator to latin and translated Nichomachus, Euclid,

SAINTS DAILY
Kings, Queens, Popes, Princes, Princesses, Emperors, Hermits, Bishops

DAILY SAINTS WHOSE ANCESTRY IS KNOWN

Pythaoras, Ptolemy, and Archimedes. He was quite an intellectual with knowledge in music, logic, theology, and astronomy. He wrote De sancta Trinitate and other theological treatises that are available today. Named consul by Ostrogoth Emperor Teodoric in 510 and then named master of the offices he was arrested when he defended Consul Albinus about overthrowing the Ostrogoth rulers. He supposedly conspired with Eastern Emperor Justin. He was imprisoned in Ticinum (Pavia) facing charges of using astronomy for impius purposes. While in prison for nine months he wrote The Consolation of Philosophy. He was tortured and executed. Cannonized in 1883 by Pope Leo XIII Saint Severinus is considered the first of the Scholastics. His translation of the Greek philosophers were the only translations available for many years.

October 23 Saint Ignatius of Constantinople

Date: b 799 d. 877 **Feastday:** October 23

Family:
Parents: Father: Michael Rangabe Mother: Daughter of Mamikonean Princessss of Byzantine Empire
Spouse: None Siblings: Theophano; Strausikios; Georgo
Children: None

Ancestry: Nicephorus I Mamikonean Byzantine Emperor was his Grandfather on his mothers side and Emperor Leo III of the Mamikonean Byzntine was his fifth generation Grandfather (Great Great).

Branch of the Tree: The Byzntine Emperors and the Mamikonean Emperors.

Biography: Saint Ignatius nickname was Niketas. In 813 he was mutilated with his brothers when his father was deposed by Leo the Armenian. They were sent to a monastery. He became a

SAINTS DAILY
Kings, Queens, Popes, Princes, Princesses, Emperors, Hermits, Bishops

DAILY SAINTS WHOSE ANCESTRY IS KNOWN

monk, and then after ordination an Abbot. In 846 was named Patriarch of Constantinople. In conflict with Bardas he was deposed and banished to the island of Terebinthos. Bardas got support from Photius who was in conflict with Ignatius. Ignatius appealed to Pope Adrian II who called a council and Photius was condemned with his supporters and was excommunicated. Later Ignatius was almost excommunicated from Rome by Pope John VIII when he claimed jurisdiction over the Bulgars, but when the legates of Pope John VIII arrived Saint Ignatius had died on October 23. Clearly he was very political.

October 23   Saint Ode

Country: Aquitaine   **Date:** c688

Family: Parents: Father-Clothaire II King of Franks Mother- Husband: Duke Boggis Of Aquitaine Gascony And Toulouse Children: King Eudes of Toulouse and Aquitaine

Ancestry: Ancestry goes back thru the Kings of the Franks back to the Cimerians and back to Zerah son of Judah. This is the same line as the ancestry of Charlemange.

Descendents: Saint Adele of Blois, Saint Louis IX of France, and Saint Fernando III of Spain are all Descendents. Also King of England Edward I and King of France Phillip IV are descendents. King Edward III Plantagenet and King Charles II of Naples are also descendents. Also Phillip II King of Germany.

Biography: Wife of the duke of Aquitaine, Saint Ode was a French princess. After her husbands death she committed her life to aiding the poor. She is a widow and servant of the poor.

October 23   Saint Clether verch Brychan

Feastday: October 23 or November 4.

SAINTS DAILY
Kings, Queens, Popes, Princes, Princesses, Emperors, Hermits, Bishops

DAILY SAINTS WHOSE ANCESTRY IS KNOWN

Family:
Parents: Father-Saint Brychan   Mother- Rigrawst b: 0450
Husband: Unknown
Children: Unknown

Biography: Listed as a Saint of Wales, also called Cleer, Clydog, Scledog, Citanus or Cleodius. Listed as descendent of a local King. Clether left Wales and went to Cornwall. Churches are built in his honor including Saint Clear in Liskeard. He was martyred. There is another Clether on November third. Saint Clether is listed as a hermit. He lived in Wales by the river Never. Later in life he settled in the remote and beautiful valley of Inny at the place that still bears his name. The finest example of an oratory and well were rebuilt in the 15th century. There is an eleventh century church built in his honor a small distance away.

October 24   Saint Maglor
Feastday: October 24   **Date:** 6th

Family:
Parents: Father: Saint Umbrafael   Mother: Saint Afrella
Spouse: None   Children: None Siblings: None

Ancestry: Saint Afrella has Saint Constantine as an Ancestor and also the Cornwall Kings of Britain are Ancestors. Therefore the Israelites Benjamin, Joseph, Levi, Zebulon, and Judah are ancestors. Bran the Blessed and Anna of Arimathea are ancestors thru their son Brons.

Branches of the Tree: This is the Branch of the Tree in the vicinity on King Arthur, son of Uther Pendragon.

Biography: It is not known if Saint Maglor is canonized, and little is known about him other than his relationship to Saint Sampson, Saint Umbrafael, and Saint Afrella and his lineage in

SAINTS DAILY
Kings, Queens, Popes, Princes, Princesses, Emperors, Hermits, Bishops

DAILY SAINTS WHOSE ANCESTRY IS KNOWN

the file Saints in the Tree. It is known that he was entrusted while young to Saint Illtud. Saint Sampson ordained Saint Maglor Deacon and took him to Brittany. Here he took charge of a monastery at Kerfunt. When Saint Sampson died Saint Maglor became bishop and abbot at Dol. However he was old so he resigned his postion to Saint Budoc. Saint Maglor went to the coast, but was troubled by all the people who came to be cured and see miracles. One chieftain of Sark was cured and gave Saint Maglor and his monks a part of his Island. Saint Maglor built a Monastery there called he seigneurie of Sark. In return for going to Jersey and defeating a "dragon" he also got some land in Jersey.

October 26   Saint Alfred the Great of England

Country: England   *Date:* 899

Family: Parents: Father- Ethelwulf   Mother- Osburh
         Wife: Ealhswith
Children: Edward; Ethelfleda

Ancestry: Saint Alfred's ancestors include the Kings of Wessex. Also King David of Judah and Israel is an ancestor thru Joseph of Arimathea and Nathan David's son.

Descendents: King Edgar the Peaceful is a descendent, as well as Edward I and Edmund I "The Elder" both kings of England. Also King Edward IV Plangagenet is a descendent.

Biography: The fifth son of the Wessex king, Saint Alfred was born in 849, became King of Wessex, a scholar, and a renowned Christian monarch. He was accepted as a godson by Pope Leo IV during a journey to Rome in 853. He translated classics for his people, being a great scholar, and seemed destined early on for a career in the Church. He became King, instead, and was forced to a conflict with the Danes during much of the reign, the

SAINTS DAILY
Kings, Queens, Popes, Princes, Princesses, Emperors, Hermits, Bishops

DAILY SAINTS WHOSE ANCESTRY IS KNOWN

Danes then threatening England. He became a beloved figure in England, due to his work as a patron of the arts, literature, and especially the Church.

October 26   Saint Evaristus 5th Bishop of Rome Pope

Date: ruled the papacy 97-105

Family: Father: Jude the son of James the Lesser Apostle   Mother: Unknown Spouse: Unknown   Siblings: unknown Children: Saint Hyginus Bishop of Rome

Country: Israel

Ancestors: See James the Lesser Apostles ancestry.

Branches of the Tree: This is the branch of the tree right on the descent of Saint James the Lesser Apostle.

Biography: Developed work of Saint AneCletus dividing Rome into Parishes (beginning of the College of Cardinals). He ordered marriage had to be made verbal in front of a Priest. He was martyred by emperor Hadrian.

October 26   Saint Eadfrid

Date: b. c 623 d. 675

Family: Father: Eadwine   Mother: Cwenburgh Spouse: Unknown   Siblings: Osfrid

Country: Briton

Ancestors: Aelli de Deira, also include Odin and Frigg.

Branches of the Tree: This is a branch of the tree at Deira.

SAINTS DAILY
Kings, Queens, Popes, Princes, Princesses, Emperors, Hermits, Bishops

313

DAILY SAINTS WHOSE ANCESTRY IS KNOWN

Biography: Saint Eadfrid genealogy relationships are found in Saints in the Tree. He was the founder of Leominster Priory. Saint Eadfrid was a priest of Mercia, England, and also Northumbria.

October 28 *Saint Jude*

Country: Israel   **Patron:** of Hopeless Causes

Family: Father: unknown   Mother: Mary Alphaews
Spouse: Unknown   Siblings: Saint James the lesser, Saint Simon the apostle, Saint Joseph Barabas the apostle

Ancestors: Saint Joseph of Arimathea is an ancestor. A little know fact of the biblical character of Joseph of Arimathea is that he is the son of Mathat, who is in the line of Nathan that is listed in the New Testament book of Luke. His ancestors then must be King David of Israel and Judah, and so the Israelites Joseph, Levi, Zebulon, and Judah. Anna married Saint Joseph of Arimathea, and her ancestry is an unbroken male line to Levi the Israelite. Saint Joseph of Arimathea's mother may have been the daughter of Eleazor, who was of the Davidic line of Solomon. Eleazor was the Grandfather of Joseph who married the Virgin Mary and this line is listed in the Gospel of Mathew. The Israelite Benjamin was an ancestor of King David's wife Maacah (Sauls daughter) whose line married in the line from Solomon joined by the marriage of Reheboam to Maacah. Therefore Saint Joseph of Arimathea has five Israelites as ancestors.

Branches of the Tree : This is a branch of the tree that has Saint Joseph of Arimathea in it. He is the Father of Cleopas who is the Father of Mary Alphaws. He is three generations the ancestor of Saint Jude. This line also marries Anna Arimathea who is the daughter of Joseph of Arimathea.

Biography: Saint Jude was the relative of the Lord. He was the son of Mary Alphaews, and the Great grandson of Saint Joseph of Arimathea. Legend says he was martyred in Armenia. He may

SAINTS DAILY
Kings, Queens, Popes, Princes, Princesses, Emperors, Hermits, Bishops

have taken part in the election of Saint Simeon to the post of Bishop of Jerusalem. He traveled to Judea, Samaria, Idumaea, Syria, Mesopotamia, and Lybia and preached the gospel.

SAINTS DAILY
Kings, Queens, Popes, Princes, Princesses, Emperors, Hermits, Bishops

DAILY SAINTS WHOSE ANCESTRY IS KNOWN

Saints of November

FEAST DAY	SAINT	COUNTRY	BORN	DIED
1-Nov	Saint Dingad	Wales		
1-Nov	Saint Cadfan	Wales	530	590
2-Nov	Saint Maura	Ireland		5th
3-Nov	Saint Hubert	France		727
3-Nov	Saint Winifred	England	565	
4-Nov	Saint Emeric	Hungary		1031
4-Nov	Saint Charles Borromeo	Italy	1538	1584
4-Nov	Blessed Francis D' Amboise	France	1427	1485
5-Nov	Saint Bertilia	Belgium		c 687
6-Nov	Saint Margaret of Lorraine	France	1463	1521
6-Nov	Saint Edwen	England		600
6-Nov	Saint Illtud Saint	Britain		c 535
6-Nov	Saint Winnoc	England		c 717
6-Nov	Blessed Nonius	Portugal	1360	1431
6-Nov	Blessed Joan Mary de Maille	France		1414
7-Nov	Saint Engelbert	England	1187	1225
8-Nov	Saint Cybi	England	490	555
8-Nov	Saint Tysilio	England		c 640
9-Nov	Saint Pabo	England		530

SAINTS DAILY
Kings, Queens, Popes, Princes, Princesses, Emperors, Hermits, Bishops

316

DAILY SAINTS WHOSE ANCESTRY IS KNOWN

Date	Saint	Country	Born	Died
12-Nov	Saint Kadwalladyr of North Wales	Wales		664
12-Nov	Saint Cadwaladr	England	c. 615	664
14-Nov	Saint Alberic	France		784
14-Nov	Saint Laurence O'Toole	England	1128	1180
15-Nov	Saint Leopold III of Austria	Austria	1073	1136
16-Nov	Saint Eucherius	France		449
16-Nov	Saint Margaret of Scotland	Scotland	1046	1093
17-Nov	Saint Gregory Bishop Of Tours	France	583	594
17-Nov	Saint Hilda	England	614	680
17-Nov	Blessed Salome	Poland	1202	1268
18-Nov	Saint Mabyn	Wales		6th
19-Nov	Saint Narses Pahlav the I	Armenia	335	373
19-Nov	Saint Ermenburga	England		c 650
21-Nov	Saint Albert of Louvain	France		1193
22-Nov	Saint Tigrida	Spain		11th
24-Nov	Saint Eanfleda	England		c 700
27-Nov	Saint Guntramus	France	c. 488	592
27-Nov	Saint Cungar	Britain	c. 488	550
29-Nov	Saint Sadwrn Farchog	Britain		6th
29-Nov	Saint Ethelwin	Britain		7th
29-Nov	Saint Egelwine	Britain		7th

SAINTS DAILY
Kings, Queens, Popes, Princes, Princesses, Emperors, Hermits, Bishops

DAILY SAINTS WHOSE ANCESTRY IS KNOWN

| 30-Nov | Saint Tudwal | Britain | 400 |

TABLE TWELVE SAINTS OF NOVEMBER

November 1 *Saint Cadfan*

Country: Brittany   **Date:** b. 530 Brittany France   d. Abt 1 Nov 590 in Bardsey Island, Carmarthenshire, Wales

Family: Father: Eneas Ledewig   Mother: Saint Gwen   Spouse: Unknown   Siblings: Eudo (Eudon) "The Grand" King of Aquitaine; Imitarius of Aquitaine

Ancestors: James the bishop of Jerusalem son on Saint Joseph. Saint Constantine the Great, Saint Darerca, Saint Ursula.

Branches of the Tree: Grandson of Budig this is near Saint Judicael.

Biography: Given Name: Latin-Catamanus, English-Gideon. St. Cadfan was a Breton nobleman, the son of Eneas Ledewig (the Breton) and Princess Gwen Teirbron (the Triple-Breasted). As a young man, he was drawn to a life in the church , probably through the influence of his elder half-brother , St. Winwaloe. He founded places of worship in Finistere and the Cotes du Nord before leading a large band of missionaries to Western Wales with his cousin, St. Tydecho, and friend, St. Cynllo. His companions are said to have included : SS. Cynan, Dochdwy, Mael, Sulien, Tanwg, Eithras, Llywen , Llyfab, Tegwyn, Padarn, Trunio and Maelrys. In Wales, Cadfan founded a renowned monastery at Towyn in M eirionydd, but later moved on to the seclusion of Ynys Enlli (Bardsey). The monastery he established on the island became a Mecca for holymen and royalty alike; and it is said that, not only his original followers, but some 20,000 further saints were subsequently buried in the Abbey's graveyard. Cadfan's confessor was St. Hywyn who lived just across the

SAINTS DAILY
Kings, Queens, Popes, Princes, Princesses, Emperors, Hermits, Bishops

DAILY SAINTS WHOSE ANCESTRY IS KNOWN

water in Aberdaron. Cadfan died on 1st November, sometime in the late 6th century. He was succeeded as Abbot of Bardsey by St. Lleuddad who buried him in the Abbey Church there. Centuries later, his body was translated to a more fitting shrine in Llandaff Cathedral.

November 1   *Saint Dingad*

Feastday: November 1

Family:
Parents: Father-Saint Brychan Mother- Prawst verch Tudwal
Wife: unknown
Children: unknown

Biography:
Hermit son. He lived in Llangingad, Llangovery in Dyfed Wales. Also called Digat. May be the patron of Dingestow (Gwent). He founded churches. These churches are in South Wales.

November 2   *Saint Maura*

Country: Ireland   **Date:** 5th Century

Family: Father: Dubtach   Mother: Unknown
           Spouse: Unknown   Siblings: Saint Brigid

Ancestors: Ancestors go back to Tuathal Teachtmar who married Baine.

Branches of the Tree: This is an early Irish branch of the tree

Biography: Saint Maura was the sister to Saint Brigid. Their bodies are enshrined in Rome, legend being that they were scottich princesses murdered by pagan outlaws. There is another

SAINTS DAILY
Kings, Queens, Popes, Princes, Princesses, Emperors, Hermits, Bishops

319

DAILY SAINTS WHOSE ANCESTRY IS KNOWN

legend about them by Saint Baya. They are also believed to be soldiers per Saint Euphronius and Saint Martin of Tours.

November 3   Saint Hubert Bishop of Liege

Country: Austrasia   **Date:** 727   **Patron**: Hunters; Hydrophobia or Rabies; Liege Belgium

Family: Father: Boggis I (Bertrand) Duke of Aquitaine
Mother: Hugbern (Afre) Princess of the Franks
Spouse: Floribanne of Austrasia   Siblings: Eudo (Eudon) "The Grand" King of Aquitaine; Imitarius of Aquitaine

Ancestors: Ancestors include Clovis, Pharamond, Dagobert I King of the Franks, and so the line to Joseph the Israelite. Also Sextus Julius Caesar was an ancestor and so many Roman rulers. Also Octavia and many Roman Emperors. Also the Britain Kings including Beli Mawr King of Britain.

Branches of the Tree: Saint Hubert's wife Floribane was the daughter of Saint Sigebert and brother to Saint Dagabert II King of the Franks.

Biography: Saint Hubert was a disciple of Saint Lambert. He was Bishop of Maastricht, Netherlands. Saint Hubert served Pepin of Herstal, France as a married courtier. It is reported he had a vison of a crucifix while hunting, between the horns of a stag. He was widowed and entered Stavelot Monastery, Belgium. Here he was ordained by Saint Lambert. In 705 he succeeded Saint Lambert as bishop. A shrine was erected by Saint Hubert for Saint Lambert's relics at Liege, France. Saint Hubert was noted for converting hundreds, and for his miracles. On May 30 he died at Tervueren, near Brussels, Belgium. Saint Hubert is the patron of Hunters.

SAINTS DAILY
Kings, Queens, Popes, Princes, Princesses, Emperors, Hermits, Bishops

DAILY SAINTS WHOSE ANCESTRY IS KNOWN

November 3   *Saint Winifred*
Country: England   **Date:** 727

Family: Father: Tyfid ap Eiludd   Mother: Gwenlo Verch Bugi   Spouse: Siblings: Saint Beuno

Ancestors: Ancestors include Saint Brychan and so all of his ancestors as well.

Branches of the Tree: This is a few generations up on her mothers side Saint Brychan of Wales area.

Biography: Saint Winifred was the daughter of Tyfid who was a wealthy resident of Tegeingl Flintshire Wales. Saint Beuno was her brother. She was supposedly beheaded on June 22 by Caradog, and her head was restored by Beuno after she refused to submit to Caradog. There was a double monastery at Gwytherin in Denbigshire where she became a nun. She became Abbess after the Abbess Tenoy and died there fifteen years after her miraculous restorationto life. Supposedly a spring welled up where Winifred's head fell, and is called Holy Well or Saint Winifred's Well. This spring has many cures reported over the centuries and has become a great pilgrimage center. Saint Winifred is also known as Gwenfrewi.

November 4   Saint Charles Borremeo
Date: b. 1538 d. 1584   **Feastday:** November 4

Family:
Parents: Father: Giberto Conte d'Arona Borromeo Mother: Margherita de' Medici
Spouse: None Children: None Siblings: Anna Borromeo

SAINTS DAILY
Kings, Queens, Popes, Princes, Princesses, Emperors, Hermits, Bishops

DAILY SAINTS WHOSE ANCESTRY IS KNOWN

Ancestry: Only a few generations are known.

Branch of the Tree: Pope Pius IV is the brother of Saint Charles Borremeo's mother Margherita de'Medici.

Biography: Saint Charles Borremeo was educated at a Benedictine Abbey os SS. Gratian and Felinus at Arona. In 1559 his uncle was elected Pope and he received his doctorate after study at Milan in Pavia. He became Secretary of State to the Pope, a cardinal, and administrator of the see of Milan. He helped resume the Council of Trent. He founded the Oblates of St. Ambrose (now the Oblates of St. Charles). In 1569 a Humiliati Priest, the order that Saint Charles was insisting reform, tried to assassinate him and he was injured. In a conflict with the Senate the Govenor that Saint Charles had excommunicated was removed by Philip, who upheld his claims. Between 1576 and 1578 he worked against the plague helping the sick and making a considerable debt after helping the thousands of dying and sick. He met many of the Priests destined for the English mission and worked against the protestant in Switzerland in 1583 when he worked against an outbreak of alleged witchcraft and sorcery. He was canonized in 1610 and was a prominent Catholic figure in the Reformation.

November 4   *Saint Emeric*
Country: Hungary   **Date:** b. 1007   d. 1031

Family: Father: Stephen of Hungary Saint   Mother: Blessed Giselle of Bavaria
Spouse: Unknown   Siblings: Hedwig of Hungary, Eminilde Arpad

Ancestors: Saint Stephen Saint Emeric's father's ancestry goes back a few generations and then is not known.

Branches of the Tree:
SAINTS DAILY
Kings, Queens, Popes, Princes, Princesses, Emperors, Hermits, Bishops

DAILY SAINTS WHOSE ANCESTRY IS KNOWN

Saint Stephen is his father and this is the branch of the tree around the Christianization of Hungary

Biography: The son of St. Stephen, Hungary's first Christian king. Born in 1007, he did not live to inherit St. Stephen's throne, as he died in a hunting accident. His tomb at Szekesfehervar was a pilgrim's site, and many miracles were reported there. He was canonized with his father in 1083.

November 4   Blessed Francis D' Amboise

Feastday: Nov 4   Date: 1427-1485

Family: Father: Louis D' Amboise   Mother: Marie De Rieux
Spouse: Peter of Brittany   Siblings: Unknown

Country: France

Ancestors: Eleven generations back King Alphonso IX of Leon and Castile is an ancestor. Also the Briene Counts are ancestors.

Branches of the Tree: This is the branch of the tree of the French and Spanish Rulers.

Biography: The house of Thouars and the house of John V, Duke of Brittany and Blessed Francis D' Amboise was sent as a four year old daughter to be raised in the court. At fifteen she married Peter, son of Duke John (his second son) and he was jealous, sulky, and sometimes violent. In 1450 Peter became Duke and Blessed Francis used her position to bless the church. She founded a convent at Nantes for Poor Clares, and gave large sums to relief of the poor. She interested herself in the cannonazation of Saint Vincent Ferrars, and in 1457 her husband died. She resisted the attempts of King Louis XI to make her his wife, and blessed the convent she had founded and blessed the Carmelite Nuns at Vannes. In 1468 Duchess Frances became a nun at Vannes. After four years she was elected Prioress for life.

SAINTS DAILY
Kings, Queens, Popes, Princes, Princesses, Emperors, Hermits, Bishops

DAILY SAINTS WHOSE ANCESTRY IS KNOWN

The house at Vannes became too small so she opened another at Couets, near Nantes. She died here in 1485, and her cultus was approved in 1863.

November 5 *Saint Bertilia*
Country: Belgium **Date:** d 705

Family: Parents: Father- Unknown Mother- Unknown
Husband: Saint Walbert
Children: Adeltrude de Hainault

Ancestry: Only one generation is known and is listed above.

Descendents: Descendents include Saint Adelaide of Italy, Saint Anglibert, Saint Lazlo of Hungary, Saint Irene, Saint Leopold III, Saint Louis IX, Saint Hedwig, Saint Isabel of Aragon, and Saint Nithard the Cronicler. Royal Descendents include King of Naples Charles II, King of France Louis VIII, Alphonso IV of Portugal, and King Edward III Plantagenet of England.

Biography: When her husband died, Bertilia lived as a hermitess near the church that she had founded at Maroeuil, France. Foundress and noble virgin, she and her bridegroom took vows of chastity and remained virgins.

November 6 *Saint Margaret of Lorraine*
Feastday: November 6 Date: 1463-1521

Family: Father: Ferri II (Frederick) of Vaudemont de Lorraine Mother: Yolanda d'Anjou Duchess Of Lorraine
Spouse: Unknown Siblings: Jeanne de Lorraine, Rene II D'anjou Duke Of Lorraine

SAINTS DAILY
Kings, Queens, Popes, Princes, Princesses, Emperors, Hermits, Bishops

DAILY SAINTS WHOSE ANCESTRY IS KNOWN

Country: France

Ancestors: Eight generations up is King Charles VI of France.

Branches of the Tree: This is the branch of the tree of the French Kings.

Biography: Duke Ferri of Lorraine had a daughter, Saint Margaret. She was ethe niece of Margaret of Anjou. Saint Margaret of Lorraine was born in Vaudement Castle Lorraine and married Duke Rene II when she was twenty-five. In 1492 whe became widowed with three children. She managed the estate at Alencon and administered acts of charity. She had an influence by Saint Francis of Paula, and when her children became of age she entered a monastery at Mortagne. She continued to care for the poor and sick at Mortagne. She founded a Poor Clare convent at Argentan Brittany but she refused the position of Abbess. She died there on November 2.

November 6   Saint Illtud

Country: Great Britain   **Date:** 535

Family: Father: Bican (Bicanus) Farchog ap Aldrien
          Mother: Rhieinwylydd verch Amlawdd Wledig
          Spouse: Tyrnihild   Siblings: Sadwrn Farchog (the Knight) ap Bican Saint

Ancestors: Saint Ursula of Dumonia and Conan are ancestors.

Biography: One of the most revered Saints of Wales Saint Illtud may have been a cousin of King Arthur of the Britain's. Saint Illtud and his wife Tyrnhild lived as members of the Army of Graham Morgan until they became hermits near the river Nadafan. Saint Illtud then studied with Saint Dudricius. The great abbey of Llanilltud Fawr in Glamorgan, Wales was founded by Saint Illtud. He was a disciple of Saint Cadoc. According to legend Illtud was one of the three Knights of the holy Grail. It was Brittany where he died.

SAINTS DAILY
Kings, Queens, Popes, Princes, Princesses, Emperors, Hermits, Bishops

DAILY SAINTS WHOSE ANCESTRY IS KNOWN

November 6   *Saint Edwen*

Country: England   **Date:** b. c 600

Family: Father: King Edwin of Northumbria
Mother: Princess Cwenburga of Mercia
Spouse: Unknown   Siblings: Princess Cynewise of Northumbria

Ancestors: Ancestors go back to the Anglo-Saxons around the year 100 AD. Also the line of the Kings of Deira lead to the Lords of the Anglo Saxons.

Branches of the Tree: This vicinity of the Branch is closest to the Northumbrian Kings.

Biography: Saint Edwen was the patroness of Llanedwen, Anglesey, Wales. She is reported to have been the daughter of King Edwin of Northumbria, the first Christian ruler there.

November 6   *Saint Winnoc*

Country: Britain   **Date:** 717

Family: Father: Judicael King of the Bretons Saint
Mother: Morone
Spouse: Unknown   Siblings: Alain II Hir King of the Bretons

Ancestors: Saint Judicael Saint Winnoc's father ancestors include Saint Patrick, Saint Cyllinus, Blessed Bran and Anna of Arimathea. Anna of Armimathea's father is Saint Joseph of Arimathea and so the Line of Nathan Son of David King of Israel and Judah. King David's ancestors include the Israelites, Zebulon, Levi, Joseph, and Judah. Also Anna of Arimathea, daughter to Joseph of Aramathea married Bran the Blessed whose line goes to Tros and so to Epraim son of Joseph the Israelite. Also the line from Anna of Arimathea's mother goes thru Simon the Just thru many High Priests to Judah the Israelite.

SAINTS DAILY
Kings, Queens, Popes, Princes, Princesses, Emperors, Hermits, Bishops

DAILY SAINTS WHOSE ANCESTRY IS KNOWN

Branches of the Tree: This is the branch of the tree of Saint Ursula and the English Kings.

Biography: Saint Winoc was a founding abbot, also called Winnoc. He was raised in Brittany France. Under Saint Bertin he became a monk at St. Peter's monastery at Sithiu (Saint-Omer). He was of the blood of King David of Israel and Judah. One tradition states he was of royal British blood. Three friends and Saint Winoc founded a monastery near Dunkirk which became a missionary center for the region. At Wormhont they labored among the Morini people. Saint Winnoc is also credited as establishing a church and a hospital.

November 6   Blessed Nonius

Feastday: Nov 6   Date: b. 1360   d. 1431

Family: Father: Unknown   Mother: Unknown
Spouse: Unknown   Siblings: none Children: Beatriz

Country: Portugal

Ancestors: None Known

Branches of the Tree: This is the branch of the tree of the Portugul Kings. Blessed Nonius daughter married the prince of Portugal Alphonzo son of John I.

Biography: Also known as Nunes and Nonius he married when seventeen and was named commander of Portugal's armies in 1383 when he was twenty-three. At the battle of Aljubarrota in 1385 they (Grand master of the knights of Aviz King John I and Blessed Nonius) defeated the Castilian army and made Portugal an independent state from Spain. When his wife died in 1422, Blessed Nonius became a Carmelite lay brother in a friary he founded in Lisbon. He died there on November 1. Blessed Nonius is called the Great Constable and is one of the National

SAINTS DAILY
Kings, Queens, Popes, Princes, Princesses, Emperors, Hermits, Bishops

DAILY SAINTS WHOSE ANCESTRY IS KNOWN

Heroes of Portugal. His story is celebrated in the sixteenth-century epic "Chronica Condestavel". In 1918 his cult was approved.

November 6   Blessed Joan Mary de Maille

Feastday: Nov 6   Date: 1414

Family: Father: Hardouin VI De Maillé   Mother: Jeanne De Montbazon
Spouse: Unknown   Siblings: Isabeau De Maille De Maillé, Hardouin VII De Maillé

Country: France

Ancestors: Not much is known, about five generations go up to the house of Dreux.

Branches of the Tree: This is the branch of the tree of the Dukes of Burgundy.

Biography: Baptized Joan and confirmed Mary, she once was said to save a playmate by her prayers when Robert de Sille had fallen into a pond. When they grew up he married her. The couple agreed to live together as brother and sister which they did for sixteen years. The war with the English caused the chateau of Sille to be captured. Robert was captured and escaped and the ransom was paid, so the couple added ransoming of prisoners to their charities. In 1362 Robert died and Blessed Joan Mary became a widow. She became a Franciscan tertiary, whose habit she always wore. She gave everything including the Chateau des Roches to the Carthusians of Liget. She returned to Tours and no one would house her. She begged her bread and lived sleeping in disused pig styes and dog-kennels. She was admitted among the servants of the hospital of St. Martin, but her holiness got her expelled. She finally found peace in the solitude of Plance-de-Vaux, near Clery. She restored a ruined chapel which later became named after her. She had a gift of prophecy which she

SAINTS DAILY
Kings, Queens, Popes, Princes, Princesses, Emperors, Hermits, Bishops

DAILY SAINTS WHOSE ANCESTRY IS KNOWN

related to the King, and had a great love for helping prisoners. She died on March 28 1414 and her cultus was approved in 1871.

November 7 *Saint Englebert*
Country: Spain **Date:** 1225

Family: Father: Unknown   Mother: Unknown
Spouse: Unknown   Siblings Unknown

Biography: Saint Englebert was slain by hired assassins and vererated as a martyr. He was Archbishop of Cologne, Germany and was the son of the count of Berg. Englebert was excommunicated but was restored into union with the Church. At the age of thirty he became the archbishop of Cologne in 1217. He became tutor to the son of Emperor Frederick II. In 1222 he crowned Henry King of the Romans. Saint Englebert was slain by his cousin Frederick. He had incurred his anger when he thwarted an attempt to steal from the nuns of Essen. Englebert was ambushed at Gebelsberg and murdered on November 7.

November 8 *Saint Cybi*
Country: Britain **Date:** b. 490   d. 555
       Patron: Cuby Cornwall, Llangibby, Monmouthshire, Wales and Llangybi, Cardigan Wales, Tregony Cornwall

Family: Father: Selyf Ap Erbin   Mother: Saint Gwen
Spouse: None   Siblings: Unknown

Ancestors: Saint Cyllus is an ancestor. Saint Helen of the Host is an Ancestor, Also Saint Brychan is an ancestor. Saint Constantine The Great is an Ancestor, as is Helen of the True Cross (Saint Helenus). Bran the Blessed is an Ancestor, as is his wife Anna of Arimathea. Saint Joseph of Arimathea and so the Line of Nathan Son of David King of Israel and Judah. King

SAINTS DAILY
 Kings, Queens, Popes, Princes, Princesses, Emperors, Hermits, Bishops

DAILY SAINTS WHOSE ANCESTRY IS KNOWN

David's ancestors include the Israelites, Zebulon, Levi, Joseph, and Judah. Also Anna of Arimathea, daughter to Joseph of Aramathea married Bran the Blessed whose line goes to Tros and so to Epraim son of Joseph the Israelite. Also the line from Anna of Arimathea's mother goes thru Simon the Just thru many High Priests to Judah the Israelite.

Branches of the Tree: Saint Non is the granddaughter of Saint Brychan and sister to Saint Gwen. Saint Dewi is in this part of the tree.

Biography: Saint Cybi was a welsh abbot. His other names he was called are Kabius and Cuby. His cousin was Saint David of Wales. He was born in Cornwall England, and is highly venerated in Anglesey. He also refused the throne of his area. He went to study under Saint Anda in Ireland to Monmouthshire and then to Avanmore. He also founded a monastery called Caer Cybi on an island near Holyhead Wales on Anglesey. Saint Cybi is the patron of Llanfebby and Llangybi, Cornwall, Landulf, Cuby and Tregony.

November 8   Saint Tysilio
Country: Great Britain   **Date:** mid 7th

Family: Father: Broche (King of Ysgithrog) ap Cyngen Saint   Mother: Unknown
Spouse: Unknown   Siblings: Cynan "Garwyn" Ap Brochwel

Ancestors: Brychan King of Brycheiniog Saint is an ancestor, and so Saint Helen of the Host.

Branches of the Tree: Because Saint Brychan is an ancestor and is the Great Grandfather of Saint Dewi, this is the Old English branch of the tree.

Biography: Saint Tysilio was the son of a Saint, Broche ap Cyngen who was also a King. He became a monk at Meifod in

SAINTS DAILY
Kings, Queens, Popes, Princes, Princesses, Emperors, Hermits, Bishops

DAILY SAINTS WHOSE ANCESTRY IS KNOWN

Powys, Wales at a young age. Later in life he served as abbot. About 617 he moved to Brittany France. This was in an attempt to pacify the widow of his brother who focused her attentions on him, and his father who demanded he return home after his brother's death. Saint Suliac was the region in Brittany he settled on. The name Saint Suliac may refer to him, or to some other person.

November 9   Saint Pabo ("Post Prydyn")

Date: 472- 530

Family:
Parents: Father- Arthwys ap Mor, King of the Pennines Mother- Saint Cywair
Wife:Unknown
Children: Arddun ("Benasgell") verch Pabo

Ancestry:
Saint Joseph of Arimathea is an ancestor and so David of Judah and Israel.
Saint Ursula is an ancestor. Saint Helenus and Saint Constantine I of the Holy Roman Empire are ancestors. King of Britain and Romans including Mark Antony and Julia of Rome. Also Saint Cyllin so Zerah thru the Kings of Siluria and Tros King of Troy.

Descendents:
Owain Prince of Wales, Eleanor Plantagenet, Rhodi King of Gwynedd, Morgan King of Morgannwg, Mawr Prince of Powys

Biography:
(Welsh-Pabo, Latin-Pabius, English-Pabio)

He divides his kingdom between his two sons: Dunaut Bwr and Sawyl Penuchel when in c.520 - King Pabo Post Prydain of the

SAINTS DAILY
Kings, Queens, Popes, Princes, Princesses, Emperors, Hermits, Bishops

DAILY SAINTS WHOSE ANCESTRY IS KNOWN

Pennines abdicates his throne in order to retire to a hermitage on Ynys Mon (Anglesey). The former founds Dunoting in the North while the latter holds the Peak District in the South. Death of King Riwal Mawr Marchou of Domnonée. King Budic II of Brittany returns to Cornouaille to claim the Breton throne. Their cousin, Cynwyd, is probably forced to seek land elsewhere and establishes his own Kingdom of Cynwydion, around the Chiltern Hills

530 - Saint Pabo Post Prydain, former King of the Pennines dies at Llanbabo. Pabo Post Prydein, earlier sources suggest that he was King Arthuis brother, is most popularly called the son of, though His epithet means *the Pillar of Britain*, said to derive from his keeping Pictish invaders at bay. In later life, Pabo turned to Christianity though his Kingdom covered the Pennines of central Britain. He abdicated the throne in favor of his sons, Dunaut Bwr and Sawyl Penuchel, and retired to Gwynedd where he founded the church of Llanabo on Ynys Mon (Anglesey). A beautiful medieval stone slab carved with his image can still be seen covering his grave. He died there on 9th November 530.

November 12 *Saint Kadwallyr*

Country: Wales   **Date:** d 664

Family: Parents: Father- Chadwallon   Mother- Daughter of Pybba Princess of Mercia
Wife: Nesta   Children: Ywrch Idwal

Ancestry: Saint Kadwallyr's ancestry is not known.

Descendents: King Edward IV Plantagenet is a descendent.

Biography: Saint Kadwallyr expanded his kingdom to Sussex, Surrey, as well as Kent. He is saint of the saxon people. King of

SAINTS DAILY
Kings, Queens, Popes, Princes, Princesses, Emperors, Hermits, Bishops

DAILY SAINTS WHOSE ANCESTRY IS KNOWN

Gwynedd, defeated and killed King Edwin of Northumbria with Penda of Mercia in 633 as he was called battle shunner because he was so peaceful. The Wessex army at Peonne defeated him in 658. Several churches are called Llangadwaladr which so bear his name. On Easter Eve in 668 he was baptized in Rome by Pope Sergius I as he had resigned his office. A few days later he died and was entombed in St. Peters.

November 12   *Saint Cadwaladr*

Country: England   **Date:** 689

Family: Father: Chadwallon   Mother: Helen (Alcfrith) of Mercia
Spouse: Nesta   Siblings: Unknown

Ancestors: Pabo ("Post Prydyn") ap Ceneu Saint is an ancestor, as is Ursula ferch Dynod Saint. Also Saint Cylinus and Saint Joseph of Arimathea, thus Nathan and the Davidic line. Blessed Bran is an ancestor and so the line to the Israelite Judah thru his son Zarah. Because David King of Judah and Israel is an ancestor the Israelites Judah, Levi, Zebulon and Joseph are Ancestors.

Branches of the Tree: Saint Cadwaladr left descendents whose line leads to the royalty of Europe thru Wales

Biography: Saint Cadwaladr is also called Ceadwalla and Cadwalla. He was born about 659 and was King of the West Saxons in 685 to 686. He also included in his kingdom as new acquisitions Kent, Surrey, and Sussex. He resigned his kingship and went to Rome where he was baptized by Pope Sergius I. A few days later he died and was entombed in Saint Peters.

SAINTS DAILY
Kings, Queens, Popes, Princes, Princesses, Emperors, Hermits, Bishops

DAILY SAINTS WHOSE ANCESTRY IS KNOWN

November 14 Saint Laurence Lorcan O'Toole

Country: Ireland   **Date:** 1180

Family: Father: Murtough Maurice Murcertac O'Toole Prince Mother: Unknown
Spouse: Unknown   Siblings: Unknown

Ancestors: Many going back to the Kings of Leinster, Ireland

Branches of the Tree: This branch is the branch of the tree strickly irish.

Biography: Archbishop Laurence Lorcan O'Toole was the son of Murtagh, Chief of the Murrays in Castledermot Kildare. He became the archbishop of Dublin, Ireland. The English invaded Ireland and he was involved with negotiating . In 1179 he attended the General Lateran Council in Rome. On a mission to King Henry II of England he died at Eu, Normandy France. He was canonized in 1225.

November 14   Saint Alberic

Feastday: November 14   Date: d. 784

Family: Father: Unknown   Mother: unknown
Spouse: unknown   Siblings unknown   Children: unknown

Country: France

Ancestors: Saint Wastrada was Saint Alberic grandmother. Saint Adele thru another line was Saint Alberics Great Grandmother. Saint Dagobert II was five generations from Saint Alberic so the line from Joseph the Israelite is true for Saint Alberic

SAINTS DAILY
 Kings, Queens, Popes, Princes, Princesses, Emperors, Hermits, Bishops

DAILY SAINTS WHOSE ANCESTRY IS KNOWN

Branches of the Tree: This is the area of the tree around Saint Dagobert II and Ragnetrude.

Biography: Friend to Alcuin and nephew to Saint Gregory of Utrecht he joined the Benedictines. He was prior of Utrectch cathedral, and in 775 was named bishop of Utrecht. This was done when his uncle Saint Gregory past to his reward. Saint Alberic is known for his successful missionary work among the Teutons. He was also known for his learning. August 21 was the date of his death.

November 15 Saint Leopold III of Austria

Country: Austria   **Date:** 1073-1136

Family: Parents: Father- Leopold II The Fair Margrave of Austria   Mother- Ida Franconia
Wife: Agnes Princess of Holy Roman Empire   Children: Agnes (Sophia) Babenberg Princess of Austria

Ancestry: Saint Leopold has Joseph of Arimathea as an ancestor. Also Saint Helena of Rome. Also King David of Judah and Israel is an ancestor thru Nathan his son. King Solomon of Israel and Judah is also an ancestor. Sainted Ancestors include Saint Ethelbert, Saint Itta, Saint Arnulf, Saint Sigebert, Saint Dagobert, Saint Beggue, Saint Liuthwin, Saint Sexburga, Blessed Pepin, and Saint Clodulf.

Descendents: Descendents include King Edward I Longshanks of England, King Charles V of France and King Charles VI of France. Also Phillippe III King of France.

Biography: Leopold was born at Melk, Austria, in 1073 of the Babenberger family. He was the Duke of Austria. He was educated by Bishop Altman of Passau, and at the age of twenty-three, he succeeded his father as military governor of Austria. He

SAINTS DAILY
Kings, Queens, Popes, Princes, Princesses, Emperors, Hermits, Bishops

DAILY SAINTS WHOSE ANCESTRY IS KNOWN

inherited the Dukedom in 1095. Known for his piety, charity, and good works in 1106 he also founded three monasteries of different orders, including Melk and Klosterneuburg, where he was buried. In critisism it is said he laid the foundation of Austria's ecclesiastical provincialism.

In 1106, Leopold married Emperor Henry IV's daughter, who bore him eighteen children, eleven of whom survived childhood. Two sons were famous, one as Archbishop Conrad of Salzburg and the other as a historian, Otto of Freising.

In 1125, Leopold refused to become German Emperor upon the death of his brother-in-law, Henry V. He died in 1135 at one of the monasteries he had founded. He was canonized by Pope Innocent VIII in 1486.

His feast day is a national Holiday.

November 15   *Saint Desiderius*

Date: d.655

Family: Father: Salvius Count of Albi   Mother: Herchenefreda
Spouse: unknown   Siblings; Rusticus Bishop of Cahors, Syagrius Count of Albi   Children: unknown

Country: France

Ancestors: Argotta of the Franks is an ancestor as is Pharamond. Saint Constantine and Saint Helen of the Cross thus the Davidic ancestry. The Franks ancestors were the line to Joseph the Israelite and so also the Greek from Priam back to Zerah son of Judah the Israelite.

Branches of the Tree: This is a branch of the tree near Saint Desideratus, and Saint Leger.

SAINTS DAILY
Kings, Queens, Popes, Princes, Princesses, Emperors, Hermits, Bishops

DAILY SAINTS WHOSE ANCESTRY IS KNOWN

Biography: Saint Desiderius brother was Saint Rusticus. Both were Bishops of Cahors France, and Saint Desiderius was his successor. In 630 he was made Bishop. As a nobleman of Albi France, he built monasteries, convents, and Churches and died near Albi.

November 16   *Saint Eucherius*
Feastday: November 16   Date: d. 449

Family: Father: Unknown   Mother: Unknown
Spouse: Galla   Siblings: Unknown Children: Saint Salonius, Saint Veranus, Tullia

Country: France

Ancestors: None known

Branches of the Tree: This Branch is three generations away from Saint Rusticus of Lyon

Biography: Saint Eucherius was Bishop of Lyon. Both his sons Saint Veranus and Saint Salonius became Bishops. He was a monk at Lerins, and then a hermit, and finally Bishop of Lyons. He dedicated a book to Saint Hilary of Arles about eremitical life and wrote letters that exist today.

November 16 Saint Margaret of Scotland
Country: Scotland   *Date:* c 1046-1093

Family: Parents: Father-Edward Atheling   Mother-Agatha of Germany
Husband: Malcolm III King of Scotland Dunkeld   Children: Matilda Canmore Of Scotland, Saint David of Scotland, Mary Princess of Scotland, Millicent Princess of Scotland

SAINTS DAILY
Kings, Queens, Popes, Princes, Princesses, Emperors, Hermits, Bishops

DAILY SAINTS WHOSE ANCESTRY IS KNOWN

Ancestry: Saint Margaret ancestors include Charlemange, Joseph of Arimathea, and Saint Helena of Rome. Also King David of Judah and Israel is an ancestor thru Nathan his son. King Solomon of Israel and Judah is also an ancestor. Sainted Ancestry includes Saint Ethelbert, Saint Arnulf, Saint Itta, Saint Sigebert, Saint Dagobert, Saint Beggue, Saint Liuthwin, Saint Bathildis, Saint Sexburga, Saint Clodulf, Blessed Pepin, Saint Matilda, Saint Elgiva, Saint Edgar, Saint Henry II, Saint Cunigunda, and Saint Stephen.

Descendents: Descendents include Louis IX of France, David of Scotland her son, and Saint Fernando III of Spain. Royal Descendents include King Edward Plantagenet III of England, King Philip IV of France, King of Naples Charles II, William I of Scotland, and Matilda Empress of Germany and Queen of England.

Biography: Margaret was an English princess named Margaret Atheling. She was the granddaughter of Edmund Ironside King of England and daughter of Edward Atheling. She and her mother sailed to Scotland to escape from the Norman king who had conquered their land. King Malcolm III of Scotland welcomed them and fell in love with the beautiful princess. Their marriage took place in 1069.

As Queen, Margaret changed her husband, church and the country for the better. Malcolm III was a good king, however he learned to listen to Margaret's advice. She founded monasteries, churches and hostels. She made the court beautiful and civilized. Soon all the princes had better manners, and the ladies copied her purity and devotion. The king and queen gave wonderful example to everyone by the way they prayed together and fed crowds of poor people with their own hands. They seemed to have only one desire: to make everyone happy and good. Margaret was a blessing for all the people of Scotland. Her private life was devoted to prayer and reading, almsgiving and needlework.

SAINTS DAILY
Kings, Queens, Popes, Princes, Princesses, Emperors, Hermits, Bishops

DAILY SAINTS WHOSE ANCESTRY IS KNOWN

Before she came, there was great ignorance and many bad habits among them. Margaret worked hard to obtain good teachers, to correct the evil practices, and to have new churches built. She loved to make these churches beautiful for God's glory, and she embroidered the priest's vestments herself.

November 17   *Saint Gregory Bishop of Tours*

Country: Germany   **Date:** b. 538 d. 594

Family: Father: Florentius Gallo Roman Senator
Mother: Armentaria
Spouse: unknown   Siblings: Unknown

Ancestors: Arthemia of Perthois who married Munderic who is the father of Saint Gondolfus.

Branches of the Tree: Saint Gondolfus is a few generations the ancestor of Saint Arnulf Bishop of Metz. Georgia is the Grandfather of Saint Gregory Bishop of Tours. Georgia married Leocardia, who had a different husband Mundéric des Francs Ripuaires. He is the father with Leocardia of Gondolfus who is a saint in his own right. Saint Gondolfus has descendents such as Saint Ladislaus of Hungary, Saint Louis IX of France, Saint Leopold III of Austria, Saint Leutwinus, Saint Margaret, Saint William of Toulouse, Saint Ansigisel, Saint Hedwig, Saint Clotilde, Saint Fernando III of Spain, Saint Ida, Saint Irene of Hungary, Saint Isabelle of Aragon, and Saint Nithard the Chronicler are all Descendents also King of England Edward III Plantagenet, King of Naples Charles II, King of France Louis VIII are also Descendents

Biography: Saint Gregorius Florentius was born of a well-known Aubergne family. He took the name Gregory. His birthplace was Clermont-Ferrand. His father died and he studied

SAINTS DAILY
Kings, Queens, Popes, Princes, Princesses, Emperors, Hermits, Bishops

DAILY SAINTS WHOSE ANCESTRY IS KNOWN

Scripture under Saint Avitus. His uncle raised him. His uncle was Saint Gaullus of Clermont. In 573 he became bishop of Tours. In 576 King Chilperic took control of Tours and Meroveus, the King's son got Saint Gregory's support. Leudastic, charged Gregory with treason. Gregory had had Leudastis who was a count of Tours removed. A council was made to investigate the charges, and the charges were proved false. Leudastis was convicted of perjury. King Chilperic died in 584. subsequent monarchs improved. Saint Gregory converted heretics, rebuilt the cathedral, and several churches. He was known for his religious fervor, and his justice and charity. Books were written by the Saint on the Gathers, the martyrs, and the Saints. He also wrote the book the History of the Franks, an outstanding source of early French History.

November 17 Saint Hilda

Feastday: November 17   **Date:** b. 614 d. 680

Family:
Parents: Father: Hereric Mother: Breguswith Spouse: Unknown Children: None Siblings: Hereswith Saint

Ancestry: Ancestors go back to the Anglo-Saxons around the year 100 AD. Also the line of the Kings of Deira lead to the Lords of the Anglo Saxons.

Branches of the Tree: Aeltheric Saint Hilda's Grandfather was brother to Saint Edwin of Northumbria.

Biography: Saint Hilda's father was the nephew to Saint Edwin. When she was baptized at thirteen it was at the same time as Saint Edwin. Her sister Hereswitha was a nun at Chelles Monastery in France. She went to the monastery at age 33. When Saint Aidan requested her return from France to Northumbria she became abbess of a double monastery at Hartleppol. Later she was transferred to the Streaneschalch monastery (Whitby). Her monasteries were renowned for the

SAINTS DAILY
Kings, Queens, Popes, Princes, Princesses, Emperors, Hermits, Bishops

DAILY SAINTS WHOSE ANCESTRY IS KNOWN

quality of her nuns and their learning. She did sponsor the Celtic customs, however when King Oswy's decree went out saying to observe the Roman usage she accepted them.

November 17   *Blessed Salome*

Country: Poland   **Date:** 1268

Father: Leszek King Of Poland   Mother: Grzymislawa
Spouse: Koloman Of Hungary   Siblings: Unknown

Ancestors: Vladimir the Saint of Russia, and the Kings of Poland

Branches of the Tree: Michael of Tschernikov Prince of Kiev Saint would be her cousin

Biography: Blessed Salome was a Poor Clare abbess. She was the daughter of Leszek the King of Poland and at age three to Prince Coloman of Hungary, son of King Andrew II. She became a widow in 1241 when Coloman was killed in battle. She then entered the Poor Clares, founding a convent at Zawichost and later moved to Skala. She later became the abbess of the convent. On November 17 she died at Zawichost. She was beatified in 1673.

November 18   *Saint Mabyn*

Date: d. Sixth   Feastday: September 21 or 18 November

Family:
Parents: Father-Saint Brychan   Mother- <u>Rigrawst</u> b: 0450

SAINTS DAILY
Kings, Queens, Popes, Princes, Princesses, Emperors, Hermits, Bishops

DAILY SAINTS WHOSE ANCESTRY IS KNOWN

Husband: Unknown
Children: Unknown

Biography:
Welsh and Cornish Saint also called Mabon and Mabenna. She is associated with Saint Teilo. She was a nun who founded the church of or lived close to St. Mabyn town. She is depicted in Stained Glass at the church of St. Neot in Cornwall in the Wives Window of 1523. Episcopal registers of the 13th century describe her church as Sancte Mabene. There is a male Malbano referred to as a Sint in the Feet of Fines (1234).

November 19 *Saint Narses Pahlav*

Country: Armenia **Date:** 335-373

Family: Parents: Father- Athenagenes Mother-Ataknines-Bambisn Princess of Armenia
Wife: Sandukht Children: Saint Isaac Pahlav

Ancestry: Saint Gregory the Enlightened is an Ancestor. Further Ancestry is unknown.

Descendents: Saint Fernando III is a descendent. Also Edward I Longshanks King of England is a descendent. Edward III and Edward IV Plantagenet are also descendents, with Thomas Prince of England. Edward Stafford 3rd Duke of Buckingham is also a descendent. Also William X Duke of Aquitane. Konstantinos Emperor of Byzantium is a descendent.

Biography: Father of St. Isaac the Great and Bishop and Martyr. He studied in Cappadocia, a native of Armenia, and he wed a princess who gave birth to Isaac. He served as a chamberlain in the court of King Arshak of Armenia after her death. He was made Catholicos of the Armenians in 353. Based on the principles he had studied under St. Basil at Caesarea Nerses devoted much effort to reforming the Armenian Church,

SAINTS DAILY
Kings, Queens, Popes, Princes, Princesses, Emperors, Hermits, Bishops

DAILY SAINTS WHOSE ANCESTRY IS KNOWN

including convening a synod in 365. His reforms and denunciation of King Arshak's murder of the queen led to his exile although he established hospitals and monasteries. After Arshak's death in battle he returned, but relations were not much better with the new Armenian ruler, Pap, whose dissolute lifestyle caused Nerses to refuse him admission into the church. Invited to a royal banquet at Khakh, on the Euphrates River, Nerses was assassinated by poison.

Saint Narses is the father of Saint Isaac Pahlav.

November 19   *Saint Ermenburga*
Country: Kent   **Date:** 700

Family: Father: Eadbald (King of Kent - 616-640) Mother: Emma de Neustria
Spouse: Merewald   Siblings Ethelred; Eanswythe Saint; Earcombryth (Earconbert) (Erconbert)

Ancestors:. .Saint Ethelbert and Saint Bertha of Paris is an ancestor, thus the Kings of Kent and the Frankish Kings are ancestors, Woden and Frigg are ancestors.

Branches of the Tree This is the branch of the tree that contains the Kings of Kent.

Biography: Saint Ermenburga was from a large family. He was the wife of Merewald King of Mercia. Saints Mildred, Milburga Ermengytha and Mildgytha were her daughters. She is also called Comna Ebba or Domneva. Her uncle, King Egbert of Kent donated some land and Saint Ermenberga founded the convent of Minster, on Thanet Isle. Ermenburga's two brothers were murdered by her uncle King Egbert of Kent so he donated this land in atonement for his crimes.

SAINTS DAILY
Kings, Queens, Popes, Princes, Princesses, Emperors, Hermits, Bishops

DAILY SAINTS WHOSE ANCESTRY IS KNOWN

November 21 Saint Albert of Louvain

Country: France   **Date:** 1193

Family: Father: Duke Godfrey III of Brabant
           Mother: Margaret Duchess of Lorraine
Spouse: Unknown   Siblings: Henry I, duke of Lorraine and Brabant

Biography: Saint Albert of Louvain was a cardinal and knight. He was the brother of Henry I Duke of Lorraine and Brabant. At twenty one years of age he became a Knight of Count Baldwin V, an enemy of Brabant. He had been made a canon of Leige France at age twelve but resigned to become a Knight. He declined going on a Crusade and became a canon again, the Bishop of Liege. Count Baldwin was not pleased and appealed to Rome. Pope Celestine III declared his appointment valid. While in Rome Saint Albert was made a cardinal by Archbishop William of Reims. Saint Albert was killed in the political struggle for Liege by a group of Knights from Emperor Henry's court. As a result Lothair was excommunicated and exiled and King Henry VI was forced to public penance for his Knights actions. Saint Albert's body was taken to the cathedral in 1612 at Reims. Then Archduke Albert of Austria had the remains transferred to the chapel of the new Carmelite convent. The cathedral of Liege has his remains since 1822.

November 22   Saint Tigrida

Country: Spain   **Date:** 925

Family: Father: Sancho Castile Cde de Castile
           Mother: Urraca Gomez of Saldana
Spouse: Unknown   Siblings: Munia Mayor Sanchez; Sancha Sanchez

Ancestors: Saint Arnulf of Metz is an ancestor, so the Israelite Joseph the Vizier of Egypt.

SAINTS DAILY
Kings, Queens, Popes, Princes, Princesses, Emperors, Hermits, Bishops

DAILY SAINTS WHOSE ANCESTRY IS KNOWN

Branches of the Tree: This is the branch of the tree of the Rulers of Spain

Biography: Saint Tigrida was the daughter of Sancho Castile and Urraca. She was a Benedictine abbess. Her father founded a convent near Burgos and she entered it. Saint Tigrida is especially venerated in Burgos.

November 24   *Saint Eanfleda*
Country: England   **Date:** 700

Family: Father: King Edwin of Northumbria Saint
         Mother: Ethelburga Saint
Spouse: Unknown   Siblings: Unknown

Ancestors: Ancestors go back to the Anglo-Saxons around the year 100 AD. Also the line of the Kings of Deira lead to the Lords of the Anglo Saxons from Saint King Edwin. Saint Ethelbert of Kent ancestry traces back to Zerah thru the Kings of Troy. His wife Saint Bertha also is traced back to the lines of the Frankish Kings to Zerah whose father is Judah. Saint Bertha's ancestor is Saint Clotilde who converted the Frankish King Clovis to Christianity. Also included is Joseph of Arimathea. Also King David of Judah and Israel is an ancestor thru Nathan his son.

Branches of the Tree: This is the branch of the tree of the English Kings.

Biography: Saint Eanfleda was the daughter of King St. Edwin and St. Ethelberga of Kent. A supporter of St. Wilfrid, Eanfleda became a Benedictine nun at Whitby as a widow. St. Paulinus had baptized her as an infant. Her daughter, St. Elfieda, was abbess at Whitby.

SAINTS DAILY
Kings, Queens, Popes, Princes, Princesses, Emperors, Hermits, Bishops

DAILY SAINTS WHOSE ANCESTRY IS KNOWN

November 27   *Saint Guntramus*

Feastday: Nov 27   Date: b c 488 d. 592

Family: Father: Clothaire I King of Franks   Mother: Ingonde
Spouse: Unknown   Siblings: Blithildis (Blithilde) Children: None

Country: Britain

Ancestors: The early Franks are ancestors and so the line to Joseph the Israelite. Saint Clothide is Saint Guntramus grandmother.

Branches of the Tree: This branch of the tree is the early Franks.

Biography: From Saint Gregory of Tours we know he was King of Burgandy and part of Aquitaine from 561. Three synods were supported to improve clerical discipline. He endowed many churches and monasteries. He divorced his wife. Of another wife he had her phusician murdered it was rumored. He spent the remainder of his life in penance for his deeds.

November 27   *Saint Cungar*

Feastday: Nov 27   Date: b c 488 d. 550

Family: Father: Gerren Llyngesog Ab Erbin, King Of Dumonia   Mother: Gwyar Verch Amlawdd
Spouse: Unknown   Siblings: Unknown Children: None

Country: Britain

Ancestors: Conan is an ancestor, and so also Saint Dareca sister to Saint Patrick. Therefore the Israelites Joseph, Benjamin, Levi, Zebulun and Judah are ancestors because Saint Patrick is a descendent of King David of Judah and Israel.

SAINTS DAILY
Kings, Queens, Popes, Princes, Princesses, Emperors, Hermits, Bishops

DAILY SAINTS WHOSE ANCESTRY IS KNOWN

Branches of the Tree: This branch is eight generations down from Conan and is two generations from Erbin Ap Custennin

Biography: Saint Cungar became a monk. He was a native of Devon England. A monstery near Yatton Somerset was founded by Saint Cungar. To escape the Saxons, he fled to South Wales. In South Wales he founded a church near Cardiff. Later he may have accompanied Saint Cybi to Ireland where a church at Llangefni was founded.

November 29   *Saint Sadwrn*

Country: Great Britain   *Date:* 6th Century

Family: Father: Bicon (Bicanus) Farchog ap Aldrien
Mother: Rhieinwylydd verch Amlawdd Wledig
Spouse: Canna verch Tewdr Marw Saint   Siblings: Illtud Farchog (the Knight) ap Bican Saint

Ancestors: Saint Ursula of Dumonia and Conan are ancestors.

Branches of the Tree: Branch of the tree of King Arthur of the Round Table.

Biography: Saint Sadwrn was a disciple of St. Cadfan and had churches dedicated to him in parts of Wales. He was a confessor and brother of Saint Illtyd. He was also known as Saturninus.

November 29   *Saint Ethelwin*

Country: Great Britain   *Date:* 6th Century

Family: Father: Cynegila Wessex   Mother: Seaxburh Cven Vvestseaxna
Spouse: Siblings: Cenwalh

SAINTS DAILY
Kings, Queens, Popes, Princes, Princesses, Emperors, Hermits, Bishops

DAILY SAINTS WHOSE ANCESTRY IS KNOWN

Ancestors: Kings of Wessex, Lines of Anglo Saxons

Biography: Monk and hermit. Founded the abbey of Athelney (Somerset) as a hermit. Suffered Ill health all his life, but to have been a healer.

November 29 — Saint Egelwine

Country: Great Britain   **Date:** 7^h Century

Family: Father: Cynegils   Mother: unknown
                 Spouse: unknown   Siblings: unknown

Ancestors: Kings of Wessex, Lines of Anglo Saxons

Biography: Saint Egelwine was a Confessor and a prince of the house of Wessex. He lived at Athelney in Somersetshire, England.

November 30 — Saint Tudwal

Country: Great Britain   **Date:** c. 500

Family: Father: Urban Meriadoc   Mother: Unknown
                 Spouse: Unknown   Siblings: Unknown

Ancestors: Conan and Saint Dareca are Grandparents.

Branches of the Tree: King Arthur is Saint Tudwal's great grandson.

Biography: Saint Tudwal father is known and his line to King Arthur is known. Other than that relationships found in the lineage tables in Saints in the Tree file are all that is known.

SAINTS DAILY
Kings, Queens, Popes, Princes, Princesses, Emperors, Hermits, Bishops

DAILY SAINTS WHOSE ANCESTRY IS KNOWN

Saints of December

FEAST DAY	SAINT	COUNTRY	BORN	DIED
1-Dec	Saint Tudwal	Britain		c. 564
4-Dec	Saint Osmund	France		1099
6-Dec	Saint Gertrude of Hamage	Prussia	540	
9-Dec	Saint Budoc	England		7th
9-Dec	Saint Ethelgiva	England		896
13-Dec	Saint Odile	France		c. 720
16-Dec	Saint Adelaide of Italy	Italy		999
17-Dec	Saint Judicael of Domnonee	Domnonee		658
17-Dec	Saint Tydecho	Britain		6th
17-Dec	Saint Begga	Landen		694
18-Dec	Saint Gondolfus Bishop de d'Aquitaine	Aquitaine	530	c 599
18-Dec	Saint Flannan	Ireland		7th
22-Dec	Blessed Jutta	Germany	1111	1136
23-Dec	Blessed Margaret of Savoy	Italy	1382	1464
23-Dec	Saint Dagobert II of Franks	Franks		679
24-Dec	Saint Irmina	France		708
24-Dec	Saint Adele of Austrasia	France		8th

SAINTS DAILY
Kings, Queens, Popes, Princes, Princesses, Emperors, Hermits, Bishops

349

DAILY SAINTS WHOSE ANCESTRY IS KNOWN

25-Dec	Saint Alburga	England	777	c 800
25-Dec	Saint Adalsind	France		c 715
27-Dec	Saint John Zebedee	Israel		1st
29-Dec	Saint Thomas Beckett	England	1118	1170
29-Dec	Blessed William Howard	England	1614	1680
31-Dec	Saint Offa	England		709

TABLE THIRTEEN SAINTS OF DECEMBER

December 1 *Saint Tudwal*

Date: c. 564   **Feastday:** December 1

Family:
Parents: Father- Hoel I Mawr ('the Great') de Bretagne Mother- Alma Pompea de Domnonée Saint
Siblings: Hoel II Fychan ('the Small') de Bretagne
Children: None

Ancestry: Saint Tudwal is eight generations the descendent of Conan and Saint Dareca. He is also descended thru Conan and Saint Ursula. Therefore Saint James the son of Saint Joseph is an ancestor and the line of David thru Solomon. Therefore the Israelites Joseph, Benjamin, Levi, Zebulon and Judah are ancestors. Also King Coel of Britain is an ancestor.

Branches of the Tree:
Saint Tudwal is located near King Budig II.

Biography:

SAINTS DAILY
Kings, Queens, Popes, Princes, Princesses, Emperors, Hermits, Bishops

DAILY SAINTS WHOSE ANCESTRY IS KNOWN

Saint Tudwal is sometimes called Saint Tugdual. He was the son of Hoel the Great King of Bretagne. King of Dumnonia Deroc was cousin to Saint Tudwal and the Saint worked to promote the faith in Dumnonia. King Childeric became his sponsor when he became Bishop of Treguier.

December 4   *Saint Osmund*
Country: Ireland   Date: 1099

Family: Father: Henry Count Of Seez   Mother: Isabella
Spouse: Unknown   Siblings: Unknown

Biography: Saint Osmund was the Bishop of Salisbury. He is credited with helping to compile the Domesday Book. Isabella, the half-sister of the King William the Conqueror was his mother and Count Henry of Seez was his father. Saint Osmund took part in the Norman Conquest and was chancellor to King William. Appointed bishop of Salisbury in 1078. He completed the cathedral there and he founded a chapter of canons regular and he founded a school for clerics. The massive census which became the Domesday Book was done with Osmunds assistance. Osmund sided with the King against Anselm in a dispute over investiture, and he later begged Anselm's forgiveness after deciding he was wrong. Saint Osmund authored a life of Saint Aldhelm, and collected manuscripts for the cathedral library. He was responsible for drawing up the books concerning the liturgical matters. These books concerned the Mass and Divine Office, and the Sarum Use. Pope Callistus III canonized him in 1457. He was the last English person to be declared a Saint until Saints Thomas More and Saint John Fisher were canonized in 1935.

December 6   Saint Gertrude of Hamage the Elder
Country: Prussia   *Date:* d. 649

SAINTS DAILY
Kings, Queens, Popes, Princes, Princesses, Emperors, Hermits, Bishops

DAILY SAINTS WHOSE ANCESTRY IS KNOWN

Family: Parents: Father- Unknown Mother- Unknown Husband: Richemeres von Franconia Children: Gerberga de Franconia

Ancestry: Parents unknown as well as any other ancestor.

Descendents: Sainted Descendents include Saint Adelaide Empress of Italy, Saint Henry II, Saint Louis IX, Saint Adele Countess of Blois, Saint Cunigunda of Luxemborg, Saint David of Scotland, Saint Margaret of Scotland, Saint Ferdinand III of Spain, Saint Leopold III of Austria, Saint Leutwinus, and Saint Raymond Berenger IV. Blessed Charlemagne, blessed Humbert III, and Blessed Gisele are also Descendents. Royal Descendents Include King of Aragon Pedro II, King of Castile Alphonso VIII, King of England William the Conqueror, King of France Hugh Capet, King of Hungary Andreas II, King of Italy Berenger I, King of Naples Charles II, King of Navarre Teobaldo, King of Jerusalem Fulk V, King of Scotland William the Lion.

Biography: Benedictine foundress and widow. She founded and served as abbess of Hamage Abbey, near Douai, France. Gertrude is six generations the ancestor of Saint Leutwinus and nine generations the ancestor of Charlemange. Feast day December 6.

December 9 *Saint Budoc*
Country: Great Britain *Date:* 7th Century

Family: Father: Alain I de Bretagne (King of Bretagne)
Mother: Azenor of Brest
Spouse: None Siblings: Hoel III de Bretagne (King of the Bretons)

Ancestors:

SAINTS DAILY
Kings, Queens, Popes, Princes, Princesses, Emperors, Hermits, Bishops

DAILY SAINTS WHOSE ANCESTRY IS KNOWN

Branches of the Tree: Paternus Pasrut (Padarn Beisrudd ap Saint) is the Saint in this branch of the tree.

Biography: He is reported to be the son of a king of Brittany and of Azenor, who was and Beuzec the daughter of the ruler of Brest, France Bishop and hermit, also called Budeux. Azenor was supposedly exiled in a cask, and attended by St. Brigid Budoc was born at sea, He became first the abbot of the house and then bishop of Dol, Brittany. He was raised in a monastery near Waterford, Ireland. For twenty-six years Budoc ruled there. Another tradition claims that Budoc was an Irish hermit who settled in Budock, near Falmouth, England.

December 9 *Saint Ethelgiva*

Country: England *Date:* 896

Family: Father: King Alfred the Great Saint
Mother: Etheldwitha Saint
Spouse: None   Siblings: Edward I King of England

Ancestors: Saint Alfred's ancestors include the Kings of Wessex. Also King David of Judah and Israel is an ancestor thru Joseph of Arimathea and Nathan David's son.

Branches of the Tree: This is the branch of the tree of the English Kings.

Biography: Benedictine abbess of Shaftesbury, England. She was a daughter of King Alfred the Great. Also a Saint was her mother Etheldwitha.

December 13 *Saint Odilia*

Country: France *Date:* 8th Century
Patron: Blind; Alsace

SAINTS DAILY
Kings, Queens, Popes, Princes, Princesses, Emperors, Hermits, Bishops

DAILY SAINTS WHOSE ANCESTRY IS KNOWN

Family: Father: Adalric I, Duke Alsace   Mother: Berswinde (Bersvinda) Duchess Alsace
Spouse: Unknown   Siblings: Adalbert Duke of Alsace

Biography: Some information about Saint Odilia is found in the lineage relationships and family information shown in the file Saints in the Tree. She was born blind at Obernheim in the Bosges Mountains, Her mother pleaded for her life and she was not put to death on the advice she would be sent away to someone who did not know her background. She was given to a peasant women. When she was twelve she entered a convent at Baume, where she was baptized by Bishop St. Erhard of Regensburg and recovered her sight when the Bishop touched her eyes with Chrism during the baptism ceremony. Adalric was told of this and angered by his prospect of her return he struck Hugh, his son and killed him. He changed his attitude and was affectionate to her until she was told to marry a German Duke. She fled and when Adalric caught her he was miraculously saved from his anger and allowed her to found a convent at his castle at Hohenburg (Odilienbeg, Alsace), and she became abbess. Another monastery was founded called Niedermunster, and she lived there until her death, venerated for her visions and the miracles attributed to her. She died at Niedermunster on December 13, and her shrine became a great pilgrimage center. Patroness of the blind and of Alsace.

December 16   Saint Adelaide of Italy

Country: Italy   **Date:** c 999

Family: Parents: Father-Rudolph II of Burgundy Mother-Bertha of Swabia
Husband: Otto I the Great Holy Roman Emperor   Children: Otto II Holy Roman Empire Emperor

SAINTS DAILY
Kings, Queens, Popes, Princes, Princesses, Emperors, Hermits, Bishops

DAILY SAINTS WHOSE ANCESTRY IS KNOWN

Ancestry: Saint Adelaide ancestors include Zerah, traceable thru the Frankish line. Also the Kings of Burgundy trace to Saint Adelaide. Also King David of Judah and Israel is an ancestor thru Nathan his son. King Solomon of Israel and Judah is also an ancestor. Sainted Ancestors include Saint Arnulf, Saint Itta, Saint Sigebert, Saint Dagobert, Saint Beggue, Saint Luithwin, Saint Bathildis, Blessed Pepin, Saint Clodulf,

Descendents: Descendents include King Edward I Longshanks of England and Joan of Acre of England. Also King Edward III of England and King Casimir of Poland.

Biography: When Saint Adelaide was two her father engaged her to Lothair of Italy and at 15 or 16 she was married to Lothair. Lothair died three years later. Saint Adelaide was imprisoned by successor and usurper to Lothair Berengar of Ivrea and he attempted to force her to marry his son. There is a legend that Adelaide escaped to Canossa, where she appealed to Otto of Germany for help. Otto conquered Italy and married Adelaide in 951. John XII crowned both Adelaide and Otto rulers of the Holy Roman Empire the following year. Adelaide quarreled with Otto II after Otto's death in 973, possibly at the instigation of her daughter-in-law Theophano, and lived with her brother in Burgundy. She became interested in evangelism and established many monasteries and churches. She became reconciled with her son before his death in 983, and she became regent for her grandson Otto III. At the convent at Seltz which she had founded Adelaide died in 999. Cluny became the center of her cult. She was canonized in 1097.

December 17 *Saint Judicael*
Country: Britain   *Date:* d 658

Family: Parents: Father- Hoel III King of Bretons Mother- Pritelle Wife: Morone
Children: Alain II Hir King of the Bretons

SAINTS DAILY
Kings, Queens, Popes, Princes, Princesses, Emperors, Hermits, Bishops

355

DAILY SAINTS WHOSE ANCESTRY IS KNOWN

Ancestry: Saint Judicael ancestors include Saint Patrick, Saint Cyllinus, Blessed Bran and Anna of Arimathea. Anna of Armimathea's father is Saint Joseph of Arimathea and so the Line of Nathan Son of David King of Israel and Judah. King David's ancestors include the Israelites, Zebulon, Levi, Joseph, and Judah. Also Anna of Arimathea, daughter to Joseph of Aramathea married Bran the Blessed whose line goes to Tros and so to Epraim son of Joseph the Israelite. Also the line from Anna of Arimathea's mother goes thru Simon the Just thru many High Priests to Judah the Israelite.

Descendents: Cadell ap Rhodri Mawr King of South Wale 861 – 910, Hywel Dda' ap Cadell Prince of Deheubarth 887 – 950, Owain ap Hywel Dda King of South Wales 913 – 987 and also King Edward IV Plantagenet of England.

Biography: King in Amorica, in Brittany. Succeeded by his brother St. Judoc, he abdicated his throne. He spent twenty years as a monk at Gael Abbey. He assumed the title of King when his father died, prince of Domnonia. After abdicating, he became a monk, again resigned and lived in the monastery of Gael the last twenty years of his life.

December 17 *Saint Tydecho*
Country: Britain *Date:* 6th

Family: Parents: Father- Amwn Ddu ap Budic , Abbot of Southill, Prince Mother- Anna verch Gwerthefyr gan Oxenhall, Princess of Wife: Unknown
Siblings: Saint Sampson, Saint Cadfan

Ancestry: Saint Tydecho's ancestors include Saint Patrick, Saint Cyllinus, Blessed Bran and Anna of Arimathea. Anna of Armimathea's father is Saint Joseph of Arimathea and so the Line of Nathan Son of David King of Israel and Judah. King David's ancestors include the Israelites, Zebulon, Levi, Joseph, and Judah. Also Anna of Arimathea, daughter to Joseph of

SAINTS DAILY
Kings, Queens, Popes, Princes, Princesses, Emperors, Hermits, Bishops

DAILY SAINTS WHOSE ANCESTRY IS KNOWN

Aramathea married Bran the Blessed whose line goes to Tros and so to Epraim son of Joseph the Israelite. Also the line from Anna of Arimathea's mother goes thru Simon the Just thru many High Priests to Judah the Israelite.

Branch of the Tree: Branch near Saint Judicael and Budig

Biography: Welsh Saint with many churches named after him.

December 17   *Saint Begga*
Country: France   **Date:** 694

Family: Parents: Father- Pepin I, Major Domus of Austrasia   Mother- Itta of Metz
Husband: Adalgiselus Major Domus of Austrasia   Children: Pepin II Count of Heristal

Ancestry: Saint Begga can trace ancestry to Pepin, but little is known past that. Also King David of Judah and Israel is an ancestor thru Joseph of Arimathea.

Descendents: Sainted descendants include Saint Adele of Blois, Saint Adelaide of Italy, Saint Louis IX of France, Saint Fernando III of Spain, Saint Cunigunda of Luxemborg, Saint Leopold III of Austria, Saint Henry II of Germany, Saint Lazlo King of Hungary, Saint Raymond Berenger IV. Saint Edgar King of England, Saint David and Saint Margaret of Scotland. Royal descendents include King Edward III Plantagenet of England, King of Naples Charles II, King of France Philip IV, and King of Scotland William the Lion. Also Casimir King of Poland, Alphonso Enriquez I King of Portugal and Henry IV Holy Roman Emperor of Germany.

Biography: With her husband Ansegilius, son of St. Arnulf of Metz, Saint Begga founded the Carolingian dynasty of rulers in France. She was the daughter of Pepin of Landen. In 691 her

SAINTS DAILY
Kings, Queens, Popes, Princes, Princesses, Emperors, Hermits, Bishops

357

DAILY SAINTS WHOSE ANCESTRY IS KNOWN

husband died and she built a church and convent at Andenne on the Meuse River and died there. Her feast day is December 17th.

December 18   *Saint Gondolphus*

Country: England   **Date:** b. 530- 588

Family: Parents: Father- Maurilion Gallo (Patrician of Roman Empire) Mother- (Daughter) of Berthar of the Thuringe Wife: Palatina de Troyes   Children: Bodegisel II Governor of d'Aquitaine

Ancestry: Only one generation is known.

Descendents: Saint Ladislaus of Hungary, Saint Louis IX of France, Saint Leopold III of Austria, Saint Leutwinus, Saint Margaret, Saint William of Toulouse, Saint Ansigisel, Saint Hedwig, Saint Clotilde, Saint Fernando III of Spain, Saint Ida, Saint Irene of Hungary, Saint Isabelle of Aragon, and Saint Nithard the Cronicler are all Descendents. King of England Edward III Plantagenet, King of Naples Charles II, King of France Louis VIII are also Descendents.

Biography: Also called Duke Saint Bodegisel I of the Franks. Born in 530 to a Patrician of Roman Empire, Maurilion Gallo, he became the Bishop of Tongres. He fathered the Governor of D'Aquitaine, and died after 599. He founded an abbey on the banks of the Meuse. He was praised by St. Gregory of Tours and St. Venantius Fortunatus as the abbot of the monastery.

December 18   *Saint Flannan*

Country: Ireland   **Date:** 7th Century

Family: Father: Tairdelbach   Mother: Unknown
Spouse: None
Siblings: Saint Aidan

SAINTS DAILY
Kings, Queens, Popes, Princes, Princesses, Emperors, Hermits, Bishops

DAILY SAINTS WHOSE ANCESTRY IS KNOWN

Ancestors: A line of Irish for nine generations ending in Conall.

Branches of the Tree: The King of Ireland Brian Boroimhe is in this branch of the tree. Saints in the branch of King Brian include Saint Flannan, Saint Breacan. A related branch of the tree of King Brian's wife Gormflaith Of Nass is the Saint Cumne, Saint Sodelb, Saint Ethne, Saint Dar-Carthaind, Saint Fedelm, Saint Coeman Santlethan and Saint Mugain, all in the branch of the tree of King Brian's wife Gormflaith Of Nass

Biography: Saint Flannan seventh century Bishop was son of an Irish chieftain. He made a pilgrimage when Pope John the fourth consecrated him. He was the son of an Irish chieftain Turlugh. On his return trip from Rome he became first Bishop of Killaloe. His feast day is December 18 in the brides he is known for his preaching.

December 22   *Blessed Jutta*

Feastday: December 22   Date: b. 1111 d.1136

Family: Father: Stephan Count Of Spondheim
        Mother: Unknown
Spouse: Unknown   Siblings: Archbishop Hugo of Koln, Count Rudolf, Count Gerhard, Meginhard I

Country: Germany

Ancestors: Nothing past the father is known

Branches of the Tree: This branch of the tree is near the Saint Eberhard. Meginhard married a descendent of Saint Eberhard V.

Biography: Sister of clount Mefingard of Spanheim, she started a community. This community was formed from the disciples she attracted when she became a recluse at a house that adjoined Saint Disibod's Monastery. Blessed Jutta was entrused with

SAINTS DAILY
Kings, Queens, Popes, Princes, Princesses, Emperors, Hermits, Bishops

DAILY SAINTS WHOSE ANCESTRY IS KNOWN

Saint Hildegard while she was a child, and was raised and educated by Blessed Jutta.

December 23 Blessed Margaret of Savoy

Feastday: Dec 23   Date: 1382-1464

Family: Father: Amadeus De Savoy Pr of Achaia
          Mother: Catherine De Geneve
Spouse: Theodore Palaeologus   Siblings: Unknown

Country: Italy

Ancestors: Saint Humbert III is eight generations her ancestor. The Palaelogus line has Daniel (Chileab) the son of King David as an Ancestor.

Branches of the Tree: This is the branch of the tree of the Lords of Savoy.

Biography: She married Theodore Palaelogous marquis of Montferrat in 1403. In 1418 she was widowed and joined as a Franciscan tertiary. She was offered marriage to Philip Visconti of Milan. On her own estate she founded a community. She founded in 1426 and in 1451 Pope Eugene IV gave her permission for the women of her community to become nuns. She was charged with being overly strict with her nuns, and she had ecstasies and it was reported she performed miracles. Her convent was charged with Waldensianism, a charge later proved false, by rumors circulated by the rejected Philip Visconti. She died on Novemeber 23, and her cult was confirmed in 1669. She died at Alba.

SAINTS DAILY
Kings, Queens, Popes, Princes, Princesses, Emperors, Hermits, Bishops

DAILY SAINTS WHOSE ANCESTRY IS KNOWN

December 23   Saint Dagobert

Country: France   **Date:** 679

Family: Parents: Father- Sigebert II King of Franks
Mother- Emnechilde
Wife: Ragnetrude   Children: Regintrud; Saint Adele of Austrasia

Ancestry: Saint Dagobert has King David of Judah and Israel is an ancestor thru Joseph of Arimathea and King David's son Nathan.

Descendents: Descendants include Saint Adele of Blois, Saint Adelaide of Italy, Saint Louis IX of France, Saint Fernando III of Spain, Saint Cunigunda of Luxemborg, Saint Leopold III of Austria, Saint Henry II of Germany, Saint Lazlo King of Hungary, Saint Raymond Berenger IV. Saint Edgar King of England and Saint David and Saint Margaret of Scotland. Royal descendents include King Edward III Plantagenet of England, King of Naples Charles II, King of France Philip IV, and King of Scotland William the Lion. Also Casimir King of Poland , Alphonso Enriquez I King of Portugal and Henry IV Holy Roman Emperor of Germany.

Biography: The son of King Sigebert II Dagobert was the martyred King of Austrasia. Forced into exile as a child he took the throne. When Childebert was named king Bishop Dido of Poitiers, France took him to Ireland. In 675 he regained his throne but after only four years he was murdered. Ebroin the mayor of the palace did the deed on December 23 while on a hunting trip. St. Wilfrid was a friend of Dagobert.

SAINTS DAILY
Kings, Queens, Popes, Princes, Princesses, Emperors, Hermits, Bishops

DAILY SAINTS WHOSE ANCESTRY IS KNOWN

December 24 *Saint Irmina*
Country: Austrasia   **Date:** 708

Family: Father: Dagobert II King Of Franks Saint
          Mother: Ragnetrude
Spouse: Unknown   Siblings: Adele Austrasia Saint, Regintrud

Ancestors: Dabobert, Walter, etc. are all ancestors, whose line leads to Joseph the Israelite. Also the line leading to Zerah, son of Judah, as well as the line leading to Levi. Thus Three Israelites are ancestors, Joseph, Levi, and Zerah. Saint Dagobert has King David of Judah and Israel is an ancestor thru Joseph of Arimathea and King David's son Nathan.

Branches of the Tree: This vicinity of the Branch is closest to the Frankish Kings, Charibert, Dagobert, etc...

Biography: Saint Irmina was the daughter of the Frankish King Dagobert II. Her father was also a Saint. He built the Oehren Convent for Irmina. She was a Benedictine abbess. The convent was built after the death of Count Herman. King Dagobert II who was a Saint betrothed her to Count Herman. For Willibrord in 698 Saint Irmina built Echternacht.

December 24 *Saint Adele*
Country: Austrasia   **Date:** 730

Family: Father: Dagobert II King Of Franks Saint
          Mother: Ragnetrude
Spouse: Unknown   Siblings: Irmina Austrasia Saint, Regintrud

Ancestors: Dagobert, Walter, etc.. are all ancestors, whose line leads to Joseph the Israelite. Also the line leading to Zerah, son of Judah, as well as the line leading to Levi. Thus Three

SAINTS DAILY
Kings, Queens, Popes, Princes, Princesses, Emperors, Hermits, Bishops

362

DAILY SAINTS WHOSE ANCESTRY IS KNOWN

Israelites are ancestors, Joseph, Levi, and Judah. Saint Dagobert has King David of Judah and Israel is an ancestor thru Joseph of Arimathea and King David's son Nathan.

Branches of the Tree: This vicinity of the Branch is closest to the Frankish Kings, Charibert, Dagobert, etc…

Biography: She was the sister of Saint Irmina and the daughter of King Dagobert II of Germany. Saint Adele became a nun when her husband died. Her son was the father of Saint Gregory of Utrecht. Saint Adele founded a convent at Palationlum near Trier. She was the abbess and ruled with compassion, prudence, and holiness. Saint Boniface did at one time write to her and there is a record of that correspondence. The Apostle of Germany Saint Boniface had many disciples, and Saint Adele appears to have been on of them. In 730 she passed, and her life was filled with good works.

December 25   *Saint Alburga*
Country: Ireland   **Date:** 800

Family: Father: Eahlmund of Wessex (Under-King of Kent)   Mother: (Daughter) of Æthelbert II (King of Kent)
      Spouse: Wulfstan   Siblings: Saint Flannan, King Egbert of Wessex.

Ancestors: A line of Irish for nine generations ending in Conall.

Branches of the Tree: The King of Ireland Brian Boroimhe is in this branch of the tree. Saints in the branch of King Brian include Saint Flannan, Saint Breacan. A related branch of the tree of King Brian's wife Gormflaith Of Nass is the Saint Cumne, Saint Sodelb, Saint Ethne, Saint Dar-Carthaind, Saint Fedelm, Saint Coeman Santlethan and Saint Mugain, all in the branch of the tree of King Brian's wife Gormflaith Of Nass

SAINTS DAILY
Kings, Queens, Popes, Princes, Princesses, Emperors, Hermits, Bishops

DAILY SAINTS WHOSE ANCESTRY IS KNOWN

Biography: Saint Alburga was an Abbess and foundress. She was the sister of King Egbert and Saint Flannan. Being a daughter of the Under King of Kent she was a princess. At an early age it was noticed she was very Pious. As part of a political alliance she was married to Wulfstan. The Abbey of Wilton was founded by Saint Alburga, and when her husband died, she retired there. Eventually she became the abbess there.

December 25   *Saint Adalsind*
Country: Franconia, Prussia   **Date:** 715

Family: Father: Adalbald I De Artois Saint   Mother: Saint Rictrudis
Spouse: Unknown   Siblings: Adalbald II De Artois, Eusebia Saint, Clotsind Saint, and Mauront Saint

Ancestors: None known

Branches of the Tree: This branch is the branch near Saint Gertrude of Hamage.

Biography: Saint Adalsind was from a family of Saints. Her siblings Saint Eusebia, Saint Clotsind, and Saint Mauront and herself were children of Saint Adalbald and Saint Rictrudis. Saint Adalsind's sister Saint Eusebia was abbess of a Benedictine convent at Hamayles-Marchiennes, near Arras, France where she joined.

December 27   *Saint John Zebedee*
Country: Israel   **Date:** 1st Century
Patron: Poison Sufferers, Taos New Mexico, Theologians, Turkey (Asiatic); Asia Minor

Family: Father: Zebedee   Mother: Mary
Spouse: Unknown   Siblings: Saint James Zebedee

SAINTS DAILY
Kings, Queens, Popes, Princes, Princesses, Emperors, Hermits, Bishops

364

DAILY SAINTS WHOSE ANCESTRY IS KNOWN

Ancestors: Saint Joseph of Arimathea is an ancestor. A little know fact of the biblical character of Joseph of Arimathea is that he is the son of Mathat, who is in the line of Nathan that is listed in the New Testament book of Luke. His ancestors then must be King David of Israel and Judah, and so the Israelites Joseph, Levi, Zebulon, and Judah. Anna married Saint Joseph of Arimathea, and her ancestry is an unbroken male line to Levi the Israelite. Saint Joseph of Arimathea's mother may have been the daughter of Eleazor, who was of the Davidic line of Solomon. Eleazor was the Grandfather of Joseph who married the Virgin Mary and this line is listed in the Gospel of Mathew. The Israelite Benjamin was an ancestor of King Davids wife Maacah (Sauls daughter) whose line married in the line from Solomon joined by the marriage of Reheboam to Maacah. Therefore Saint Joseph of Arimathea has five Israelites as ancestors.

Branches of the Tree: This is a branch of the tree that has Saint Joseph of Arimathea in it. He is three generations the ancestor of Saint John. This line also marries Anna Arimathea who is the daughter of Joseph of Arimathea.

Biography: Saint John is the apostle that is mentioned in various places in the bible. His grandfather was Saint Joseph of Arimathea, and so was related to the house of David. He is called Saint John the Evangelist, and was one of the two "Sons of Thunder". Saint John is credited as writing a gospel, three epistles, and the book of Reveleation. Saint John was the only one of the apostles to stand by the Lord on Calgary standing at the cross and was given the charge of his Mother by the Lord.

December 29   *Saint Thomas Becket*

Country: England   **Date:** b.1118 d.1170

Family: Father: Gilbert Beckett   Mother: Matilda Rosea
Spouse: Unknown   Siblings: Unknown

SAINTS DAILY
Kings, Queens, Popes, Princes, Princesses, Emperors, Hermits, Bishops

DAILY SAINTS WHOSE ANCESTRY IS KNOWN

Ancestors: Saint Thomas Becket's father Gilbert had a sister, whose name is not known. This sister left descendents.

Branches of the Tree: Hervey Walter Fitz Gilbert De Clare married the sister of Gilbert Beckett. This line goes thru many noble houses until a marriage is made to Joan Beaufort, who was the granddaughter of King Edward III Plantagenet of England.

Biography: Saint Thomas Beckett was the son of Gilbert Beckett and Matilda Rosea. Gilbert Beckett was the sheriff of London. Saint Thomas went to France to the University of Paris. He became friends with King Henry II of Engand and was the Archbishop of Cantebury and eventually the Chancelor of England. This created conflict between the King and his wishes and Saint Thomas Beckett's obligation to the Church. The Pope was Alexander III and of course sided with Saint Thomas Beckett. King Louis VII got involved when Saint Thomas came to France in opposition of King Henry's attempt to pass judgement on the temporal Bishop, a subject of the Pope, not the King. Saint Thomas eventually hid in the Church, and King Henry died. His son Henry the new King sent four Knights, whose names where Reginald Fitzurse, William de Tracy, Hugh de Morville, and Richard le Bret. They met with Saint Thomas and eventually chased him in the Church. He stood between the altars of Our Lady and Saint Benedict. He was accompanied by his teacher and confessor William Fitzstephen, and a monk Edward Grim. Although Grim tried to defend him the Archbishop was killed in the Church. His
feast day is observed by the Holy Roman Catholic Church.

SAINTS DAILY
Kings, Queens, Popes, Princes, Princesses, Emperors, Hermits, Bishops

DAILY SAINTS WHOSE ANCESTRY IS KNOWN

December 29   Blessed William Howard

Country: England   **Date:** 1680

Family: Father: Sir William Howard Blessed
        Mother: Alathea Talbot
Spouse: Mary Stafford   Siblings:

Ancestors: Saint Phillip Howard is an ancestor who was also a Martyr of England.

Branches of the Tree: This is the line of the Howards, who where English Knights.

Biography: Blessed William Howard was a Martyr of England. He was the son of Thomas Earl of Arundel and was raised a Catholic. Blessed William held the title of Viscount Stafford. King Charles I made him a Knight of the Bath and he married Mary Stafford in 1637. In 1640 he was named Baron Stafford. The so called Popish Plot was found out and he was falsely accused of complicity. He was beheaded on Tower Hill on December 29. There is a county in Virginia in the United States that bears his name. In 1929 he was beatified.

December 31   Saint Offa Of Essex

Country: Leinster, Ireland   **Date:** 1070

Family: Father: King Sighere of Essex
        Mother: Osyth of the Roman Catholic Church Saint
        Spouse: Unknown   Siblings: Princess Osyth of Essex

Biography: Saint Offa of Essex was the abbess of the Benedictine convent of St. Peter's, near Benevento, Italy. Her Mother was also a Saint, and her father was a King of Essex.

SAINTS DAILY
Kings, Queens, Popes, Princes, Princesses, Emperors, Hermits, Bishops

DAILY SAINTS WHOSE ANCESTRY IS KNOWN

List of Sources for Saints and Blessed For Further Reading

1) Oxford Dictionary of Saints published by Doubleday c. 1983 Author David Farmer
2) Butler's Lives of the Saints published by Burns and Oates c. 1956, 1991 Author Alvin Butler
3) Engleberts Lives of the Saints published by Barnes and Noble Inc. c. 1994 Author Omer Englebert
4) Dictionary of Saints published by Doubleday c. 1980, 1983 Author Delaney (book alphabetical order)
5) Catholic Online Saints and Angels (Internet Site)
6) Saints Preserve Us published by Random House c. 1993 Authors Sean Kelly and Rosemary Rogers
7) Family Forest CD (CD family tree of famous people)
8) Encyclopedia of Saints published by Our Sunday Visitor Publishing Division c. 1998 Author- Bunson

Other works by the Author on the same subject

Saints Who Left Descendents and Their Ancestry
……first published in November 2003 as CD eBook, published in print November 2005

Tree of Saints
…………………………………………………… first published in June 2005 as CD eBook, published in print April 2006

SAINTS DAILY
Kings, Queens, Popes, Princes, Princesses, Emperors, Hermits, Bishops

DAILY SAINTS WHOSE ANCESTRY IS KNOWN

Calendar of Saints
....first published in December 2005 as CD eBook, published in print May 2006
Lineage of Saints
....first published in 2007 as CD Published in Print August 2007
Major Saints Ancestry
....first published in 2007 as CD Published in Print July 2007
Ancestral Secrets of Knighthood
....first published in 2007 as CD Published in Print November 2007
Ascent of the Saints..first published in February 2007 as CD eBook Published in Print January 2010
Complete Saints Ancestry
......................................first published in May 2007 as CD eBook
Daily Calendar of Saints
....first published in May 2007 as CD eBook Published in Print January 2010
The Five Generation Genesis of God
....first published in May 2007 as CD eBook Published in Print January 2010
The Saintly Defense
....first published in May 2007 as CD eBook Published in Print January 2010
The Answer to the Generations of Galilee
...........................first published June 2010
The Saints of the Five Generations of Galilee
........................first published June 2010
The Book of the Priest...............first published July 2010

SAINTS DAILY
Kings, Queens, Popes, Princes, Princesses, Emperors, Hermits, Bishops

369

DAILY SAINTS WHOSE ANCESTRY IS KNOWN

The
KnightMaker..
...............first published July 2010

Additional Information Gedcom Offer.

This book was written with the aid of a genealogy program. The file this program generates is called a Gedcom. I am making the research Gedcom available to the public. The relationship is shown for each generation mother or father to son or daughter. All the Saints in this book are in the Gedcom, and their relationship to each other is shown. In other words the line is complete for each Saint in the Gedcom. Better genealogy programs can show how many generations are between members of the file, and the relationship to two members, either cousin, second cousin or twenty fifth cousin!!! Also from the internet it is possible to obtain free genealogy programs to view the file. For a copy of the Gedcom that contains the full lineage's listed please write to

Brian Starr
117 Redbud Drive
Hendersonville TN 37075

Please include 9.95 for the CD with the Research Gedcom. Also found on the CD is a computer generated copy of this book in portable document format (pdf), a pdf reader, and a copy of a review of the book Saints Who Left Descendents. Please also include 2.95 shipping in the USA and 5.95 shipping in the remainder of the world

The Gedcom shows complete lineage of the Saints found in this book to royal or noble people who lived about the year 1400 or before. If a trace can be made of your ancestry to almost any royal noble of any European country, the lineage is almost

SAINTS DAILY
Kings, Queens, Popes, Princes, Princesses, Emperors, Hermits, Bishops

DAILY SAINTS WHOSE ANCESTRY IS KNOWN

certainly to link to a part of this tree, and the lineage to the Saint can be found

Please also feel free to write with any comments, corrections, or additions that could be incorporated into the book and released with the second printing of this work.

NOTE: Tree on cover of book is actual photograph of a tree or large bush found at the Hermitage near Nashville Tennessee, the home of Past President Andrew Jackson.

SAINTS DAILY
Kings, Queens, Popes, Princes, Princesses, Emperors, Hermits, Bishops

17807685R00210

Printed in Poland
by Amazon Fulfillment
Poland Sp. z o.o., Wrocław